This is our Home

A History of Trinity Lutheran Church
Keyser, West Virginia

Compiled and Written by
Carl D. Avers

Trinity Lutheran Church
76 North Davis Street
Keyser, West Virginia

2019

© 2019 Trinity Lutheran Church
All rights reserved

ISBN 978-1-7335866-1-0

Contents

Preface 5

Prologue 7

Genesis 13

The House of the Lord 19

The Founding Saints 31

The Shepherds 91

The Music 109

Chronicles 125

Epilogue 141

Appendices 143

Preface

IT WAS LATE SUMMER OF 2017 when I received the call from Keyser.

"The pastor wants to honor the charter members, the founding saints of Trinity Lutheran Church, at the All-Saints Day service." My reaction was, of course, very positive. Then came the next few words that set everything in motion.

"We don't know the names of the charter members. We do know that you are very interested in history and your grandparents were charter members. Would you help us?"

About two months later, the names of the founding saints of Trinity Lutheran Church were individually recognized, in print and spoken from the pulpit, at the All-Saints service. It was an inspirational experience.

But the story doesn't end there. First, I must digress.

As a child of Trinity Lutheran, it was there that I was Baptized, attended Sunday School and Church, was nurtured and Confirmed in Faith, was a Luther Leaguer and attended Camp Luther. I'm still a member of the congregation, even though I now live in Virginia. As my research uncovered the names of the charter members, I realized that I had known several of them while growing up. They were memorable to me as wonderful people and faithful Lutherans.

Interested in history? My professional life was closely tied to computer engineering and project management. But I always remember, while still a young child, those two worn pages of family history that were the words of my great-grandfather, written before his death in 1916. They told of life in Germany, marriage, immigration to America and Preston County in 1854 and raising a family there. In 1976 I travelled to North Horn, Germany, and discovered the church where they were married. The nearly five-hundred year old church has kept detailed records of ecclesial events for many generations of the congregational families.

John and Geertjen Avers were charter members of Holy Trinity Lutheran Church in Newburg in 1870. It was their third child Jacob Avers and his wife Christina, my grandparents, who were charter members of Trinity Memorial Lutheran Church in Keyser in 1903.

Back to the original telephone conversation in 2017. I immediately seized upon the notion that I would need to study the early church records, especially the registry books. The response was disheartening. "They are either lost or never existed."

And so, my research began. Inspection of the newspapers of 1903 revealed that there were forty charter members. Various articles helped me identify more than half. Then the breakthroughs: copies of booklets distributed to the congregation – a brief history of the congregation (1936) and an updated version (1973) that included a list of the same forty names! Transcriptions of the booklets are included in this publication.

After the All-Saints service, I continued to expand my knowledge of the lives of the forty. Over a period of months, research and writing produced profiles of each of the charter members; they were distributed to the congregation in a serial-like fashion. One thing led to another and my research was extended to include the clergy, facilities, worship, music and fellowship at Trinity. I was motivated by the notion that the information presented herein needed to be written and widely distributed, so the early history of the congregation is never lost again.

In June, 2012, my wife was diagnosed with pancreatic cancer. I made the trip to Keyser to inform friends and begin preparations for the worst. That day, during my visit to Trinity Lutheran, Pastor Sally and I prayed in the sanctuary. Moments later, as we rose from kneeling, I was moved to say with considerable emotion, "This is my home." While briefly addressing the congregation on All-Saints Sunday 2017, it became clear to me that all who were present, the living saints of Trinity Lutheran, share the exhilarating bond of Faith; we cherish our relationship with Trinity Lutheran Church. Indeed, "This is our home."

I dedicate this book to the forty charter members, the founding saints of Trinity Lutheran, and to my wife and love of my life, Nancy Avers, who died on August 9, 2018.

– Carl D. "Denny" Avers

Chapter 1 – Prologue

PERHAPS THE BEST PLACE TO BEGIN this narrative is to present a few facts to set the formation of Trinity Lutheran Church in the proper historical context. The history of Keyser, West Virginia, has been well-documented by a son of Trinity Lutheran, Mr. William W. Wolfe; it will not be repeated here.

The earliest presence of non-native people was certainly that of trappers and hunters who pushed through the wilderness in pursuit of their trade in the early years of the 18th century. They traveled along the Hunter's Trace trail and the Potomac River valley. Early records document their presence along the South Branch, Patterson Creek and even Pine Swamp, atop the first ridge of the Alleghenies that frames the western side of the New Creek valley.

The first Lutheran congregation in Virginia, Hebron Lutheran, was formed in 1717 by a group of German colonists brought to America by Gov. Alexander Spotswood to live and work at Fort Germanna, by the Rapidan River. They later settled near today's Madison, Virginia, and built their church in 1740. It is the oldest Lutheran church in continuous use in the United States. The congregation recently celebrated its 300th anniversary.

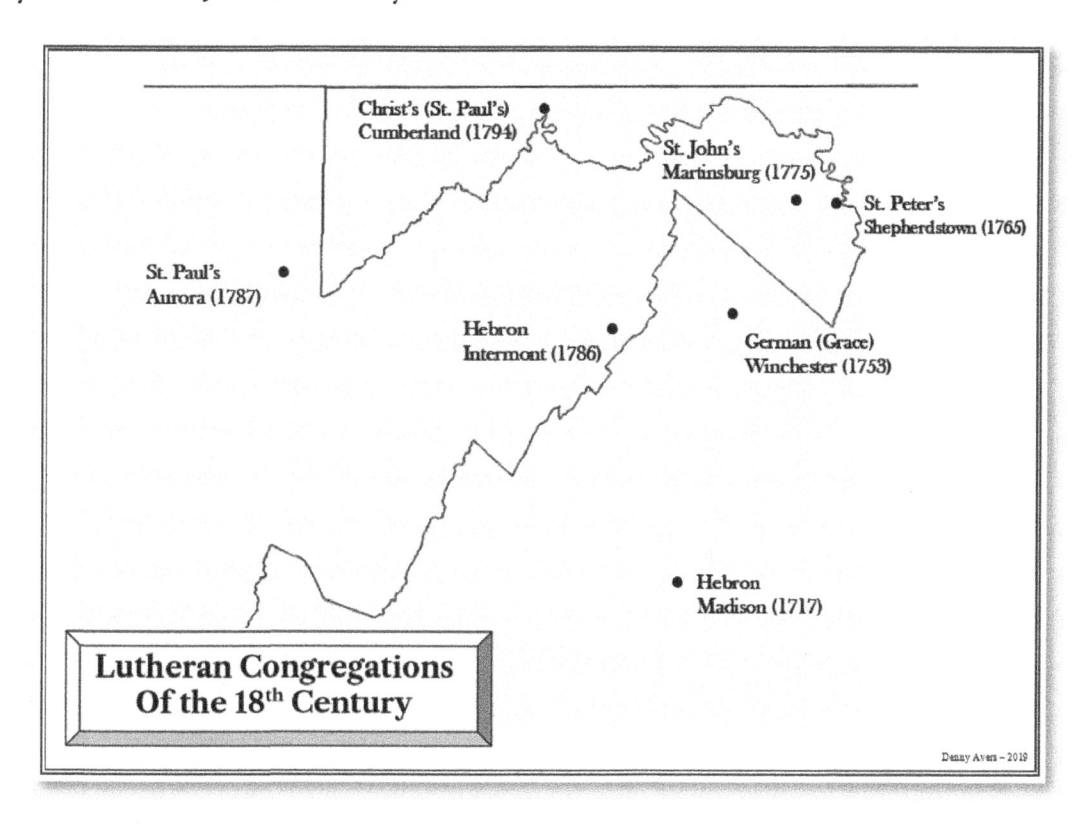

Lutheran Congregations Of the 18th Century

- Christ's (St. Paul's) Cumberland (1794)
- St. John's Martinsburg (1775)
- St. Peter's Shepherdstown (1765)
- St. Paul's Aurora (1787)
- Hebron Intermont (1786)
- German (Grace) Winchester (1753)
- Hebron Madison (1717)

Denny Avers – 2019

The Potomac's North Branch was first surveyed in 1736 by a party that measured and mapped from Harper's Ferry to the source of the Potomac, high atop the Allegheny mountains, where the Fairfax Stone was placed in 1747. The 1736 surveyors reported they saw evidence of only five settler cabins upriver from present-day Hancock, and none beyond the abandoned Shawnee town near present-day Oldtown.

The New Creek valley was first surveyed by Mr. Guy Broadwater in 1749. Immediately thereafter, Lord Fairfax made the first land grant in the valley to John Lindsey – 400 acres that are roughly bounded by New Creek, Hoover's Hollow, and today's Lincoln, Cross and Baker streets. The 333 acres that are now much of downtown Keyser, the college campus and the west end of town were granted to Christopher Beeler in 1752, the same year that the 182 acres of the eastern side of present-day Keyser, out to Limestone Run, were granted to Peter Peterson. Early settlement was interrupted by the French and Indian War and the area remained sparsely populated. Obviously, there were no churches. The first permanent church congregations in Keyser were not established until 1850 (Methodist) and 1853 (Presbyterian).

In Winchester, after receiving a patent given by Lord Fairfax, dated May 15, 1753, the Lutherans built a log schoolhouse to educate their children. It was not until April 16, 1764, that the cornerstone for the German Lutheran Church of Winchester was laid. The building was destroyed by fire in 1854. The remains of the stone walls are standing today in Winchester's Mount Hebron Cemetery. The congregation changed its name to Grace Lutheran in 1877. The present location of Grace Lutheran Church was secured in 1840 and a new church was built in 1842. During the Civil War it was used by both Southern and Northern forces. To get a better idea of regional Lutheranism during this period, we can read from Samuel's Kercheval's landmark *History of the Valley of Virginia*, published in 1833, Winchester:

> The German Reformed and Lutheran churches in our country, as far as I know of them, are doing well. The number of the Lutheran congregations is said to be at least one hundred; that of the Reformed, it is presumed, is about the same amount.

It is remarkable that throughout the whole extent of the United States, the Germans, in proportion to their wealth, have the best churches, organs and grave-yards. It is a fortunate circumstance that those of our citizens who labor under the disadvantage of speaking a foreign language, are blessed with a ministry so evangelical as that of these very numerous and respectable communities.

St. Peter's, Shepherdstown, was present-day West Virginia's first Lutheran church, Established in 1765, the congregation built its first church in 1795, a brick structure on East German Street near the old Lutheran graveyard.

St. John's Lutheran, Martinsburg was founded in 1775 and formally organized in 1790. It was one of the earliest and largest congregations in the Lower Shenandoah Valley. Dr. Charles S. Trump, the pastor of St. John's from 1888-1919, served as head of the Maryland Synod and was the senior pastor in the region when Trinity Memorial Lutheran Church at Keyser was founded.

At Intermont, in Hampshire County, Hebron Church was founded in 1786 by settlers in the Cacapon River Valley, making it the first Lutheran church west of the Shenandoah Valley.

St. Paul's Lutheran, Aurora was founded in 1787. It has the honor of being the first Lutheran Church founded in the first settlement in the western Allegheny Mountains. While other Lutheran congregations have come and gone, St. Paul's is once again the only congregational beacon of the Lutheran faith in Preston County.

Christ's Lutheran (now St. Paul's Lutheran) was founded in Cumberland in 1794, followed by St. Luke's (1848) and St. John's (1893).

St. Paul's Lutheran, Frostburg, dates back to the beginning of Frostburg as a town, about 1812. It may have been the first church in Frostburg. The church was part of the Cumberland English Lutheran charge during that time up to 1842. Ministers of this congregation did mission work along George's Creek.

In 1852, the Baltimore & Ohio Railroad was extended up the river from Cumberland to the village that became known as New Creek Station, then on to Piedmont and up the famous Seventeen Mile Grade, and down to the Cheat, reaching Wheeling and the Ohio River in 1853. After the Civil War, the B&O sought to expand its operations. New Creek Station was considered ideal, but local leaders rebuffed the notion and the B&O focused on Piedmont as a center of its operations. The English Evangelical Lutheran Church of Piedmont was organized in 1869. The congregation met in several locations until a church sanctuary was built in Westernport and dedicated on November 9, 1879. Today, we know it as Mount Calvary Lutheran. There was also a short lived Lutheran congregation in Barnum (1901-1904).

Realizing the enormity of their error, New Creek officials began to encourage the railroad to come back to New Creek. Success was theirs; railroad yards, shops and other facilities created an economic boom, even in the face of a severe national economic depression. The town was re-named Keyser, in honor of a senior B&O official.

On November 7, 1874, *The Frostburg Mining Journal* informed its readers:

Keyser City – During a visit to Keyser, Mineral Co., W. Va., this week we were astonished at the rapid and substantial manner with which it is building up. A number of magnificent brick edifices, recently erected, and many others in various stages of completion, exhibit a near, prosperous and important future. The sound of the hammer which binds piece to piece until the city is built, is heard in all parts of the town. Everything and everybody are instinct with life and energy, and permanent growth, improvement and enhanced values must result.

The location at Keyser of important Baltimore and Ohio Railroad works will be of incalculable benefit to the town. These must bring large numbers of workingmen and artisans, who must have homes, goods and provisions, thus increasing population growth and trade. The erection of these works is in progress. The wall of the roundhouse is completed; the roof will shortly he put on. This immense structure is 912 feet in circumference, which gives it capacity for the shelter of forty-four locomotives. Another of the same dimensions will he erected next spring. The freight depot, 102x46, and the passenger depot, main building, 42x36, wing, 32x25 feet, two stories high, are going up rapidly. Besides these the Company is building large barns, stables, cattle-pens, immense water-tanks, and a beautiful residence for their agent. Of the style of architecture and the general arrangement it is needless to say more than that all is being done after the manner of the Baltimore and Ohio Railroad Company – a sufficient guarantee both of the elegance and magnitude of these important additions to Keyser.

A prominent fleet of this fortunate accession to the business interests of the town is already seen in the numerous real estate transactions in and around the place.

On June 5, 1875, *The Frostburg Mining Journal* reported on the progress being made on the railroad-related work in Keyser:

Keyser, W. Va.: Railroad Improvements – Among a number of important improvements being perfected by the Baltimore & Ohio Railroad Company for the more expeditious transaction of its great and growing freight traffic, the following program for Keyser, W. Va., is put down by the Baltimore Sun for inauguration early this month:

The next and most extensive of these improvements is at Keyser, formerly New Creek. W. Va., where the company has purchased nearly one hundred acres of land for the purpose of establishing a great central station, and which it proposes, upon the change of time-table, to make the end of the second division. It has recently erected at this point a fine brick and stone station, the lower portion for the accommodation of passengers, and the upper for the offices of its employees. It has also erected an engine-house of forty-four stalls, similar to the one at Riverside, and is constructing machine and blacksmith shops capable of doing the running repairs for this station. It has also just finished extensive stock-yards, with ample stabling for horses, houses for sheep, and pens for cattle and hogs. In the construction of these yards all the latest improvements have been adopted, insuring the convenience of the drovers and stockmen, as well as the cleanliness and comfort of the animals.

Owing to present and prospective growth of the company's business, its managers, foreseeing that its terminal facilities at Washington and Baltimore, while large and conveniently arranged, would soon be taxed to their utmost capacity, have decided to relieve these points by the establishment of a great drill-yard at Keyser, where cars from all parts of the West, as well as the coal regions, would he made up into trains for the different stations and points of delivery to which they are destined, thus obviating the necessity of separating trains and distributing the cars upon their arrival here. To accomplish this the company has just completed two additional tracks between Piedmont (its intersection with the Cumberland and Pennsylvania railroad, leading into the coal-fields) and Keyser, to be devoted exclusively to its coal traffic, thereby securing four tracks between these important points.

The great drilling ground at Keyser will be more than one mile long, and wide enough to accommodate fourteen side tracks its entire length, and here trains will be made up for direct delivery to all points east and west. This arrangement is designed to prove of great advantage to the company as well as to its patrons, increasing the promptness and dispatch with which goods will reach their destination.

People came flocking to Keyser for jobs, while none were available where they had been living and working. Advertisements appeared in newspapers throughout the region:

The Keyser Land and Improvement Company at Keyser City (late New Creek), Mineral County, W. Va.:

This Company have decided to offer for sale for a few days only, 200 building lots situated about 200 yards of the Court House, Post Office, Churches, school houses, stores, depots, round houses, machine shops, etc. These lots are pleasantly situated, command fine scenery, have an abundance of good water, ease of access, and in every way desirable for homes. Will sell at the following prices and easy terms, believing the improvement of these will largely enhance the value of their [investment of] $75, $100, $150 per Lot, according to location – $25 down and $5 per month until paid for, without interest. A discount of 10 percent, allowed when the whole purchase money is paid at the time of sale.

Insurance benefits – Any person buying a lot on the above terms, and making one payment, if they should die, we will cancel all claims, and give legal heirs a clear title, thus becoming a Home Insurance Company, without cost to the insured.

This will afford people of limited means an opportunity to buy a house, and thus become independent of exacting and exorbitant landlords. Why pay heavy rents for poor tenements, when the same money will buy you a home in a desirable locality? If you haven't the money now, the sacrifice of a cigar or two or a glass of beer a day will make your payments. No excuse to be without a home of your own. What better investment for any person, old or young, man or woman, than to buy one of these lots on the above terms?

The location of natural surroundings of Keyser City, affording such unusual facilities for manufacturing, cheap coal, large quantities of timber and iron, the outlet of the richest farming section of West Virginia, which for years has shipped more produce than any other point on the line of the road, are so advantageous and without rival, that the B. & O. R. R. Co. have purchased 100 acres offered for the purpose of making this a manufacturing and supply point, and end of the Second Division of their road, where they must employ thousands of men to relieve the now overcrowded shops and yards at Baltimore, Martinsburg, Piedmont, Grafton, and other points. They are already erecting large round houses, (the largest in the country), Passenger and Freight Depots of large capacity, Machine Shops, Cattle Pens and Stables to accommodate their extensive cattle traffic, making this a 'resting place'. All point to a very rapid and immediate increase of population and corresponding increase in the price of building lots.

Among the new families that came to Keyser were highly dedicated Lutherans: farmers and craftsmen from the Shenandoah Valley, railroaders from Preston County, shopkeepers and entrepreneurs, physicians and teachers.

In early 1884, Rev. William Stoudenmier, Pastor of St. Mark's Lutheran in Oakland, visited

Baltimore with a view of inaugurating steps leading to the building of a Lutheran Church in Keyser. He left his charge later that year and nothing substantial came of his effort.

Records at Mt. Calvary, Westernport, make vague reference to requests for assistance to organize a Lutheran congregation in Keyser during the early 1890s, noting that the Ohio synod was somehow involved. Mr. Calvary, affiliated with the Maryland synod, declined the overtures from Keyser, wishing to avoid any territorial entanglements.

At the turn of the 20th century, the time to establish a Lutheran congregation in Keyser was approaching.

Chapter 2 – Genesis

The beginning...

THE GENERAL SYNOD HERALDED THE FORMATION of a new congregation in Keyser, West Virginia, in its official newsletter, published in Philadelphia on September 18, 1903.

Lutheran Observer.

Unless with proofs of Holy Writ, or with manifest, clear and distinct principles and arguments, I am refuted and convinced, I can and will recant nothing.—Luther

In Essentials, Unity; in Non-Essentials, Liberty; in all Things, Charity.

VOL. LXXI. NO. 39.   LANCASTER AND PHILADELPHIA, FRIDAY, SEPTEMBER 18, 1903.   WHOLE NO. 3784

ORGANIZATION AT KEYSER, W. VA.

It is a known fact that there are less than six thousand Lutherans in the state of West Virginia. The various towns and villages, it seems, in the past did not attract the wide-awake workers and advance couriers of our denomination. Here and there were families of our faith, but scarcely enough to organize, knowing, too, that it would be difficult to secure a preacher and maintain church life. These families with few exceptions have entered other denominations which occupied the territory. But today our own church is waking up to the claims upon it, through increased population and many Lutheran families entering this state, and we trust not too late for efficient work.

There are a dozen and more growing towns and even cities where our Church has no representation. Members of the Maryland, Virginia and Ohio synods are seeing what marvelous developments are taking place and how cities are springing up, and have conceded to investigate, doing what they can, along with our General Synod Secretary, to establish churches and send forth the missionary.

The little yet growing city of Keyser, W. Va., on the B. & O. railroad, one hundred miles west of Martinsburg and twenty west of Cumberland, Md., was selected as a field for work. Our young brother, William Ney, of the junior class in our Theological Seminary, Gettysburg, was appointed for the undertaking. A wise choice was made in him, for the work performed was almost phenomenal. In less than three months he gathered together into a congregation forty Lutherans. Beside this, a Sunday-school numbering eighty was organized. He preached the Word Sabbath morning and evening in a hall over a store.

At the request of the missionary and some of the members, Rev. C. S. Trump, of Martinsburg, was invited to organize this congregation. The time appointed was August 16th. The weather was unfavorable, yet the enthusiasm of the members brought together a large assembly. Forty charter members subscribed to the constitution and polity of the Lutheran Church, and adopted the name "Trinity Memorial Lutheran Church." After organization, the Holy Communion was administered, after which four elders were installed. The writer preached a sermon on the theme, "A Model Congregation," based upon Acts x. 33. A session of the Sunday-school was held in the afternoon, when 78 members were reported. In the evening Rev. J. W. McCauley, of Cumberland, preached on the theme, "My Church." Dr. L. A. Mann, of Cumberland, was also present, conducting the evening communion and addressing the organization. Rev. Luther Miller, of Piedmont, was present also and took part in the services.

It was a day of rejoicing for this organization, which has indeed a bright future. Many professional and representative men of Keyser, with their families, compose this congregation. A lot will be purchased in the near future, and a chapel, if not church, be erected.

Brother Ney, through his untiring energy and genial manner, together with his wisdom and ability, has done an excellent work, endearing himself to the people whom he has encouraged to work. We trust the right man will be appointed or selected to continue this work, as Mr. Ney will pursue his studies for the next two years at the Seminary. There is "much land yet to be possessed" in this state for Christ through our Lutheran Zion.

– C. S. T.

―――――――○ ○―――――――

The author, the Rev. Charles S. Trump, was the "dean" of Lutheran ministers in the area. Under the auspices of the Rev. Dr. A. Stewart Hartman, General Secretary of the Board of Home Missions, Rev. Trump played an active role in the efforts leading up to the formation of the congregation. Both were present in Keyser to participate in the events on the day the charter of Trinity Memorial Lutheran Church was signed.

The culminating events of August 16, 1903, were enabled by the efforts of a small group of faith-filled Lutheran activists in Keyser. Canvassing the community for adherents to the Lutheran denomination, they found that some were journeying to Westernport to attend services at Mt. Calvary Lutheran, while others were attending non-Lutheran services in Keyser. The number of potential members, coupled with their enthusiasm and commitment to support a congregation in Keyser, provided the evidence needed to approach the Board of Home Missions of the General Synod with a request for support. After careful consideration and expressions of support from other Lutheran ministers and their congregations in the area, the Board of Missions agreed and selected Gettysburg Divinity student William C. Ney as their home missionary for Keyser. He accepted the calling to become the full-time pastor upon his graduation and ordination in the late spring of 1905.

From time to time, *The Lutheran Observer* published updates on the progress of the new congregation: "The mission at this place has promise of rapid growth. An urgent call to Mr. W. C. Mann to serve it as supply has been accepted." (December 25, 1903); "Rev. Wm. Ney, pastor of the Keyser, W. Va., mission, reports the work there encouraging, and under his able supervision we hope to have a strong church in Keyser in the near future." (June 24, 1904). Dr. Peter Bergstresser also assisted as a supply pastor.

Local newspapers chronicled events, as well. On June 18, 1903, *The Cumberland Evening Times* informed its readers:

Mr. Ney has only been in Keyser a few days, but is very much pleased with the outlook in his field of labor so far.

On August 19, the *Evening Times* reported the formational events that had taken place on August 16:

Keyser, W. Va. – A new Lutheran church has been instituted at Keyser, W. Va., with 40 charter members. It will be known as Trinity Memorial Lutheran Church. Mr. W. C. Ney, of the Gettysburg Theological Seminary, has charge. He was assisted in the organization by Rev. C. S. Trump, of Martinsburg, W. Va., Rev. Luther F. Miller, of Westernport, Rev. J. William McCauley and Rev. Luther A. Mann, D. D., of Cumberland. It is the first Lutheran church to be organized in Keyser. John T. Sincell, Augustus S. Wolf and Dr. J. W. Hall were elected elders and William Boehmes, John G. Koelz, Jacob Avers and P. M. Spangler were elected deacons. All the deacons and elders were installed according to the rules of the church.

The Rev. Dr. Trump preached on this text from the Book of Acts, 10:33: "Immediately therefore I sent to thee; and thou hast well done that thou art come. Now therefore are we all here present before God, to hear all things that are commanded thee of God.

And thus, it began.

Early Records

No formal or comprehensive record of membership, births, baptisms, confirmations, marriages, transfers and deaths from the earliest days of Trinity Lutheran's existence has been found. A ledger-style book containing a chronological record of Minutes of church council meetings 1903–1928 has been rediscovered. On two central pages of this book are some fascinating facts about the first two years.

At services conducted by Rev. L. A. Mann on May 8, 1904, the first new members were admitted after opening of the charter: Mr. Albert Steiding, Miss Rose Shafferman, and Miss Charlotte Shafferman. Mrs. Christina Avers was also recognized. Although she was one of the forty individuals noted on the charter of August 16, 1903, Mrs. Avers missed the service that day, having given birth to her son Carl one day before. The first two Confirmands, Miss Gertrude Wolf and Miss Icy Avers, were admitted to full membership.

Holy Communion was celebrated at the morning and evening services. Those receiving the Sacrament were: Mr. & Mrs. Sincell, Mr. & Mrs. Wolf, Miss Jennie Wolf, Miss Gertha Wolf, Miss Annie Carl, Mr. & Mrs. H. W. Baker, Miss May

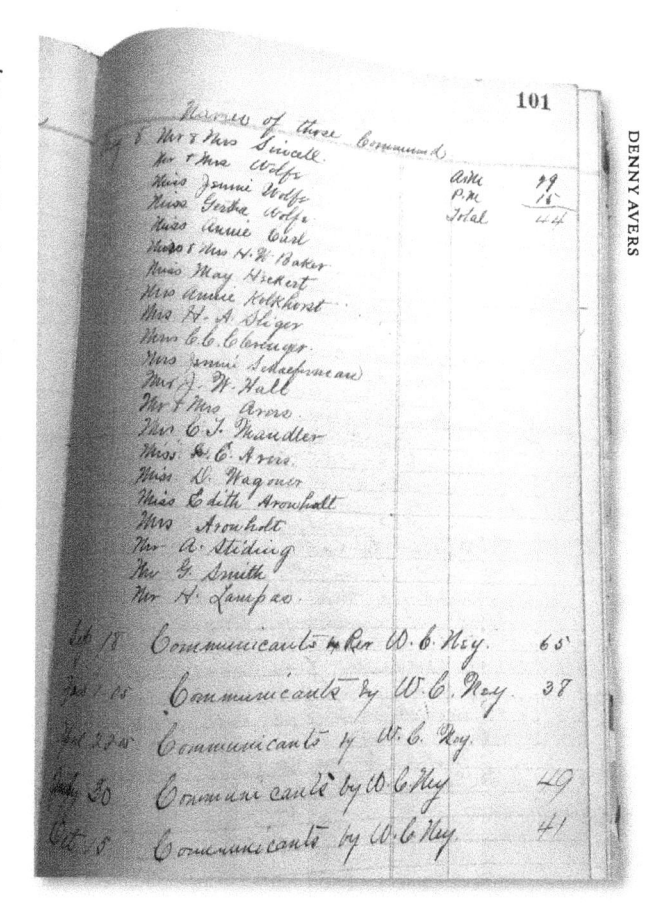

15

Heckert, Mrs. Annie Kolkhorst, Mrs. H. A. Sliger, Mrs. C. C. Clevenger, Mrs. Jennie Shafferman, Mrs. J. W. Hall, Mr. & Mrs. Avers, Mr. C. T. Mandler, Miss Icy Avers, Mrs. D. Wagoner, Miss Edith Aronholt, Mrs. Emily Aronholt, Mr. A. Steiding, Mr. G. Smith, Mr. H. Lampas

On August 21, 1904, five new members were added: Mr. Henry Neuhauser, Mrs. H. Neuhauser, Miss K. Neuhauser, Mrs. F. W. Davis and Mr. George Loy.

On September 18, 1904, W. C. Ney celebrated the Sacrament with 65 communicants.

On January 1, 1905: W. C. Ney welcomed Mr. William E. Lawrence as the congregation's newest member and 65 individuals received the Sacrament of Holy Communion.

On April 23, 1905, W. C. Ney presiding, Miss Ella Wolf and Mr. John Gank were added to the membership roll and Communion was celebrated.

On July 30, 1905, W. C. Ney and the congregation welcomed new members Mr. David Kesner, Mrs. Susan Kesner, Mr. Lee Kesner, Miss Eva Kesner, their housemaid Miss Ella Lough, and Mrs. Marie [Steiding] Gank. The Sacrament was given to 49 communicants.

When the first sanctuary was dedicated on October 14, 1906, the number of Confirmed members had grown to seventy-eight, nearly double the number of the original saints of Trinity Lutheran Memorial Church on August 16, 1903.

The 1936 History Pamphlet

Thankfully, many details regarding the early days of Trinity Memorial Lutheran were documented in a twelve-page history pamphlet that was written and distributed in 1936

The Origin of Trinity Memorial Lutheran Church was compiled by eyewitnesses Mrs. P. M. Spangler and Miss Martha Watson. They were among the members of the Ladies' Aid Society, including Misses Anna Carl and Margaret Koelz, who led the initial canvassing to identify other Lutheran adherents in the community. We are filled with gratitude for their efforts to support the notion and establishment of a Lutheran Church in Keyser and to sustain the congregation with their devoted service and gifts.

Although it is well documented by multiple sources that there were forty Lutherans who signed the August 16, 1903 charter, *The Origin of Trinity Memorial Lutheran Church* is the definitive source of the names of those individuals. It is a treasure.

Few copies of the 1936 history pamphlet are known to exist today. To ensure it remains available for future reference, a complete transcription of this documented history is provided in Appendix I herein. Electronic scanned images of the original document are available from the church business office.

Coda

Searchable images and text of local and regional newspapers are now accessible on-line to facilitate further research and casual reading about events related to Trinity Lutheran and other local history. Of particular interest are files of Keyser and Piedmont newspapers that are available on-line as a service to the community by the Potomac State College of WVU library. Other regional newspapers are available on-line through the *Chronicling America* project, sponsored by the Library of Congress and the National Endowment for the Humanities.

Chapter 3 – The House of the Lord

This is our Home...

UNTIL OCTOBER 14, 1906, when the first Trinity Lutheran Church building was dedicated, church activities took place in three public locations.

On Thursday, June 18, 1903, the *Cumberland Evening Times* reported: "William C. Ney, of the Evangelical Lutheran Mission, has rented the **Odd Fellows Hall** and the denomination will hold its Sunday meetings there until a church can be built."

Several buildings in the downtown area had large rooms on the floors above street-level storefronts. The owners often rented these facilities to churches, fraternal and social organizations. The Odd Fellows Hall was located at 32 N. Mineral Street, across from the Keyser Electric & Light Company.

After three Sunday evening services, the place of worship was moved. On July 5, 1903, the worship service and the first Sunday School were held at **Carskadon's hall**. On July 11, 1903, the *Evening Times* noted: "The Lutheran Mission has rented Carskadon's hall and will hold regular services there hereafter." It was at Carskadon's hall, upstairs on the corner of Main and Center streets, that Trinity Memorial Lutheran Church was formally organized by the signing of its charter on August 16, 1903.

| Johnson's hall Pharmacy | View at intersection of Main/Center Streets (note clock beside auto on left) | Carskadon's hall |

Minutes of Trinity's Church Council indicate dissatisfaction with the maintenance of Carskadon hall; the assembly hall and stairwell were being left in unkempt conditions by fraternal organizations that also used the facility. The congregation chose to move across Main Street to **Johnson's hall**, above the Keyser Pharmacy that was operated by charter member Dr. J. W. Hall and then Henry Grusendorf following Dr. Hall's retirement. Trinity worshiped at Johnson's hall for three years until construction of the first church sanctuary building was completed in 1906.

Johnson's hall was opened in 1880 by Mr. J. H. Johnson and described as a "neat and commodious" place, with hand-painted stage scenery and drop curtain. Even after the new church building was opened for worship, Trinity continued to use Johnson's hall for social functions until 1911, when the space was rented by the local school district to provide much needed classroom space. Perhaps that was the impetus that led to the construction of the Lutheran club house in back of the church building about that time. In 1939, when the Main Street storefront was then pharmacist Dr. Harry Kight's drugstore, local businessman Henry Grouden opened "Henry's" in the upstairs hall. It immediately became a very popular place for its duckpin bowling alleys, pool tables, sports and social events. It was re-named the "Sports Center" in 1941 and continued to operate for several decades under that name. By the way, Dr. Kight was married to Myra Elizabeth Kight, the youngest daughter of charter members Augustus and Christina (Head) Wolf.

Of the three public spaces used by Trinity Lutheran as temporary places of worship, only Johnson's hall remains standing today.

Abounding in faith, the fledgling congregation embarked on an effort to erect a house of worship. On June 22, 1905, a lot on North Davis Street was purchased for $1,250. The Ladies' Aid Society once again stepped forward to lead the way by providing the $500 down-payment. The design of the church and fundraising began almost immediately. With hard work and a spirit of generosity, the loan of $750 for the purchase of the lot was completely paid by January 1906.

In the spring of 1906, construction of the new edifice began, and on June 17 the congregation gathered about the foundation to celebrate the laying of the corner stone. By early fall, the church was ready for use.

The last service at Johnson's hall, with Holy Communion, was on October 7, 1906. On October 14, 1906, the new church was dedicated in the name of the Father, and of the Son, and of the Holy Ghost. Trinity Lutheran had seventy-eight confirmed members, nearly double the original forty founding saints of Trinity Lutheran.

Concurrently, it was announced that Rev. Ney had accepted a call to the Lutheran mission charge in Elkins and would assume his new duties about November 1. The congregation continued to grow during the ensuing pastorates of Rev. C. P. Bastian and Rev. Harry F. Baughman.

During the morning service of August 5, 1918, the "Burning of the Mortgage" was celebrated. Here's how the *Mineral Daily News* reported the story:

> Yesterday was a day of great joy to the members of Trinity Lutheran Church as they burned the mortgage that has rested on the church since [1906].
>
> The exercises were held at the morning service at which time a large audience was present. The Congregation was organized [fifteen] years ago with 40 charter members. Twenty-eight of the charter members were at the service, and were brought to the church in autos.
>
> The addresses of the occasion were made by the present pastor, the Rev. H. F. Baughman and by Mr. J. M. Shaffer, financial secretary, Mr. George M. Loy on behalf of the trustees of the Church and Mr. John T. Sincell on behalf of the Charter members.
>
> When the mortgage was called for by the pastor it was delivered to him by Mr. A. S. Wolf, one of the trustees who signed the document. He in turn delivered it to Mr. J. C. Kephart, acting president of the Church Council, who placed it on the tray on which it was to be burned.

Mr. Henry W. Baker, the contractor who built the church was called upon to set flame to the document. Mr. Baker, in a few well chosen words, delegated the duty of striking the match to his grandson, Master Luther Ney, the son of Rev. W. C. Ney, who organized the congregation and under whose pastorate the church was built. Master Ney applied the match and while the mortgage burned the congregation sang, "Praise God from Whom All Blessings Flow."

The Lutheran congregation was organized with 40 members. It owned no property, but since that time it has acquired the lot and church building, has erected a club house, and is about to purchase the parsonage property. The mortgage was to cover a loan of $2,000. At the same time this was being reduced another loan of the same amount was paid off and the church re-[frescoed] and renovated at a cost of about $400. A thing that this congregation should be more than proud of is that all these obligations have been met without any solicitation from those not members of the church. However, a few outside contributions have been received, which are highly appreciated. But they were all voluntary. The [funding] was raised without fairs or sales or suppers.

After the services a congregational meeting was announced by a councilman and the pastor exited and they increased his salary $250. He had refused to raise his salary until the church was free of debt.

Further descriptions of these events may be found in *The Origin of Trinity Memorial Lutheran Church – Keyser, West Virginia* (1936).

Sunday School Room

Sanctuary

Piano

Altar

Console

Choir

Organ

Narthex

Davis Street

Trinity Lutheran Church
Keyser, West Virginia

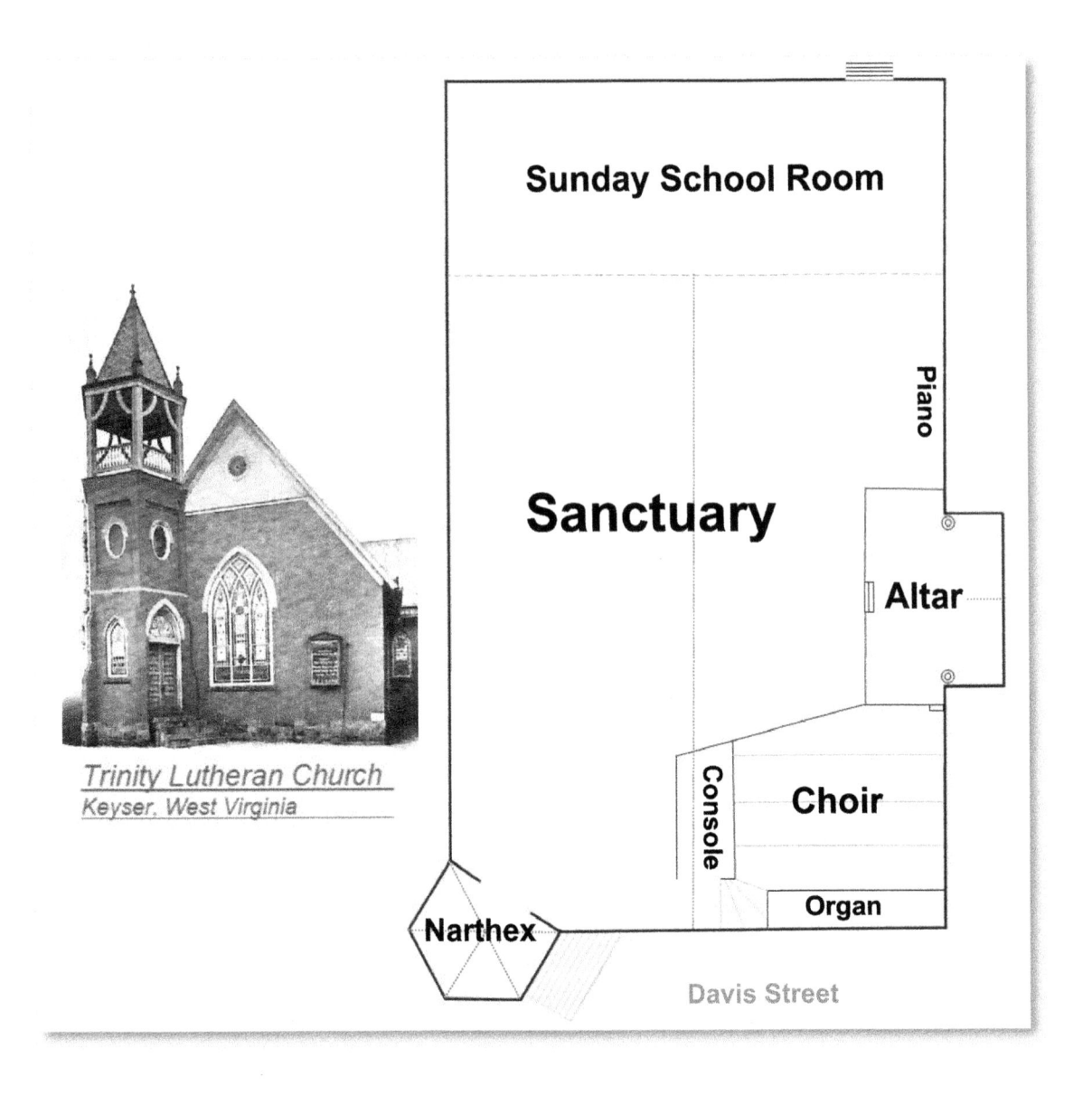

    The church building was a rectangular red-brick structure with a hexagonal narthex and bell tower on the left of the building front (Davis Street), an extension on the right (Center Street side) for the altar alcove, and a rather spacious room at the rear (alley side) to house Sunday School classes, meetings and events. Partitions between the sanctuary and classroom area were raised vertically to expand the size of the sanctuary when additional seating was required for services. Entry to the sanctuary building required climbing steps in the front or back of the building.

    The church was filled with light. Beautiful stained glass windows decorated the sanctuary and bell tower. The organ console, choir loft and sanctuary were brilliantly illuminated by a magnificent large window at the front facing Davis Street – a gift to the congregation presented by Rev. William Cramp Ney, in memory of his maternal grandparents, Jacob and Elizabeth (Fisher) Cramp.

WEST VIRGINIA AND REGIONAL HISTORY COLLECTION – MORGANTOWN

The earliest known photograph of the church exterior dates to about 1908. Looking south from the intersection of So. Davis and Armstrong streets, the hexagonal bell tower of Trinity Memorial Lutheran stands tall. One of the oval stained glass windows from the Lutheran bell tower is still displayed in the modern sanctuary. In the background is the First M.E. church; the old Davis mansion sits atop the hill where the old Keyser High School was erected in the 1920s. In the left foreground is the building shared by the Sincell Company and the U. S. Post Office..

The photographs that follow illustrate the church interior are from more recent times. The first is almost certainly the one mentioned in a letter to Rev. William C. Ney, written by George Loy in December, 1950, which began:

William C. Ney, D.D.
Brookline, Pa.

Dear William C.,
You are about to see a picture of a group that has developed from your first pastorate. Emmett Kolkhorst and my son William could not be present for the picture – hence they said I should robe for my son's chair. We are very fond of this group and their accomplishment.

23

(1st row) Laura Lea, Eliz. Stoutamyer, Virginia Kolkhorst, Beverly Bowne, Evelyn Shinn
(2nd) Wanda Watson, Anna Montgomery, Rena Mott, Clara Kauffman, Marie Farley
(3rd) Martin Watson, Don Heare, Abe Goldsworthy, Bob Coffman, Arnold Sliger
(4th) Harry Stoutamyer, Fred Athey, Robert Lee Fisher, George Loy

Choir director Leonard Withers and organist Mary Evelyn Coffman were preparing the choir for an upcoming Christmas cantata when the above photo was taken. Three groups of beautiful wooden pews faced the altar. The largest of these was directly in front of the altar. Another, in front of the opening to the classroom area, was angled slightly to face the altar. The smallest, only two short pews, was just inside the entrance, between the door from the narthex and the organ console. The stained glass window in the choir loft was donated by charter members Mrs. Jennie Arnold and her daughter, Mrs. Bertha Sliger, in memory of their deceased children – Laura Arnold (1876-1882), Harry Arnold (1887-1904) and Elizabeth Sliger (1903-1904).

The altar area, on the left where Mr. Withers is standing, was a raised platform. An alcove was framed in lush dark wood and supported by two floor-to-ceiling columns. The formal altar in the alcove was illuminated by two stained glass windows.

In 1911, a large painting was donated to the congregation and placed immediately above the altar. This scene formed an indelible memory in those who came here to worship in The House of the Lord. The following was published in the 11 August 1911 edition of the *Keyser Tribune*:

> A Work of Art and Genius – At the forenoon services of the Keyser Lutheran Church last Sunday, the Greenwade and Newhauser families presented to the church a very handsome hand-painted picture representing Christ praying in the garden of Gethsemane the night of his betrayal. The picture, which is a masterpiece, was painted by Miss Cora Reed, of Keyser, and we call special attention to the artist because many of our people do not know that we have such a genius in our community.

COURTESY OF DINAH COURRIER

The orchestra was seated in the area to the left of the altar. It is thought that Mrs. Virginia (Knott) Kolkhorst is the piano accompanist in this photograph. The stained glass window was donated by Mr. and Mrs. Henry Baker in memory of their son John. In the background is the Sunday School area and the door at the back of the church, Steps from this doorway led to the parish Club House that was constructed during the 1907–1912 pastorate of Rev. Bastian. Affectionately known for years as the "green house" or "Sunday School building," it was razed after the construction of the new Parish House.

This 1949 Sunday School class was photographed on the front steps that led to the narthex and sanctuary. A small corner of the large stained glass window is visible.

(1st row) Robin Blackburn, Steve Heare, Susie Manns, John Hussen
(2nd) Martha Athey, Mark Ginn, Linda Smith, Mike McDonald, Patty Kephart, Mrs. Coffman
(3rd) Janet Staggs, Vickie Ginn, Karen Heare, Ann Ebert, Diane Manns
(4th) Lilly Pat Golden, Carol Athey, Missy Ebert, Barbara Coffman, Terry Lancaster

This much later photograph of the Junior Choir further illustrates a larger portion of the same window and the organ pipes.

Coda

The first parsonage owned by the congregation was located on Davis Street, adjacent to the north side of the sanctuary; it was purchased in 1919 at a cost of $2,900. In 1926, the congregation took advantage of an opportunity to purchase a home at 47 South Main Street for $9,250. This lovely residence served as the Lutheran parsonage until 1964 when the present parsonage on Valley View Avenue was completed.

After it was vacated in 1926, the original parsonage was intermittently rented as a private residence and used for congregational activities. The building was sold in 1943, moved across the street and placed to face Center Street at the back of the W. W. Long property at 73 N. Davis Street. All three parsonages remain standing today.

The new Parish House was erected in 1953 at a cost of $46,000. It was located immediately adjacent to the sanctuary on the lot where the original Parsonage had been situated. Rev. Harry Baughman returned to Keyser for the formal dedication of the building on January 31, 1954. Over two hundred people attended the reception that followed.

COURTESY OF TRINITY LUTHERAN CHURCH

The present church sanctuary was built and dedicated on the site of the original 1906 building. The blessing of the site and groundbreaking took place on August 2, 1969; the cornerstone was laid on October 12. Rev. C. Gerald Huhn conducted the cornerstone dedication service and the Rev. William C. Hankey, president of the Western Pa. – West Va. Synod addressed the congregation. Bible lessons were read by Romaine Kephart, chairman of the building committee, and Donald P. Heare, lay president of the congregation. Former pastor, Rev. Donald D. Anderson and Rev. Hankey were present for the Service of Dedication of June 12, 1970; a reception followed, chaired by Mrs. A. D. Wells, assisted by church women.

More about these later events may be studied in the transcription of Part II of *The Origin* that may be found in Appendix II. Published at the time of Trinity's 70th anniversary in 1973, Part II was compiled by Mrs. Anna (Kolkhorst) Montgomery-Mott, assisted by Mr. William Wolfe, Mr. W. E. Coffman and Mr. Walter Kephart.

DENNY AVERS

Those who worshipped in the original building are reminded of the history of Trinity Lutheran Church when they encounter the cherished painting now found at the center of a small altar in the Parish House. May all who pass this way be similarly inspired.

The artist, Cora Alice Reed, the child of Walter and Martha (Hays) Reed, was born near Greenland Gap, Grant County, on July 18, 1872. She never married, lived alone, and was the subject of several local legends, few of which were true. She suffered a debilitating stroke a few days before Christmas, 1947. Lee Shepp, a local grocer, who was making a delivery to her home, broke down two barricaded doors to reach the small room where Miss Reed was lying.

The *Cumberland Times* newspaper of July 27, 1948, noted: "The small wooden house on New Creek Drive, which was the residence of Miss Cora Reed, painter and recluse, is being razed. The home, a half mile from Keyser, was sold at a public sale recently, after Miss Reed suffered a paralytic stroke. She is now a ward of the county at the Old Homestead Hotel, Burlington."

Miss Reed then left Burlington to reside in Emoryville at the home of her brother, Clarence Reed, before moving back to Keyser to live with Mrs. Sally Hood. She died March 30, 1953, and was buried in the IOOF Cemetery in Elk Garden. In 1976, the Mineral County Bicentennial Commission named her as one of 76 people who shaped Mineral County history as "a painter in the early 1900s."

Chapter 4 – The Founding Saints

Faith, hope and strong Lutheran backgrounds brought them together...

As one learns about the history of Trinity Lutheran Church, distinct impressions are formed regarding the remarkable growth of the congregation during its early decades.

- The Charter members all came from strong Lutheran backgrounds. The strength of their beliefs, their love of the Lutheran liturgy, and their knowledge of Lutheran tradition rubbed off on those who later joined them as members of the congregation.
- Trinity's pastors were strong preachers and teachers who excelled in fostering congregational fellowship and community outreach.
- Music played a major role in worship and outreach. Trinity was widely recognized as the musical center of the community. On June 15, 1914, the local newspaper said: *"The Lutheran Church seems to be filled with music."*
- Fellowship among members was unusually stout, for adults and children alike, at congregational events and in their everyday social lives.

Many upon many individuals and families have contributed mightily to the ever evolving story of Keyser's Trinity Lutheran Church and its enduring success. In this Chapter, you will be introduced to the forty faithful and dedicated Lutherans who were at the core of the formation of the congregation and the early decades of its congregational life. In the Chapters to follow, you will learn about its pastors, worship and music, outreach to the community, and the great fellowship among its members.

One might wonder why the spouses and older children of several charter members were not among those who signed the charter. A careful reading of the 1936 *The Origin of Trinity Memorial Lutheran Church* reveals that the individuals who canvassed the community were seeking those who were already "adherents to the Lutheran denomination" or "of the Lutheran faith."

Of the forty who signed the formative charter of August 16, 1903, thirty-nine have been definitively identified and are profiled herein. The identity of "Mrs. F. Moffitt" has been elusive; there are clues, but clearly documented evidence has not yet been found.

Trinity Memorial Lutheran Church
Charter Members

Mrs. Virginia Arnold

Mr. Jacob Avers &
Mrs. Christina Avers

Mr. Henry W. Baker &
Mrs. Jane E. Baker

Mr. Charles W. Balthis &
Mrs. Mary Alice Balthis

Mr. F. W. Boehmes &
Mrs. Louisa Boehmes

Miss Anna Carl

Mr. James Monroe Clem &
Mrs. Catherine Isabelle Clem

Mrs. Mary Katherine Clevenger

Mrs. Ida May Gerstell

Mrs. Nancy Emma Gull

Dr. James W. C. Hall

Mr. John C. Kephart &
Mrs. Elizabeth Kephart

Mr. John G. Koelz

Mrs. Anna Kolkhorst

Mr. Louis Herman Lampas

Mr. Conrad T. Mandler

Dr. Ephraim T. Martin

Mrs. F. Moffitt

Mrs. Bettie Lee Newhouse

Mr. Charles P. Pifer &
Mrs. Emma Elizabeth Pifer

Mr. William C. Pifer

Mrs. Margaret C. Shaffer

Mrs. Virginia H. Shafferman

Mr. John T. Sincell &
Mrs. Valetta Irene Sincell

Mr. Harry A. Sliger &
Mrs. Bertha Sliger

Mr. Benjamin Souder

Mr. Parker M. Spangler &
Mrs. Laura Bertha Spangler

Mrs. Diana Wagoner

Mr. Augustus S. Wolf &
Mrs. Christina Jane Wolf

August 16, 1903

Name		Born	Place	Death	Place	Burial
Arnold	Virginia (Young)	Mar 1845	Winchester, VA	24 Aug 1918	Keyser	Queen's Meadow Point
Avers	Jacob	22 Apr 1858	Rodemer	22 Dec 1925	Keyser	Queen's Meadow Point
Avers	Christina (Miller)	01 Sep 1861	Preston Co.	11 Mar 1922	Keyser	Queen's Meadow Point
Baker	Henry W.	18 May 1839	Shenandoah Co., VA	24 Jun 1934	Keyser	Queen's Meadow Point
Baker	Jane E. (Feely)	28 Jul 1844	Shenandoah Co., VA	10 Jun 1923	Keyser	Queen's Meadow Point
Balthis	Charles W.	Jun 1843	Loudoun Co., VA	25 Jan 1909	Charles Town	Fairview Lutheran Bolivar, WV
Balthis	Mary Alice (Loman)	30 Apr 1853	Jefferson Co.	30 Oct 1905	Keyser	Fairview Lutheran Bolivar, WV
Boehmes	Frederick Wm.	17 Mar 1842	Germany	13 Sep 1906	Keyser	Queen's Meadow Point
Boehmes	Louisa (Kimmerling)	18 Jun 1842	Germany	23 Jan 1917	Keyser	Queen's Meadow Point
Carl	Miss Anna	16 Sep 1866	Plainfield, PA	10 Jun 1910	Pittsburgh, PA	Bethel Church Plainfield, PA
Clem	James Monroe	19 Mar 1859	Shenandoah Co., VA	09 May 1927	Keyser	Queen's Meadow Point
Clem	Catherine (Wiles)	17 Mar 1858	Preston Co.	05 May 1931	Keyser	Queen's Meadow Point
Clevenger	Mary "Kate" (Avers)	25 Mar 1880	Independence	13 Aug 1938	Painesville, OH	Evergreen Painesville, OH
Gerstell	Ida May (Fleming)	01 May 1859	Shepherdstown	24 Apr 1950	nr. Keyser	Gerstell Family Farm nr. Keyser
Gull	Nancy Emma (Poling)	16 Apr 1873	Mineral Co.	01 Dec 1953	Keyser	Queen's Meadow Point
Hall	Dr. James Wm. C.	23 Feb 1844	Nr. Winchester, VA	04 Feb 1909	Keyser	Queen's Meadow Point
Kephart	John Conrad	11 Dec 1858	Leadmine	23 Nov 1931	Keyser	Queen's Meadow Point
Kephart	Elizabeth (Geldbaugh)	19 Nov 1863	Newburg	27 Sep 1947	Keyser	Queen's Meadow Point
Koelz	John G.	06 Oct 1846	Mühlhausen, Germany	09 Feb 1925	Keyser	Queen's Meadow Point
Kolkhorst	Anna (Geldbaugh)	14 Feb 1868	Barrackville	23 Oct 1937	Keyser	Queen's Meadow Point
Lampas	Louis Herman	03 Aug 1839	Germany	09 Jul 1912	Martinsburg.	Philos. Westernport, MD
Mandler	Conrad Thomas	30 Jan 1867	Baltimore, MD	12 Jul 1941	Philadelphia, PA	West Laurel Hill Bala Cynwyd, PA
Martin	Dr. Ephraim T.	Oct 1866	Preston Co.	24 Feb 1938	Seattle, WA	Calvary Seattle, WA
Moffitt	Mrs. F.					
Newhouse	Bettie Lee (Everett)	11 Aug 1876	Milroy	27 Jul 1914	Keyser	Queen's Meadow Point
Pifer	Charles Preston	09 Jan 1870	Edinburg, VA	26 Feb 1947	Martinsburg	Green Hill, Martinsburg
Pifer	Emma Eliz. (Crisman)	20 Aug 1870	Kernstown, VA	09 Mar 1957	Martinsburg	Green Hill Martinsburg
Pifer	William Custis	03 Jul 1878	Stephens City, VA	01 Sep 1961	Keyser	Queen's Meadow Point
Shaffer	Margaret (Geldbaugh)	23 Apr 1870	Newburg	16 Aug 1923	Keyser	Queen's Meadow Point
Shafferman	Virginia (Heetlage)	23 Jan 1850	Nordhorn, Germany	19 Feb 1920	Keyser	Queen's Meadow Point
Sincell	John Thomas	08 Sep 1866	Frederick, MD	19 Mar 1937	Keyser	Oakland Garrett Co., MD
Sincell	Valetta Irene (Brown)	14 Feb 1881	Washington, DC	29 Mar 1961	Mt. Lebanon, PA	Oakland Garrett Co., MD
Sliger	Harry A.	18 Jun 1876	Piedmont	24 Mar 1966	Keyser	Queen's Meadow Point
Sliger	Bertha Caudy (Arnold)	30 Jan 1884	Keyser	25 Nov 1966	Keyser	Queen's Meadow Point
Souder	Benjamin	30 Jun 1853	Bergton, VA	12 Mar 1929	Pendleton Co.	Queen's Meadow Point
Spangler	Parker M.	24 Apr 1863	Westernport, MD	26 Nov 1943	Waynesboro, PA	River View Williamsport, MD
Spangler	Bertha (Bomberger)	11 Jan 1865	Williamsport, MD	29 Aug 1942	Pen Mar, MD	River View Williamsport, MD
Wagoner	Diana (Troutman)	26 Feb 1852	Wellersburg, PA	20 May 1934	Keyser	Queen's Meadow Point
Wolf	Augustus S. "Gus"	04 Apr 1852	Boalsburg, PA	08 May 1921	Keyser	Queen's Meadow Point
Wolf	Christina Jane (Head)	09 May 1861	Cameron	15 Nov 1936	Keyser	Queen's Meadow Point

The average age of the charter members in 1903 was forty-three. Twelve were born in the Shenandoah Valley of Virginia, seven in Preston County, five in Germany, three in Mineral County, four elsewhere in West Virginia, four in Maryland, three in Pennsylvania, and one in the District of Columbia.

A slight majority, twenty-two, were women. Three were sisters: Mrs. Elizabeth (Geldbaugh) Kephart, Mrs. Anna (Geldbaugh) Kolkhorst and Mrs. Margaret (Geldbaugh) Shaffer. Two were daughters of charter members: Mrs. Kate (Avers) Clevenger and Mrs. Bertha (Arnold) Sliger.

Three of the men were veterans of the Civil War in service to the Confederate States of America: Henry Baker, Charles Balthis and James Hall. Mrs. Arnold's husband John also served the CSA. Mrs. Shafferman's husband Frank served in the Union army.

Three were college graduates: Mrs. Ida May Gerstell, Dr. James W. C. Hall and Dr. Ephraim T. Martin.

At the age of sixty-five, Mr. Baker was the oldest to sign the charter; Mrs. Sliger was the youngest, at the age of nineteen; Mrs. Sincell and Mrs. Clevenger were twenty-three.

Mrs. Mary Alice Balthis was the first to die, in October 1905. Mr. Boehmes died in 1906. Mr. Harry Sliger and his wife Bertha Sliger both died in 1966. The death of Mrs. Sliger on November 25, 1966 marked the passing of the last remaining charter member.

At the time of death, the average age was seventy-three. Among the charter members, Mr. Baker lived the longest life, passing to his eternal reward at the age of ninety-five. Of those who later became members, Mrs. Edith (Steiding) Workman (1897–2000) lived an exemplary Christian life of 103 years, 5 months, and 17 days. Mrs. Otie (Davis) Neville (1888–1991) was with us for 103 years and 7 days.

Among the immediate families of the charter signees, Carl Edward Avers, the youngest child of Jacob and Christina Avers, was born on August 15, just one day before the charter was ratified.

No children of the charter members are still alive; scant few of the grandchildren remain.

Mrs. Virginia Arnold

Mrs. Virginia "Jennie" (Young) Arnold was born in Winchester during the early spring of 1845, innocent of the hardships that would soon engulf her birthplace and childhood home. Oh, the events she must have witnessed during the War Between the States, as she would have described it. She was the youngest child of Phillip Young, a tailor, and his wife Julia (Ryan) Young. Phillip and Julia Young are buried in the grave yard of Winchester's historic German Lutheran Church in Mt. Hebron Cemetery.

Her future husband-to-be, John Wesley Arnold, was born in Winchester on August 9, 1843. He was the child of John and Mary Arnold and had at least five siblings. Less than a week after the Confederate artillery fired on the Union garrison at Ft. Sumter and not yet eighteen years old, he enlisted in the Confederate States Army on April 18, 1861. He served in Company A, 5th Infantry Regiment, a unit that participated in the battle of First Manassas in July 1861 as part of the 1st Brigade of Gen. Thomas J. Jackson that distinguished itself to become known as the Stonewall Brigade. During the first six weeks of 1862, the 5th Infantry participated in the Romney Expedition, Jackson's attempt to recapture western Virginia. In May-June of 1862 came Jackson's highly successful Valley Campaign. After the conclusion of the Valley Campaign, the 5th Virginia immediately moved east to assist Gen. Lee during the Seven Days Battles. After seeing action at Malvern Hill, Cedar Mountain, Second Manassas, and the siege at Harper's Ferry, the unit entered the Battle of Antietam in mid-September. On October 11, 1862, while in camp just north of Winchester, Arnold mustered out of the 5th Infantry and mustered-in to the 39th Cavalry, also known as Richardson's Battalion of Scouts, Guides and Couriers. The 39th was Gen. Lee's personal cavalry command. He served throughout the war and was honorably discharged on April 17, 1865.

After the war, Mr. Arnold returned home and followed in his father's footsteps as a butcher. Jennie Young and John Arnold were married in Winchester on November 26, 1868. Their first child, Mary Juliet, was born in Winchester, before the family moved to Piedmont c.1871 to join the economic boom triggered by the B&O railroad, mining and timber industries. As the B&O shifted the center of its operations to Keyser, the family moved here in 1877. Mr. Arnold became the county jailer and remained in that position for more than a decade. In the Census of 1880, two incarcerated men were listed as members of the Arnold 'household', rather strong evidence that the family, father, mother and five children, were living at the Mineral County jail. The family eventually established a household on nearby Sharpless Street and then moved to 33 N. Water Street. When Mr. Arnold left the jailer's position, he returned to the meat-cutting business and became a merchant. Mrs. Arnold and her husband were very active in church activities and the social life of the community. Proud of her southern heritage, Jennie was a charter member of the local McNeill Chapter of the United Daughters of the Confederacy.

John and Jennie Arnold had eight children.

Mary Juliet Arnold (1869–1931) married Andrew Wesley Stanhagen (1866–1943). They raised their family in the Arnold family home on Water Street.

John Luther Arnold (1872–1937) was born in Piedmont, married Janice 'Janie' Peake (1879–1965) and was a B&O locomotive fireman and engineer.

Charles P. B. Arnold (1874–1930) was the first sibling born in Keyser. He was twice married: in 1897 to Mary Stewart (1880–1916), a girl from Claysville, and to Edith Smith in 1919, following the death of his first wife. He worked various jobs on the railroad and operated a restaurant for a time. Charles died in Washington at age 56.

Laura Clayton Virginia Arnold (1876–1882) was only six years of age when she died of the croup.

Stewart Baldwin Arnold (1879-1941) married Marguerite Cockey and lived in Baltimore and Towson for many years, where he worked as a road contractor.

William Thomas Arnold (1881-1932) married Hazel Crabtree (1886-1951). He operated the meat market following his father's death and later was a salesman for the Marietta Chair Company. After her first husband's death, Hazel married Willis Keller.

Bertha Caudy Arnold (1884-1966) married Harry Sliger (1876-1966); both were charter members of Trinity Lutheran. Another article in this series will provide more details on their lives.

The youngest child, Harry Arnold (1887-1904) died a tragic death. While fishing in the Potomac River with his friends, Bill Woods and Charlie Spotts, on August 2, 1904, their frail canoe overturned. His companions were unable to save Harry, who could not swim.

At the age of 73, Mrs. Virginia "Jennie" Arnold died on August 24, 1918, at the home of her daughter, Mrs. A. W. Stanhagen. Her husband preceded her in death on September 15, 1913. Both funeral services were conducted by the pastor of Trinity Lutheran Church, Rev. Harry F. Baughman.

Mr. Jacob Avers & Mrs. Christina Avers

Charter members **Mr. Jacob "Jake" Avers** and his wife **Mrs. Christina (Miller) Avers** were children of German immigrants who came to Preston County in the mid 1850s. Their parents were charter members of Holy Trinity Lutheran Church in Newburg. The history of several previous generations of the Avers family is recorded in the registry of the Evangelical Reformed Church in North Horn, Germany.

The History of West Virginia, Old and New (The American Historical Society, 1923) notes: "John Avers [the father of Jacob Avers] was a farmer in Germany and brought his family to the United States, arriving in very straight forward circumstances financially. After purchasing a cow he had only seven dollars left. At Terra Alta he began with a small parcel of ground and farmed it. Later he moved to Independence, West Virginia, and entered the railroad employ, and after many years of service in the Newburg, West Virginia, shops of the Baltimore and Ohio he retired. He died at the age of eighty eight. He had a large family, and some of his sons became prominent in railroad circles."

Jake was born on April 22, 1858, in Rodemer; Christina was born on September 1, 1861, near Newburg. Both experienced the difficulties of life and endured tragedies among their siblings. One of Jake's brothers, age 17, was killed in a mining accident at Irondale Furnace in 1883; one of Christina's brothers (age 43) and his son (age 15) were among the thirty-nine killed in the Newburg mine disaster of 1886.

Following their 1879 marriage by the local Lutheran minister, Jacob and Christina had eight children, one of whom died shortly after birth. Their first three children were born in Independence; the remaining five were born after the family moved to Keyser c.1885 to establish a household on Spring Street.

Icie, William, Kate, John, George, Clifton, Carl, Christina & Jacob Avers

Their first child, Kate Avers (1880-1939) was also a charter member of Trinity Lutheran. She married Claude Clevenger (1877-1952) in 1902. Another article in this series will provide more details on their lives.

John Avers (1882-1962) was a faithful member of Trinity Lutheran. He married Sallie Borror (1907-1990). They lived on Center Street, opposite the north end of Sharpless Street. Their marriage was childless.

Icie Avers (1884-1947) was a member of the first confirmation class at Trinity. She married Alex Miles (1867-1952), who was born at Bloomery, Hampshire County. They had eight children, only two of whom lived to adulthood.

William Avers (1887-1936), the happy-go-lucky favorite son, died suddenly of a heart attack in the prime of his life. He never married.

George "Dusty" Avers (1891-1951) married Ethel Mae Harmison. He lived in the Avers home at 32 Spring Street until his death. They had one daughter.

Clifton Avers (1899-1979) moved to Illinois during the Great Depression. Twice married, he and his second wife had one son. Clifton Avers died in Granite City, Illinois.

Carl Edward "Chicken" Avers (1903-1975) was born on August 15, 1903, the day before the formal organization of Trinity Lutheran Church. It is likely that he was the first to be baptized at Trinity, but records have not been found to confirm this notion. He began his work at the B&O while still in high school, picking up fire-box tiles, sand and other debris along the tracks in the Keyser yard. Known as an excellent baseball player, he enrolled at Potomac State to become a member of its team. He married Sarah Elizabeth Dennison (1910-1997) in 1937. He worked in the B&O car shops and in 1968 retired from the railroad as a locomotive engineer with fifty years of overall service. Carl was a faithful and active member of the congregation throughout his life. Sarah transferred her church affiliation from Grace M.E. to Trinity and contributed much to the life of the congregation. Their son maintains the presence of grandchildren of charter members as a member of the congregation.

Jacob Avers was elected as a Deacon of Trinity Lutheran upon its formation in 1903. The entire family was engaged in the social, civic and fraternal life of the community, especially those with whom they shared a bond in Trinity Lutheran Church. He was twice elected as Councilman for the Town of Keyser.

Christina Avers died on March 11, 1922, a victim of influenza. *The Baltimore and Ohio Railroad Magazine* reported in its April 1922 issue:

> It is with deepest sympathy that we report the death of another one of our "Baltimore and Ohio Mothers." Mrs. Christine Avers, wife of engineerman Jacob Avers, passed peacefully at her home on Spring Street, on March 11. We refer to her as a "Baltimore and Ohio Mother," and do so because of the sons she gave to our Company and who are now in its employ. She was the mother of John and William, west end engineermen, Clifton and Carl, shopmen, and George, clerk, Master Mechanic's Office. She was also the mother of Mrs. Claude Clevenger and of Mrs. Alex Miles, both of Painesville, whose husbands are loyal employees of our Company. A real Baltimore and Ohio Family.

Jacob Avers was at the old Keyser post office, quite close to the church, on December 22, 1925. He was mailing Christmas packages to his two daughters and his grandchildren in Painesville when he suffered a fatal heart attack.

Mr. Henry W. Baker & Mrs. Jane Baker

Henry William Baker was born near Strasburg, Shenandoah County, Virginia on May 18, 1839. His parents, Lewis and Anna (Dellinger) Baker were members of St. Stephen Lutheran Church, built in 1842 on land donated by Lewis Baker. As a young man of twenty-one, Henry came to Hampshire County, where relatives lived, to learn architecture and the building trade.

While he was building a home for Isaac Carskadon at Headsville, the Civil War broke out. He returned to the Shenandoah Valley and enlisted in Company E, Virginia 17th Virginia Cavalry Battalion on October 24, 1862, a unit that was on the field at Second Manassas and Antietam. On February 5, 1863, that unit was merged with others to form Company E, Virginia 11th Cavalry Regiment. The 11th Cavalry saw service throughout the remainder of the war until the surrender at Appomattox Court House on 9 April 1865.

After the war, he returned home to marry Miss Jane Feely. **Mrs. Jane (Feely) Baker**, born on July 28, 1844 in Shenandoah County, was the child of Alexander and Elva (Kackley) Feely, who were also Lutherans and are buried in Lebanon Lutheran Church Cemetery. The couple moved to Burlington, joining several other members of the extended Baker family who had migrated to that community. In 1873, Henry and Jane moved to Keyser. Mr. Baker became a preeminent architect and builder. He built numerous commercial buildings and homes, many that are still standing today. He designed and built Trinity's first church sanctuary, dedicated in 1906.

Henry and Jane Baker had seven children: Hannah Francis Baker (1873-1876) died of diphtheria before reaching her third birthday and is buried near Burlington in the Peerce Cemetery. Mary Effye Baker (1876-1965), the only child that survived their father, married Harry Welch (1871-1923). John W. Baker (1878-1905) married Gertrude Taylor (Caldwell); he died an accidental death in 1905 during the construction of the Richardson residence on South Mineral Street. Elsye West Baker (1882-1918) married Rev. William Ney, Trinity's first pastor, on June 12, 1907. The marriage was performed by Rev. William A. Wade, pastor of Mt. Calvary Lutheran from 1905-1909.

Mrs. Jane Baker died at their home on Main Street on June 10, 1923.

The newspaper account of Henry's ninety-first birthday illustrates the reach of his family ties in Mineral County: "Henry Baker celebrated his 91st birthday Sunday with a family reunion and an indoor picnic in the home or Dr. and Mrs. F. L. Baker at Burlington. There were nieces and nephews of three generations present. A large three tier birthday cake with ninety-one candles adorned the centre at the table. Mr. Baker was on May 18, 1839 at Strasburg, Va. and came to Keyser in 1874. Those attending the celebration were his daughter, Mrs. Effye Baker Welch; his grandson, Luther Ney; Miss Lena Troutman, Mrs. Rebecca Homan and daughter Jane, of Keyser; … Dr. and Mrs. F. J. Baker, Lucy Baker, David Baker, John Baker and Phillip Baker, Burlington."

When Henry Baker died on June 24, 1934 at age 95, newspapers recounted that he was the town's oldest resident, its oldest Confederate veteran, and Keyser's last remaining soldier of either side who saw active duty during the Civil War. Funeral services were held at Trinity Lutheran Church, Rev. Felix G. Robinson officiating.

Mr. Charles Balthis & Mrs. Mary Alice Balthis

Charles Balthis (sometimes spelled Balthus), the child of Joseph and Rebecca (Grim) Balthis, was born in Loudon County, Virginia, probably in June, 1843. While living in Martinsburg, he enlisted on September 13, 1862 to serve the Confederacy as a member of Company A, 6th Virginia Calvary, a unit known as the Loudoun Dragoons. This unit fought throughout Virginia. At the war's end and their unit severely depleted, most of the remaining cavalrymen escaped through enemy lines. Only three members of the 6th Cavalry surrendered at Appomattox. Charles Balthis returned to Martinsburg and on December 14, 1871, married **Mary Alice (Loman) Balthis.** Her parents were John Loman, a miller, and his wife Sarah Ellen, who lived at Bolivar Heights, near Harpers Ferry, where Mary Alice was born on April 30, 1853.

Their first child, Charles Luther Balthis, was born in Westernport on September 12, 1875. It appears that the family moved to Keyser shortly thereafter, because the B&O car shops, where Charles worked, moved from Piedmont to Keyser in 1874–1875. There is a record of a one-year old daughter who died of meningitis in Keyser on February 26, 1901

Charles and Alice Balthis continued to reside in Keyser, where Charles worked as a car inspector at the B&O Railroad shops. They became charter members of Trinity Memorial Lutheran Church in 1903.

Alice died in Keyser on October 30, 1905. Her obituary noted the following: "Mrs. Alice Balthus, wife of Charles Balthus, died at her home on Main Street Thursday evening after a long illness. Mrs. Balthus was a good, Christian woman and a member of the Lutheran church, loved and admired by all who knew her. She was a loving and devoted wife and mother. Besides her sorrowing husband, she leaves one son, one granddaughter, a number of relatives and a host of friends to mourn her. The remains of Mrs. Balthus will be taken to her former home at Harper's Ferry for burial Saturday morning on train No. 2."

In late January, 1906, Mr. Balthis was painfully injured in an accident while working as car foreman in the Keyser yards. He was taken to the Hoffman hospital, where he remained for more than two months. He sold off his household goods, retired in July 1907, and left Keyser. On January 26, 1909, near Charles Town, Charles W. Balthis died at the home of George W. Marlow, a dear friend and fellow veteran of Company A, Virginia 6th Cavalry. Charles and Mary Alice Balthis' remains were interred at the Fairview Lutheran Cemetery, Bolivar, where her parents were also buried.

Their son Luther lived in Hagerstown, where he was visited by his mother on several occasions. Twice married and estranged from both, Luther died on June 17, 1938, in Scranton, Pennsylvania.

Mr. F. W. Boehmes & Mrs. Louisa Boehmes

This harrowing report was published on page 1 of *The Cumberland Daily Times* on June 22, 1888:

BLOWN INTO ETERNITY – Another Baltimore and Ohio Engine Explodes, this Time at Keyser

Another tale of horror comes from the Baltimore and Ohio railroad near here. Another of those terrible boiler explosions has hurled one more brave man into eternity and dangerously wounded others. Is there no explanation known to science, no remedy to mechanical skills?

At 6 o'clock this morning Capt. John McNabb, accompanied by his next neighbor Wm. Boehmes, fireman, and Joe Bell, engineer, left his family. At 6:35 he was brought home severely wounded and Boehmes lay writhing in agony next door and poor Joe had been hurried across the great divide.

How did it happen? Ah, that's it. Was the engine unsafe, the company to blame, or did Bell neglect some fundamental duty? The Times' bulletin quickly announced the sad occurrence and a reporter was sent to the scene of the catastrophe. He was accompanied by James McNabb, watchman at the Baltimore and Ohio rolling mill gate, a brother of the wounded conductor. There was nothing, save a few splinters and a split rail or two, to indicate the scene of the explosion.

Hurrying to the bedside of the wounded men the Times man found Capt. McNabb propped up with pillows at his home. A man of grand physique he yet suffered terribly from scalds and cuts in the head, a severely cut and possibly broken left shoulder and some very painful injuries in the right side and back. While in great pain, Mr. McNabb will recover. He is a native of Winchester, Va., was born in June 1849, has worked for the road for 25 years in various capacities, is now and has been for the past 8 years, conductor of the yard engine on which he was so nearly killed this morning. He is married, and has two children.

The Conductor's Story – In talking to the reporter, he said: "I was on the front of the engine. We had just come out of the siding with two loaded cars for the west way freight. I don't remember anything further until I was found sitting on the north track some distance from the engine. I thought I was in Piedmont. Yes, I suffer very much, but will soon be alright. Something hit me from behind. I don't know what or how."

The Fireman – Next door lay poor Boehmes scalded from head to foot, his head cut and terribly bruised; he was in terrible agony. The steam had scalded him internally and he could scarcely speak above a whisper. There he lay, matted in oiled cloths and much disfigured. The flesh comes off his legs at the touch. He may recover but is not likely. He said he had just put in coal and had his left hand on the furnace door when the explosion occurred and the hot water and steam went all over him. He is 46 years old, married and has 7 children living; recently he lost a pair of twins. He came to Martinsburg from Germany 19 years ago. He has been at Keyser for 7 years.

The Engineer – Joseph Bell was 42 years old. He had been a railroad man all his life. He leaves a wife and five children. He had been in many wrecks, and was blown up in the Rowlesburg explosion. He will be buried at Westernport on Sunday. Joe Bell was a very good fellow, a skilled engineer and very popular, and was well known in Cumberland.

An Eye Witness Account – An eye witness says he "was on top a car not over 70 yards away. The old camel back No. 122 had just passed me. Boehmes was on the foot board of the tender with one hand on the braces. Bell had 'shut off' and was leaning out of the cab window. I did not notice McNabb. The explosion was terrible. The cab was blown into a million pieces. I saw what seemed a black ball shoot up with the steam. It went 50 or 60 feet in the air and as it descended it took the shape of a man – it was poor Joe. Boehmes was blown from the tender. He was crying with pain, giving a shriek he started for his home, running like mad."

McNabb was found sitting on the wide track 60 feet from the engine. Bell's body fell 100 feet from the engine. He gasped twice and was dead. The engine was on the north track and was backing east, it was 100 yards west of the station when it exploded. It did not leave the track but drifted up to the station.

The wrecked engine was an eight-wheel "camel-back" No. 122, and was used only for yard service. It had been in use for about ten years at Keyser. The outer boiler sheet gave way directly under the engineer. This liberated the flues from the fire-box and they turned out like a peacock's tail, remaining fast under the dome. The outer sheet curled up and was blown clear off the engine. The truck was uninjured. As the flues gave way the fire-box dropped, and stopped the engine, after it had run some 150 yards.

Agent Woodward said he was at breakfast and it was 6:30 o'clock: the explosion was terrific. "I thought that lighting had struck the house. The windows and glass rattled and the building shook. Bell was a good man and competent engineer." The track was quickly cleared and the engine taken into the Keyser round house.

Eighteen years later, on September 20, 1906, the *Cumberland Alleganian* newspaper published the closing chapter of this sorrowful story:

Keyser, W. Va., Sept. 14 – A very sad accident which resulted in death occurred in the Keyser yards this morning. Mr. William Boehmes, an old citizen, who for a number of years, resided on St. Cloud street, was struck by one of the large engines while walking along the track, Nearly two years ago Mr. Boehmes was compelled to give up work on account of trouble with his eyes. His body was very much cut up and bruised by the engine and he died on the way to the Hoffman hospital. He leaves a wife, four sons, three daughters besides other near relatives and number of friends. Mr. Boehmes was born in Germany and was 64 years of age.

Keyser, W. Va. – The funeral services of Mr. F. W. Boehmes were conducted at his late home on B street Sunday afternoon at two o'clock by Rev. W. C. Ney, pastor of the Lutheran church, assisted by Rev. Dr. A. M. Cackley, pastor of the Southern Methodist church, after which the body was laid to rest in the Queen's Point cemetery.

Mr. Boehmes was an old railroad man and for some time has been on the retired list. He was injured on June 22, 1888, when an engine blew up in the Keyser yard. At that time he was a fireman on the engine No. 122. Since then his eye sight has been very bad.

Frederick William Boehmes, a Deacon of the congregation, was the second charter member of Trinity Memorial Lutheran church to pass from this life. His wife, **Louisa (Kimmerling) Boehmes**, also a charter member of Trinity, followed him to the grave on January 23, 1917.

Both were born in Germany, probably in the Coburg-Gotha region, but they first met in Martinsburg. Frederick was born in February 1842; Louisa was born in June of that same year. It appears she came to America with her parents, Anton and Christine Kimmerling, who lived on a farm in Morgan County, near Martinsburg.

Miss Anna Carl

Miss Anna Carl was among the forty who signed the Charter of August 16, 1903. Miss Carl was born on September 16, 1866, in Plainfield, Pennsylvania. He parents were Henry Carl and Sarah Ann Watson. She joined her first cousins of the Watson family when they came to Mineral County.

James Calvin Watson (1856-1932) came to the area from Central Pennsylvania in June, 1887, just a year after marrying Naomi Katherine Trout (1860-1945), to develop a timber and sawmill business on the North Branch of the Potomac at Barnum, a few miles up-river from Piedmont. With them came his sisters, Martha and Ella, and Miss Anna Carl, their first cousin. Subsequently, Mr. Watson and Mike Masteller, who married Miss Ella, went into partnership to build a highly successful coal mining company along the upper Potomac River. Mr. George Loy later joined them as Secretary of the Masteller Coal Company; his father, William H. Loy, was associated with Mr. Watson from the very beginning of his business ventures here; early on, the company was known as the Watson-Loy Coal Company.

Miss Carl moved from Barnum to Keyser with the Watson family in 1903. In Keyser, she was active in social and church activities, especially the Ladies' Aid Society, until she fell ill in 1909. After an extended stay in the Hoffman hospital, she was moved to Pittsburgh, where she passed away at the relatively young age of forty-three on June 10, 1910.

Mr. Watson's sister, Miss Martha Ziegler Watson (1859-1946), who came to Barnum with her brother in 1887, was a deeply loyal member of St. Matthew Evangelical Lutheran Church in Plainfield. Miss Martha Watson and Miss Anna Carl were leaders among a small group who organized the Ladies' Aid Society on March 5, 1903, to promote the idea of a Lutheran Church in Keyser. Although she was not a charter member, Miss Watson did transfer her membership to Trinity during the early days. She spent considerable time in Fredericksburg with the Mastellers and at Maplewood, the Watson family summer home at Claysville. In 1921, she moved back to Pennsylvania to live with her sister Ella and Mike Masteller on their "Ellen Dale Farm" and transferred her church membership back to Plainfield at that time. After Mr. Masteller's death in early 1930, the sisters returned to Keyser. With Mrs. Bertha Spangler, Miss Watson co-authored the 1936 brief history of Trinity Lutheran. Miss Martha Watson died in 1946. Her obituary suggests that she had chosen to retain her church membership in Plainfield, where her remains were interred in the Lutheran cemetery. Nevertheless, she was always very involved in the congregational life of Trinity Lutheran.

James Calvin Watson and his wife Naomi were committed members of the Reformed Mennonite faith. Nevertheless, their acts of kindness and support for Trinity Lutheran abound.

They had only one child, Martin Loy Watson (1894-1951), who was Confirmed in the Lutheran faith at Trinity Lutheran on March 28, 1920.

Martin Loy Watson married Tabitha Thompson (1897-1961) and followed his father's footsteps at Masteller. Tabitha's father was the president and operator of the Thompson Furniture Company. Tabitha was accessioned to membership of Trinity by Letter of Transfer on April 16, 1922. They had two sons and three daughters: Naomi Harriett, James Thompson, Martin Taylor, Susanna Katherine, and Martha Ellen.

Naomi Harriett Watson (1921-2007) and Richard Bruce Dellinger (1912-1982) were married in 1948 by Rev. C. K. Spiggle. They maintained enduring relationships with Trinity Lutheran and Mt. Calvary Lutheran, Westernport.

James Thompson Watson (1925-2009) married Wanda Tasker (1921-1988) and followed his father and grandfather as the owner and operator of the coal company. Jim and Wanda were deeply devoted to Trinity Lutheran Church. Their son, J. T. Watson, who served as an Army pilot in Vietnam, was only 24 years old when he was tragically killed in the crash of an airplane he was piloting near Spruce Knob. Their daughter, Mrs. Melinda Chaney, is still an active and highly supportive member of the congregation.

Martin Taylor Watson (1926-2001) married Beverly Bowne (1924-2011), a music instructor at Potomac State College, in 1952. They lived in Texas and Michigan, returned to Keyser in the late 1970's and reestablished strong bonds with Trinity Lutheran. They had three children.

Susanna Katherine Watson (b.1928) and Charles Leonard Coffman (1925-2011) were also married by Rev. Spiggle. They had four children. Dr. Coffman was a highly regarded public school administrator.

Martha Ellen Watson (b.1931) and George Hampton Harris (b.1929) were married by Rev. Donald D. Anderson in 1953.

There is another bit of local Lutheran history that has a likely connection to Miss Carl and the Watsons – a short-lived Lutheran congregation in, of all places, Barnum.

In the *Centennial History of the Evangelical Lutheran Church of Maryland 1820-1920*, Rev. Prof. Abdel Ross Wentz wrote: "in a nearby mining village, Barnum, West Virginia, a small congregation was formed and a frame church built. This congregation has since been disbanded due to changes in population and mine ownership."

In 1991, B. B. Mauer and Mary Miller Strauss wrote about the Barnum church in their wonderfully useful book *Lutherans on the Mountaintop – in West Virginia and Western Maryland*:

HARMONY CHAPEL (Union)

Barnum, West Virginia

1901—1904

The minutes of the July 5, 1901 meeting of the Church Council of Mt. Calvary Evangelical Lutheran Church, Westernport, Maryland record the granting of permission to Pastor Luther F. Miller to be absent from his pulpit January 20, 1901, in order to participate in the opening services of a new congregation at Barnum, West Virginia. At the following meeting February 2, 1901, Pastor Miller was granted permission to conduct services at Barnum on the fourth Sunday evening of each month.

Barnum was a coal mining town on the West Virginia Central and Pittsburgh Railroad of Henry Gassaway Davis, about four miles up the North Branch of the Potomac River from Piedmont, in Mineral County, West Virginia.

On September 17, 1902, the new Barnum Harmony Chapel costing $1,000 was dedicated debt-free. The Chapel was built for the use of a union of Lutheran and Methodist Episcopal South congregations.

There is no record of any formal relationship between Mt. Calvary, Westernport and the Harmony Chapel congregation at Barnum. Pastor Miller terminated his service at Mt. Calvary July 10, 1904, and Harmony Chapel faded from the records. The site of the church has been located and the building is no longer in existence.

Mr. James M. Clem & Mrs. Catherine Isabelle Clem

James Monroe Clem, the son of Solomon Clem and Sarah (Hall) Clem, was born in Shenandoah County, Virginia, on March 19, 1859. The Clem home at Maurertown was known for many years as "The Brick House", one of the few brick residences remaining on that section of the Valley Pike after Sheridan's ruthless campaign of 1864. His father served in the same unit as Trinity member John Arnold, the Virginia 5th Infantry Regiment. Records show that the Clem family was affiliated with the St. Peter's Lutheran congregation of Toms Brook, Virginia.

His wife, **Catherine Isabelle (Wiles) Clem** was born in Preston County on March 17, 1858. Her parents David and Eliza (Wotring) Wiles lived at Lantz Ridge, about halfway between Aurora and Rowlesburg, where the family worshipped at Mt. Olivet Lutheran.

In 1880, James Clem, a skilled carpenter, was working in Preston Co., single, and renting a room in the household of David and Eliza Wiles. A year later, he and Catherine were married in a ceremony performed at the Wiles home by the minister of St. Paul's Lutheran of Aurora. Incidentally, St. Paul's, once among many, is now the only remaining Lutheran congregation in Preston County.

The family moved from Preston County to Piedmont c.1887 and to Keyser shortly thereafter. It seems the family attended the Grace M. E. South church until the formation of Trinity Lutheran in 1903. It was during that period, in 1893, that Mr. Clem, Dr. C. E. Hoffman and J. H. Markwood observed a modern water system while attending a church conference in Front Royal. Shortly thereafter, a devastating fire destroyed the store operated by J. C. Kephart in the old Carskadon building on Main Street. The lack of sufficient water was responsible for huge losses. In addition, the death rate from typhoid fever had been rising steadily. Romig and Hoffman invited the designer of the Front Royal system to come to Keyser. Mr. Clem guided the expert all over the area for several days, and a site on Limestone Run was selected for what became Keyser's first reservoir in 1894. A larger reservoir was completed in 1911, just behind the 1894 structure – coexisting for many decades thereafter and known as the 'upper' and 'lower' dams.

Mr. and Mrs. Clem had nine children, the first three of whom were born in Preston County: Jesse Clay Clem (1882-1942) married Barbara Bane (1879-1963) and lived in Keyser; David Solomon Clem (1884-1959) married Sarah Maberry (1882-1967) and lived in Schuylkill Haven, Pa.; Milo Henry Clem (1886-1967) first married Pearl Reed (1887-1913). After her death, he married Mary Reed (1890-1982) and lived in Wiley Ford and Cumberland, where he was a yard foreman for the B&O.

Sadie Ellen Clem (1888-1888) was the first child to be born in Mineral County. Omer Melville Clem (1890-1955) married Mary Lee Bland. He was a machinist by trade and reached the rank of M. Sgt. during a long career in the U.S. Army, AAF and USAF that spanned World Wars I and II. His body rests in the Hampton National Cemetery. Frank Hall Clem (1891-1986) married Ruth Snyder (Menefee), lived in Morgantown and followed in his father's footsteps as a carpenter. Alvan B. Clem (1893-1924), married Maude Crabtree and became a B&O car repairman in Cumberland. Robert Dewey Clem (1898-1974) married Pearl Mae Michaels (1897-1965). They were the parents of long-time Keyser chief of police, Guy Clem. Ada Elizabeth Clem (1899-1986) married Albert Morris and lived in Keyser.

James M. Clem died in Keyser on May 9, 1927 as a result of a cerebral hemorrhage. Catherine died of influenza on May 5, 1931. Both funerals were conducted by Rev. Robert T. Vorberg, Trinity's pastor from April 1926 until his death on July 8, 1933.

Mrs. Mary Katherine Clevenger

Mrs. Mary Katherine "Kate" (Avers) Clevenger was the eldest child of charter members Jacob and Christina Avers. She was born on February 25, 1880, in Independence, Preston County. The Avers family moved to Keyser in the mid-1880s and lived at 32 Spring Street.

She married Claude Cinclare Clevenger in 1902. Born in Winchester to William Hardesty Clevenger and Mary Virginia "Mollie" (Merryman) Clevenger, his entire family came to Keyser in 1882, about the same time as the Avers family, with whom they shared deep friendships. Claude had five siblings.

Mr. Clevenger's eldest sister, Catherine Leone (Clevenger) Wolfe (1871-1949), married Charles Clinton Wolfe (1871-1901). They were the parents of William Wayne Wolfe (1900-1979), a cherished son of Trinity Lutheran. Ernest Merryman Clevenger (1873-1950) married Miss Maggie Siever (1872-1961). Lena Bell "Nellie" Clevenger (1874-1874) died of typhoid fever, as did her father, just a few days before his death. Jared Thomas Clevenger (1879-1939) married Miss Grace Halbritter (1879-1939). Esther Pearl Clevenger (1886-1945) married Willis Keller (1883-1951).

Claude Clevenger worked as a carpenter and for the railroad before purchasing the general store at the corner of Spring and W. Piedmont streets in April, 1909. Kate was a very talented musician. They were socially and culturally involved in the community and deeply committed to Trinity Lutheran.

COURTESY OF KAY LUCAS

Kate and Claude Clevenger had five children, all of whom were born in Keyser: Christine Virginia Clevenger (1904-1943) married Col. Donn R. Austin, USAF (1902-1954); Catherine Clevenger (1906-1982) married Bernard M. Toan (1903-1960); Alice Elizabeth "Bea" Clevenger married Waldmar M. Ruetenik (1888-1970); Claudia Clare Clevenger (1912-1980) married Col. Paul Lord, USA (1910-1986); Carl Courtney Clevenger (1916-1931), dearly adored as their first male child, died of a mastoid infection at age fifteen.

Claude left the mercantile business in early 1917 to work briefly for the Western Maryland Railway in Cumberland. Within a few months, the family moved to Painesville, Ohio, where Claude worked as a general car foreman for the B&O railroad until his retirement. As an aside, the general store was taken over by the twin brothers John and James Rogers, natives of Antioch. John Dye Rogers died in 1941; his brother, James Sanford Rogers, continued to operate the store until his death in 1955.

Mrs. Clevenger's sister, Icie (Avers) Miles (1884–1947), wife of Alexander Miles (1867–1952), migrated to Painesville in 1916, where Mr. Miles worked for the B&O. He was born in Bloomery, Hampshire County, and was the son of John Loy Miles and Elizabeth Jane Powell. Icie and Alec had seven children. Only two lived to adulthood: Mildred (1908–1975), who married Walter Frederick Suess, and Betty Jane (1922–2009), who married Edward Michael Safick.

In Painesville, Claude Clevenger and Alex Miles both worked for Harry Geldbaugh, General Car Foreman, another young man from Keyser, who was the brother of Trinity Lutheran charter members Elizabeth (Geldbaugh) Kephart, Anna (Geldbaugh) Kolkhorst, and Margaret (Geldbaugh) Shaffer.

Kate (Avers) Clevenger suffered a stroke in 1926. Despite her affliction, illnesses and tragic death of their son Carl Courtney Clevenger at age fifteen in 1931, she struggled on until her death on August 13, 1938. Claude Cinclare Clevenger died on March 8, 1952, in Painesville.

Mrs. Ida May Gerstell

A native of Shepherdstown and graduate of Shepherd College, charter member **Ida May (Fleming) Gerstell,** born May 1, 1859, was a child of Joseph Shindler Fleming (1829-1911) and Catherine (Hawn) Fleming (1831-1910). Following her 1877 graduation at Shepherd, Miss Fleming came to Mineral County to teach in the small rural schools at Ridgeville, Headsville, and Waxler. It is likely she met her future husband while teaching at Waxler.

To discover her Lutheran ties, one has to go back in time. Her mother was baptized in the Old Reformed German church in Frederick, Maryland, where Reverends Heinrich Melchior Muhlenberg and Michael Schlatter, the organizers respectively of the Lutheran and German Reformed churches in America, preached in 1746-1747.

Eugene Harold Gerstell (1854-1948) was the son of Dr. Arnold Frederick Gerstell, MD (1818-1896) and Hannah Cresap (1820-1910).

Arnold Frederick Gerstell, the son of a physician, was born in Germany. Young Arnold trained at the University of Göttingen and came to America in 1842. He practiced medicine in Lonaconing for several years. He then relocated his practice to Piedmont and also took on the responsibilities of surgeon for the Baltimore and Ohio Railroad division between Cumberland and Grafton. In 1870, he moved his practice to Keyser. He retired in 1885 due to failing eyesight. He remained a valued consultant for the leading physicians in the area. His wife, Mrs. Hannah (Cresap) Gerstell, was a descendent of the very earliest settlers of Western Maryland. Two of Dr. and Mrs. Gerstell's children, Robert and Richard, also became medical practitioners; their son Arnold, Jr. became president of Alpha Portland Cement Co.

Their son Eugene Harold Gerstell, born in Westernport, married schoolmarm Ida May Fleming in 1885. They were married in Shepherdstown by the Rev. D. M. Moser, pastor of St. Peter's Lutheran, West Virginia's oldest Lutheran church, founded in 1765. Ida May and Eugene Gerstell lived on and operated the large and productive Gerstell farm, bounded to the west by the Potomac River, to the east on Knobley Mountain, and bisected by the now abandoned Western Maryland Railway tracks. The Gerstell heirs deeded ground on the mountainside at the intersection of Gerstell and Waxler roads where Fairview Chapel Methodist Church was built in 1925. John Barger, editor of the *Mineral Daily News-Tribune* told a Gerstell-related story in his daily must-read "Colyum" of July 27, 1955:

> Miss Hannah Gerstell [daughter of Eugene and Ida May] had a narrow escape the other day when she was almost run down by a Western Maryland Railway locomotive while crossing the Western Maryland bridge over the Potomac from Dawson. Miss Hannah was walking to her home at Gerstell from McMullen Highway, and while crossing the railroad bridge she suddenly heard the locomotive behind her. She started running and finally reached the end of the bridge where she stumbled and toppled over a bank. The train crew stopped the locomotive and offered to take her to Cumberland for examination by a physician. But Miss Hannah said

she was only slightly bruised and shaken. So the crew put her on the train and took her the rest of the way to Gerstell station, from where she walked home.

The Gerstell farm eventually came into the hands of the Mineral County Commission and was leased to Potomac State College for many years. The college purchased the property in 1991. The farm was recently reacquired by a Gerstell descendant, J. Duncan Smith, a major benefactor of Potomac State College.

Ida May and Eugene Gerstell had three children: a son and two daughters.

Joseph E. Gerstell (1886-1944) married Miss Myrtle E. Masteller (1896-1950) in 1918. He was a machinist at the paper mill.

Hannah Katherine Gerstell (1888-1979), like her mother, was a public school teacher earlier in her life. Miss Gerstell, who never married, remained a member of Trinity Lutheran. Miss Hannah Gerstell died at Hopemont State Hospital at age 90. Her funeral was conducted by Rev. Donald W. Moore.

Her sister, Elsie May Gerstell (1891-1978), married Rev. Edgar Harrison Showacre (1884-1949), a Methodist minister.

COURTESY OF GERSTELL FAMILY

Mrs. Ida May Gerstell died on April 24, 1950. Her grave is aside that of her husband in the family cemetery on the Gerstell farm. Funeral services were conducted by Rev. Louis E. Bouknight, pastor of Trinity Lutheran Church.

Mrs. Nancy Emma Gull

Mrs. Nancy Emma "Nannie" Gull, daughter of Isaac T. Poling and Amelia (Shirley) Poling, was born in Mineral County on April 16, 1873. In 1900, she married Harry George Gull, who was born at Newburg on March 7, 1874. Harry's parents, George Gull and Elizabeth (Brown) Gull brought their family to Keyser from Preston County. George Gull had served in the Union army for three years as a Private, Company D, West Virginia 3rd Infantry Brigade. He was wounded at the Battle of McDowell on May 8, 1862, while his unit was assigned to Gen. Milroy's brigade. When Milroy's forces were defeated at McDowell and retreated toward Franklin, they were pursued up the valley by a confederate cavalry unit led by Capt. George Sheetz, who was a resident of New Creek Station (Keyser) before the war.

While Harry was growing up, his mother cooked for Col. Thomas B. Davis at his mansion, originally built in the 1850s by William McCarty Armstrong at the most prominent location in the town, on the site now occupied by the old Keyser High School building. Still a teenager, Harry began working for Col. Davis as a horse trainer. William W. Wolfe, a son of Trinity Lutheran, recorded in his 1974 book, *History of Keyser, West Virginia 1737-1913*:

> Col. Thomas B. Davis made Keyser his home and lived in the Armstrong mansion until his death in 1911. He was the son of Caleb and Louisa (Brown) Davis of Baltimore. He and his brothers [Henry Gassaway Davis and William Davis] were early developers of Piedmont. The colonel was a banker, coal and lumber magnate, railroad developer, race horse owner and millionaire." Mr. Wolfe also wrote: "[Col. Davis] had been very ill for some time. A few days before his death, he said to his attendant, Mr. Harry Gull, "Harry, are you going to the funeral?" Harry asked, "Whose funeral, Colonel?" "My funeral, Harry, my funeral, damn it!" "Colonel, let's not talk about that." "Don't you go to it, Harry. You stay here and watch the house to see that no one steals anything."

When Col. Davis died, Harry went to work as a car painter, and ultimately as a foreman, for the B&O Railroad. Mr. Gull passed away on December 7, 1931. Mrs. Gull was dedicated to raising her family and to Trinity Lutheran. She and Harry were blessed with three children.

Elsie Elizabeth Gull (1900–1975) married Emmett Kolkhorst (1898–1957) in 1918. Prior to her marriage she was an "accommodating and popular" telephone operator for the Chesapeake and Potomac Telephone Company. Their only child, Emmett, Jr. (1919–1998), was a World War II veteran and long-time Baltimore County police officer.

Elizabeth Davis Gull (1907–1985) married Reuben Stoutamyer (1892–1965) in 1928. She was employed as a floor lady for the G. C. Murphy Company. Their only child, Harry (1934–2008), worked for the United States civil service in the Washington area.

Louise Amelia Gull (1911–1985) married Roy Leatherman. Mrs. Leatherman worked at the People's drugstore as a bookkeeper and at the Kessel News Agency, located in the space previously occupied as pharmacies operated by Dr. J. W. Hall, Dr. H. C. Grusendorf and Dr. Harry Kight.

Mrs. Nannie Gull and daughter Elsie

Mrs. Gull was present for the celebration of Trinity Lutheran's 50th Anniversary. She is standing between Rev. and Mrs. Anderson and Rev. Ney in this old photograph. In the back are Mrs. Bertha Sliger, W. C. Pifer and Harry Sliger, the other charter members who were present on that memorable day. Mrs. Nannie Gull died on December 1, 1953 – three months after the anniversary celebration.

Mrs. Gull and her three daughters were exceptionally active members of the congregation throughout their lives, serving the congregation in many, many ways.

Dr. James W. C. Hall

James William Clay Hall was born near Winchester on March 23, 1844. He was a son of Col. James B. Hall, a wealthy land owner in Frederick County, and Mrs. Margaret (Rosenberger) Hall. It was reported at the time of his death that he was a direct descendent of Lyman Hall, one of three Georgians to sign the Declaration of Independence, who served as a representative to the Continental Congress and was governor of Georgia (1783-1784).

Dr. Hall enrolled as a student at Roanoke College in 1859, but left to join in the Civil War. He served in the Virginia 33rd Infantry Regiment, CSA. Fighting in the front lines of many engagements, he was twice wounded. After the war, he resumed his studies at the University of Virginia and then at Bellevue Medical College, where he received his medical degree in 1869. He returned to Winchester to open a medical practice. In 1872, he married Elizabeth Clara "Lizzie" Ewing of Berkeley Springs, the daughter of Dr. J. W. Ewing, a celebrated Methodist minister. Not long thereafter, the couple came to Keyser.

Dr. Hall practiced medicine and surgery for a while, but his primary focus soon turned to pharmacy. He operated the Keyser Pharmacy for nearly thirty years. It was located at the northwest corner of Main and Center streets, in the storefront directly below Johnson's hall, where Trinity Lutheran held its services for three years. Dr. Hall sold his business to Dr. E. V. Romig in 1903. Rather than renting this space, Dr. Romig chose to locate his drugstore about a half-block north, near the Reynolds (Corwin) Hotel, on the same side of Main Street. Dr. Henry Grusendorf then opened a drugstore in the space previously occupied by Dr. Hall. Years later, Dr. Harry Kight operated a Walgreen pharmacy in this space. Eventually, Dr. Kight built a larger store a half-block south. After Dr. Kight's death in 1952, the larger store was purchased by Dr. E. V. Romig and his son, Dr. Richard Romig. Quite a circle of history, and confusion!

Dr. and Mrs. Hall had eight children. James Ewing Hall (1876-1912), who had been breaking on the 3rd Division of the B&O railroad only two months, met with an accident that caused his death on September 10, 1912. He was flagman on a freight train, and after coupling a car at Newburg, stepped back, and passenger train No. 4 struck him. He was hurried to the hospital at Grafton, where he died that night. Hallie Hall (1877-1931) married D. T. Greenwade, Jr. in 1901. After his death in 1909, she and their son Bruce moved to Montana and then to Oakland, California, where she died. Frederick Hall (1879-1944) moved to Montana, married, and became president of a bank. Bennett Clay Hall (1880-1933) worked for the B&O Railroad in Newark, Ohio. Emily Hall (1883-1936) earned an AB degree from West Virginia University and taught school until her marriage to Joseph Helm. She was active in the Woman's Club, the DAR, and the United Daughters of the Confederacy. She died in Clarksburg. John Wotring Hall (1886-1965) was a civil engineering graduate of West Virginia University and practiced engineering in Montana. Bee Barto Hall (1887-1964) lived in Ohio, Montana and Oakland, California; he was employed as a bookkeeper and bank teller. Franklin Ewing Hall (1893-1942) lived in New Jersey and worked for the NJ Central Railway.

Dr. James William Clay Hall, one of the original church Elders of 1903, died on February 4, 1909. The funeral was officiated by Rev. C. P. Bastian, pastor of Trinity Lutheran Church. His wife Clara died in November 1916. Both are buried in the central circle of Queen's Meadow Point Cemetery.

Dr. Hall's sister, Sarah Hall, was the wife of Solomon Clem. They were the parents of James Monroe Clem, also a charter member of Trinity Lutheran Church.

The Hall family lived in a beautiful home on Main Street, adjacent to the old Presbyterian Church that can be seen on the left side of the photograph. Some years after the Halls were gone, the house fell into disrepair and was removed. Newt Carskadon erected the New Keyser Theatre here. It was a modern marvel for its day, including a geothermal air conditioning system – in 1939!

Mr. John C. Kephart & Mrs. Elizabeth Kephart

The *Mineral Daily News* edition of June 22, 1931, provided a worthy encapsulation of the lives of **John Conrad Kephart** and his wife Elizabeth **(Geldbaugh) Kephart**:

> On June 23, 1881, fifty years ago tomorrow, the Reverend Mr. Shipman united J. C. Kephart and Miss Elizabeth Geldbaugh in the bonds of Holy Matrimony in Newburg. [Rev. Shipman was the pastor of Newburg's Holy Trinity Lutheran Church.] It was a happy young couple that started out to face life together, willing to share each others joys and sorrows alike.
>
> Both of the young people were from Newburg, but the young groom was faced with the desire to do something big for his bride. They moved to Keyser shortly after the wedding and set up house keeping on Spring Street. The Baltimore and Ohio being the biggest industry in Keyser, the young man went in search of work there and found it as a fireman.
>
> After a few years of firing he became an engineer. But railroad life palled on him and he decided to go into business for himself. Accordingly, the old Carskadon building on Main Street had a new tenant. J. C. Kephart had started in the general merchandise business.
>
> That was in 1892. One year later [the night of April 20, 1893] a fire burned Mr. Kephart out of business. He lost almost all he owned. Nevertheless, he decided to start out on his own again. This time he purchased some land on Limestone and started into the fruit business.
>
> Ever since that day he has been in the fruit business. Today it is known as J. C. Kephart and Sons.

COURTESY OF KEPHART FAMILY

> Today Mr. and Mrs. Kephart are living on Spring Street. They are making plans for the celebration of their Golden Wedding at Van Myra Camp grounds tomorrow.
>
> To celebrate with them will be six children with their husbands, wives and children. There were seven but the eldest, a boy, died at the age of six. The children are Raymond A., Luther A.,

Walter G., Mrs. Franklin Lark, Mrs. Kimmill Purgitt, all of Keyser, and Mrs. Roy Markley, of Columbus, Ohio. There are twelve grandchildren, nine boys and three girls.

According to official Tucker County birth records, John Conrad Kephart, child of Joseph and Gese Kephart, was born at Leadmine on December 11, 1858. This date is at variance with the date of November 17, 1859 that was recorded when he died. His mother Gese "Tracey" Hüseman (often recorded in America as "Hieselmann") was born on December 23, 1813 in Bakelde-Nordhorn, Germany, immediately adjacent to the Dutch border. Mr. Kephart's mother had first married Lambert Heetlage in 1845 and had three children. Two of the children were born before the family came to America in 1851, including Mrs. Virginia "Jennie" (Heetlage) Shafferman, a charter member of Trinity Lutheran. Following the death of her first husband, Mrs. Heetlage married Joseph Kephart, a native of Holland. Their child John Conrad Kephart was left fatherless at a very early age when Joseph Kephart passed away on October 1, 1861, after which the family, the twice-widowed mother and four children, moved to nearby Preston County.

Elizabeth (Geldbaugh) Kephart was born in Newburg on November 19, 1863. She was the first of eight children born to Jacob Geldbaugh, an immigrant from Darmstadt, and Christina Nightingale, an immigrant from Alotshouser-Hessia. Two of her sisters, Mrs. Anna Kolkhorst and Mrs. Margaret Shaffer, were also charter members of Trinity Lutheran in Keyser. Two Geldbaugh brothers also became active members of the congregation.

John Conrad and Elizabeth Kephart had seven children.

Their firstborn, Harry, died as a young child in 1887.

Their son Raymond Alton Kephart (1886-1951) wed a Tucker County girl, Donna Maude Shrader (1892-1967); they had four children: Romaine, Gail Keith, Norman and Beverly.

Luther Aaron Kephart (1889-1973) married Louise Haines (1895-1990); they had two children: Luther Neil and Melba.

Walter George Kephart (1892-1981) married Mary Georgiana McGee (1901-1987); they had four children: Walter Galen, Mary Elizabeth, Frederick and Harold John Conrad.

Eva Esther Christine Kephart (1894-1940) married Franklin Lark (1897-1977) and they had one son, Franklin.

Ruth M. E. Kephart (1899-1985) married Roy Markley (1900-1978); they had one son, Donald.

Lena Margaret Naomi Kephart (1902-1982) married Kimmel Purgitt (1904-1968).

Following the 50th anniversary, the same newspaper summarized the festivities:

Mr. and Mrs. J. C. Kephart celebrated their golden wedding with an all day outing at the Van Myra campgrounds, Tuesday, June 23. Forty-three relatives and friends were present at the happy occasion.

The morning hours were spent in games and other activities. At one o'clock the guests were called to one of the cottages where a large table was laden with good things to eat. In the center of the table was a large bridal bouquet of rambler roses, gold and white honeysuckles and white Madonna lilies, which had been gathered out of the flower gardens at the home place on Limestone.

Mr. Ray Kephart acted as toastmaster and called on the different folks to express their thoughts of the happy occasion. Mr. Edward Geldbaugh recited a poem, "The Golden Wedding," which was highly enjoyed by all. Mr. J. B. Gillum and Mr. John Shafferman gave very interesting talks. The following songs were sung after all had partaken of the delicious eats: "On our Golden Wedding Day," Silver Threads Among the Gold," and "When Your Hair Has Turned to Silver."

The afternoon was pleasantly spent in talking over old times. At 4:30, Coyd Yost came over to the camp and took several pictures of the group. At six o'clock the group was again called to the dining cottage and another feast. After supper the folks joined in singing some favorite hymns. After singing "God Be with You Till We Meet Again," the happy crowd started for home.

Mr. and Mrs. Kephart were very pleased to have with them on the occasion, Mr. and Mrs. John Shafferman of Fairmont, who acted as best man and maid of honor at the wedding in 1881. Mr. and Mrs. Kephart received many beautiful gifts. Mr. Kephart presented his wife with a Town Sedan. The sons and daughters gave a diamond ring to their mother and a gold watch to their father.

Those participating in the happy affair were: Mr. and Mrs. J. C. Kephart, Mr. and Mrs. Ray Kephart and family, Mr. and Mrs. Luther Kephart and family, Mr. and Mrs. Walter Kephart and family, Mr. and Mrs. Franklin Larke and son, Mr. and Mrs. Roy Markley and son, Mr. and Mrs. Kimmel Purgitt, Mr. and Mrs. J. B. Gillum, Mr. and Mrs. Edward Geldbaugh, Mrs. Emily Aronholt, Mr. and Mrs. John Geldbaugh, Mr. and Mrs. Charles Geldbaugh and daughter of Newburg, Mr. and Mrs. Ed Bolen and Miss Lottie Shafferman, Mr. and Mrs. John Shafferman of Fairmont, Mr. Wm. Salyards and Mrs. Warren Lane of Cleveland, Mrs. Henry Shrader and granddaughter of Parsons and Mrs. Clyde Hoffman of Clarksburg.

During World War I, Mr. Kephart demonstrated his patriotism by walking to church from the farm on Limestone Road. And John and his boys knew how to raise peaches on that farm. At the peak of the picking season in 1913, the editor of the local newspaper wrote: "Mr. J. C. Kephart made this office a very pleasant call yesterday, and knowing the editor's weakness for good things to eat, brought him a half-dozen peaches, for which he has sincere thanks. They were the finest peaches we ever saw, and during the excitement of weighing and measuring them, we forgot to ask the variety, but nevertheless they were fine. The six weighed 3 lbs and 10 oz., and the largest one measured 10 inches around the small way. The firm of J. C. Kephart & Sons took last year both first and second prizes for their peaches, and after seeing these he brought us we do not wonder at it."

After his retirement, the boys stayed at Limestone and John and Lizzie moved back to Spring Street. On November 23, 1931, less than six months after the celebration of fifty years of marriage, John Conrad Kephart died suddenly. It was reported that he was feeling quite well, attended Sunday school, remained for the sermon, and then returned for the evening service before going to bed. At about 2:30am, he awoke, complaining about a pain in his cheek. Within the hour, he passed into the afterlife. Rev. C. P. Bastian, an early pastor at Trinity Lutheran (1907–1912), returned to Keyser to officiate at the funeral.

Mrs. Elizabeth Kephart died on September 28, 1947, in her home at 19 Spring Street. Her funeral was conducted by Trinity's pastor, Rev. C. K. Spiggle, and the pastor of Southern Methodist Church, Rev. Harry Myerly.

Not enough can be said of the impact the Kephart family had, and continues to have, on the life of Trinity Lutheran Church: teachers, musicians, lay leaders, exemplars of hard work and sources of inspiration. We rejoice in the legacy of the Kephart family and their continuing presence among us.

Mr. John G. Koelz

John George Koelz was born on October 6, 1846 at Mühlhausen, Germany, and baptized in the Lutheran Church. Although he often told the story of being on the train to Parkersburg during the John Brown raid at Harper's Ferry in 1859, records indicate he came to America in 1862 and became a citizen of the United States in 1868. He met and married his wife, Anna Rost (1851-1891), in Parkersburg. Anna's father, John Rost, who served in the 6th WV Artillery during the Civil War, was a skilled cooper. Anna was born in Albany, New York.

John and Anna Koelz moved from Parkersburg to Keyser in 1873. He operated a bakery and confectionary for thirty-five years until his retirement in 1908. It seems Mr. Koelz sold an amazing variety of items, but was especially famous for his "Koelz cookies", loved by everyone in the community, especially the youngsters.

Success in the early years enabled him to construct a new building on Main Street to house his growing business. After the bakery closed, the building has seen numerous tenants, including Kaplon's Men's Shop. The building finally passed from Koeltz family ownership when Margaret Koelz sold the building to Jacob and Ada Shear in 1960.

Mr. Koelz's brother, William Koelz (1848-1926), was a baker in Grafton and married Miss Anna Geldbaugh, the aunt of Trinity's three charter-member "Geldbaugh Sisters": Mrs. Lizzie Kephart, Mrs. Anna Kolkhorst, and Mrs. Margaret Shaffer.

John and Anna Koelz had six children. Paulina and John, Jr. died as infants. Their daughter, Margaret Frederica Koelz (1876-1964), never married. She lived in Baltimore for many years, traveled extensively and remained quite close to her brothers. She was living in a Meyersdale nursing home when she died at age 87.

The lives of sons William, Herman, and Fred tell us that this was a family that placed a high value on education.

William Jacob Koelz (1880-1954) graduated dental school in Baltimore in 1904 and practiced dentistry in Keyser for many years. With his brother Herman, he purchased the old 'race track field' from the T. B. Davis estate in 1913. He was active in local politics and served as the elected Mayor of Keyser. Dr. Koelz was twice married: in 1907 to Dawn Hollen Mohler, a Keyser native who was living in Parkersburg at the time, whom he later divorced, and then to Mrs. Verna (Liller) Woy, a widow, in 1952. When Dr. Koelz passed away in 1954, his "Trouten Holler" farm of nearly 460 acres was sold at auction for $15,500 to Congressman Harley O. Staggers.

Herman Charles Koelz (1882-1977) received a Bachelor of Science degree in civil engineering from West Virginia University in 1909. He practiced as a design and construction engineer for the Atlantic Coast Railroad. He married Miss Louise Grimes.

> **J. G. Koelz,**
> **BAKER AND CONFECTIONER**
> Keeps Constantly on Hand
> **Fresh Bread,**
>
> Rolls, Cakes of all kinds, Pies, etc. Also a choice and fresh stock of French and American Candies, Foreign and Domestic Fruits, Nuts, Raisins, Figs, Citron, Currants, etc. A general assortment of
>
> **TOYS AND FANCY ARTICLES**
>
> Just received. Also Accordeons, Harmonicas, Pipe Cigars, Tobaccos and Smokers' Articles, all of which will be sold at lowest cash prices.
>
> **FRESH OYSTERS**
>
> Of the best quality received regularly and served either at saloon, or furnished by the quart or gallon, at reasonable rates.
>
> **PARTIES, WEDDINGS, Etc.**
>
> Supplied at short notice, and all orders promptly attended to.
> J. G KOELZ,
> Main Street, Keyser, W.Va

Frederick Rost Koelz (1887–1983) graduated from the Keyser Preparatory School of WVU in 1906, went on to Morgantown where he received a Bachelor of Arts degree in German and became a highly respected educator in Keyser, Baltimore, Maine, and Pennsylvania. For a time in the early 1920's, he was principal of Keyser High School.

John George Koelz died in 1925, outliving his wife Anna by almost thirty-five years.

Mrs. Anna C. Kolkhorst

Although the footprints of the Kolkhorst family on the doorstep of the sanctuary have lightened in recent years, they were heavy indeed for many decades. Charter member **Mrs. Anna Christine (Geldbaugh) Kolkhorst** (1868–1937) was born in Barrackville, Marion County. Her parents, Jacob Geldbaugh and Christina (Nightingale) Geldbaugh, immigrants from Germany, were among the fifteen families that formed Holy Trinity Lutheran, Newburg, in 1870.

The family story, written by Mrs. Kolkhorst's daughter Anna, was published in *Mineral County, West Virginia: Traits, Tracks and Trails*, compiled, edited and published by Robert L. Rummer, Sr. in 1980. Lightly edited, the chronicle provides an insider's view of the Kolkhorst family of Keyser:

Anna Geldbaugh Kolkhorst (c. 1880)

> My father and mother were married in Baltimore on September 15, 1889. My father, Henry Kolkhorst was a professional wood carver. He carved a piano for the White House and was commissioned by President Grover Cleveland to make furniture for the Blue Room of the White House. He came to Keyser to carve the stairways and other details of the Markwood and Crooks (Buckeye Cottage) mansions on South Mineral Street..
>
> From the marriage of Henry Kolkhorst and Anna (Geldbaugh) Kolkhorst, six children were born: William and Henrietta, who died at an early age; Lawrence (1892–1951); Warren (1894–1948); Emmett (1897–1957); and Anna (1900–1986).
>
> Mrs. Anna Kolkhorst was made a widow in 1901 while living in Parkersburg. She then moved to Keyser because many of her family lived here: her sisters Mrs. Konrad Kephart and Mrs. Joseph Shaffer, also brothers Harry and Edward Geldbaugh lived in Keyser. She settled on Spring Street and ran a boarding house for B&O men in order to raise her family. Mrs. Kolkhorst was very active in church work, having had a lot to do with the building of the first Lutheran Church on Davis Street, which was built by Henry Baker, a contractor who lived on Main Street. The children attended public school and WV Prep School and studied music under Professor McIlwee, who was also director of the Keyser Concert Band. Lawrence, Warren and Emmett were outstanding musicians and played in the Concert Band for many years.
>
> When Prof. McIlwee left Keyser for Winchester, Lawrence took over directing of the band. When Lawrence moved to Cumberland, Warren directed the band; he was also director of the American Legion Drum and Bugle Corps. The band played for many outstanding events such as Apple Blossom Festivals and Presidential Inaugurations.
>
> All of the Kolkhorst family sang in the Lutheran Choir throughout their lifetimes. Out of this choir came the American Legion Ladies Quartette composed of Marie (Knott) Farley,

Virginia (Knott) Kolkhorst, Anna (Kolkhorst) Montgomery and Nyta (Shaffer) Greenwade. This quartette won National Honors for three consecutive years and for Quartets and Trios. They travelled extensively all over the United States singing at conventions, etc. They were entertained at the White House by Mrs. Eleanor Roosevelt.

Mrs. Kolkhorst's first husband, Heinrich "Henry" Kolkhorst (1860-1901), was born in the Hannover region of Germany. He died tragically. While working as the superintendant of the Brumby Chair Company in Marietta, Georgia, he was killed by a disgruntled former employee. In 1916 Mrs. Anna (Geldbaugh) Kolkhorst, then a widow for fifteen years, married the widower Joshua Gillum (1871-1946).

Lawrence, Warren, Emmett & Anna Kolkhorst (1905)

Lawrence Edwin Kolkhorst (1892-1951) married Minnie Bright (1891-1962). He was general foreman of the B&O Bolt and Forge Shop in Cumberland at the time of his death. They had three children: Lawrence Arden Kolkhorst (1916-1984), a long-time and highly respected employee and manager for Potomac Edison in Keyser and at its headquarters in Hagerstown; Julia Henrietta Kolkhorst (Allen) (1919-1992), a public health nurse and administrator for the U.S. Dept. of Health and Human Services; Bernard Edwin Kolkhorst (1921-1998), a graduate of the U.S. Coast Guard Academy who retired with twenty-two years service at the rank of Captain.

Henry Warren Kolkhorst (1895-1948) married Virginia Knott (1902-1977). He worked as a carman and became supervisor of the paint shop at the B&O. Mrs. Virginia Kolkhorst was an accomplished instrumentalist, vocalist and member of the famed ladies quartette, who, for a time, directed the church choir. She was preceptress at Potomac State College for many years and was known as a competitive bridge player with partners "Sleepy" Stanhagen and Leonard Withers at the old PSC Student Center.

Emmett Carriens Kolkhorst (1898-1957) married Elsie Gull, child of charter member "Nannie" Gull. He was a carman and car inspector at the B&O. They had two children Emmett C Kolkhorst, Jr. (1919-1988), a Baltimore policeman, and Beverly Lou (DeVore) (1926-2014).

Mrs. Kolkhorst's daughter and namesake, Miss Anna Kolkhorst (1900-1986), who chronicled the family history, married Clem Edward Montgomery, Sr. (1895-1957), a rural mailman for the U.S. Postal Service. They had two children: Dr. Clem E. Montgomery, Jr. (1918-1994), a local dentist, and Warren Montgomery (1920-1997), a 1943 graduate of the U.S. Naval Academy. She gave freely of her great musical talents to the choir and ladies quartette. Following the death of her first husband in 1957, Mrs. Anna (Kolkhorst) Montgomery married Walter Mott (1897-1988). Anna Montgomery-Mott died in Keyser on July 11, 1986, at age 86.

Anna Kolkhorst and grandson Arden

Charter member Mrs. Anna Kolkhorst-Gillum died on October 23, 1937. She was survived by four children, her second husband, one sister, Elizabeth (Mrs. J. C. Kephart), of Keyser and four brothers; Edward Geldbaugh, Keyser; Harry Geldbaugh, Painesville, Ohio and John and Charles Geldbaugh, of Newburg, and seven grandchildren. Mrs. Kolkhorst, her children and their families were important contributors to the religious, musical and social lives of the community. Their gifts to Trinity Lutheran will never be forgotten.

Mr. Louis Herman Lampas

Louis Herman "Henry" Lampas, a child of Luther Lampas, was born in Germany on August 3, 1839, and immigrated to America in 1869. While living with relatives in Martinsburg, he met another young German immigrant, Miss Mary Paulina Zwing (1850–1897). He found employment with the railroad in Piedmont and returned to marry Paulina in Martinsburg on June 3, 1873. They settled in Westernport, where he worked as a machinist and as a painter. It was there that Kathryn Lampas, their only child, was born on October 23, 1877. It was a deeply committed Lutheran family.

The Piedmont Herald reported the death of Mrs. Lampas as follows:

> Mrs. Mary P. Lampas, wife of Mr. Herman Lampas, of Westernport died at her home March 8, 1897 after a lingering illness, aged 46 years eight months and eight days. Mrs. Lampas lived at Martinsburg a short time but soon moved to this place twenty-odd years ago, where she has since resided. She has long been connected with the Evangelical Lutheran church of which she was a very devoted member. Her funeral took place from Mt. Calvary Lutheran church Tuesday, Rev Engle, Presbyterian pastor at Oakland officiating for the pastor Rev J. W. Butler, who was sick at his home in Oakland. A husband and one daughter survive her.

Alone, following his wife's death and his daughter's absence to study nursing at Kings Daughters Hospital in Martinsburg, Mr. Lampas moved to Keyser and continued to work as a painter at the B&O car shops. In 1903, he transferred his membership from Mt. Calvary, where he served as an Elder, to become a charter member of Trinity Lutheran. Then, in October 1905, the Keyser newspaper reported that Mr. Lampas "was hurt last week painfully, but not seriously, in the Keyser yards, is getting along nicely at the Hoffman Hospital." Shortly thereafter, he retired. In February, 1907, it was reported: "Mr. Lampas, a retired employee of the B&O car shops, who for sometime has lived in our town [Keyser] left this week for Martinsburg, W. Va., where he will make his future home with his daughter, Miss Katie Lampas."

Then, on July 12, 1912, the *Keyser Tribune* published the details of his death:

> Herman Lampas Killed – L. Herman C. Lampas, a well known retired employee of the Baltimore and Ohio Railroad, who for some time made his home on Center Street, Martinsburg, W. Va., died Sunday night at 12:45 o'clock in the Kings Daughters Hospital, Martinsburg, as the result of internal injuries received last Friday morning when struck by B&O fast freight No. 97 at the Queen Street crossing, Martinsburg. He had never regained consciousness after the accident. He would have been 73 years old had he lived until August 3. He is survived by one daughter, Miss Catherine Lampas, a well known trained nurse of Martinsburg, and two sisters: Mrs. Adam Schuckman, Chambersburg, Pa., and Mrs. Charles Bentz, of Marion, Pa. For a number of years he was employed as a painter by the B&O Railroad. Mr. Lampas was a member of the Lutheran Church. The funeral will be held there this morning and the remains will be taken to Westernport, Md., for burial, leaving Martinsburg on train No. 55.

Following her father's death, their daughter Kathryn lived with her aunt, Mrs. Rosa (Zwing) Sakeman, for several years and continued to work as a nurse until her death in Martinsburg on July 28, 1941. She never married.

Yes, the names associated with Mr. Lampas are a bit tangled. The 1936 history booklet gives his name as "Mr. Henry Lampert." Recently re-discovered handwritten records of Trinity communicants in 1904 give his name as "Mr. H. Lampas". Census records and newspaper articles are consistent in the use of the surname "Lampas", but the given name varies as Herman, Harman, Hiram, and Henry. Official records and proven associations with the Mt. Calvary and Trinity Lutheran congregations leave no doubt that this is 'our' Mr. Louis Herman "Henry" Lampas.

Mr. Conrad T. Mandler

Conrad Thomas Mandler, the child of German immigrants John and Barbara (Schmidt) Mandler, was born in Baltimore on January 30, 1867. The family worshiped at English Evangelical Lutheran. About 1890, he married Ruth Cofran (1871-1958) and for a few years engaged in the grocery business. Later that decade they moved to Keyser.

After living on Gilmore Street, the family moved to North Water Street, where they were close neighbors and friends of the Arnold and Sliger families.

Mr. Mandler was foreman of the B&O carshops in Keyser and was elected to the Keyser City Council in 1907.

It was during his term on City Council that the first public bridge was built between McCoole and Keyser. There was, of course, the Western Maryland Railway bridge that spanned the river just east of present-day N. Main Street. The 1908 vehicular bridge was a low, wooden structure that was replaced by an iron bridge in 1942 that met Main Street at the river's edge.

Mr. Mandler was an active member of Trinity Lutheran and member of the Church Council. In 1909 he was transferred to Philadelphia to become foreman of the B&O carshops there. Nevertheless, he held on to his innate desire to once again become an independent businessman. His father had owned a shoe store and his brother Charles had operated Mandler's German Restaurant in downtown Baltimore. After several years, he returned to the retail business as the owner of a grocery store. He then engaged in the real estate business as a salesman and Broker.

Mr. and Mrs. Mandler had two children: John Elmer Mandler (1892-1968), who was born in Baltimore, and Ruth Mandler (1902-1998), who was born in Keyser in 1902.

Conrad Mandler died in Philadelphia on July 12, 1941. He and his wife are buried in West Laurel Hill Cemetery, Bala Cynwyd, Pennsylvania.

Dr. Ephraim T. Martin

A surgeon, **Dr. Ephraim Thurman Martin**, born near Rowlesburg in October 1866, was the son of Milton and Lydia (Forman) Martin. He worked in the railroad office and taught school until he enrolled in medical school in the fall of 1891. Dr. Martin was a graduate of the College of Physicians and Surgeons, Baltimore, Class of 1893. Returning home, he established a medical practice in Cranesville, near Terra Alta.. Evidence has been found that indicates that he married Mary E. "Mollie" Michael, the daughter of Phillip and Lavinia (Parsons) Michael and she gave birth to a son, Carroll Martin, on June 5, 1894. Mollie Martin died the following day; their son died four months later on October 7. Both were buried near Bruceton Mills in the Sugar Valley Cemetery, where, years later, her parents were buried.

The December 14, 1899, issue of the *West Virginia argus* newspaper (Kingwood) reported that Dr. Martin had been charged with a misdemeanor offense for selling fourteen cases of liquor without a license to do so! This brings to mind Martin Luther's Latin phrase, "*Simul justus et peccator.*" With these words, Luther captured the essence of Lutheran theology – that Christians are "*simultaneously, saints and sinners.*"

Dr. Martin then came to Keyser to practice. He had a brief association with Dr. James W. C. Hall at the Keyser Pharmacy. Dr. Martin was elected as a member of the West Virginia State Medical Society on May 23, 1901. He was here for only a short time.

After leaving Keyser, he established a general medical practice in Acme, Washington, a small picturesque town near the Cascade Mountains, about one hundred miles north of Seattle. He married Miss Alice Timeson, a native of Davenport, Iowa, in Seattle on December 16, 1905. They had three children. The family relocated to Seattle in 1911, where Dr. Martin died on February 24, 1938.

Mrs. Bettie Lee Newhouse

Bettie Lee (Everett) Newhouse was one of eleven children born to William and Hannah (Ketterman) Everett. She began life on August 11, 1876, in a rural area near Petersburg. At the time, the family name was often recorded as "Ebert" or "Evert", rather than the "Everett" that was consistently used in later years. Her father farmed and did day-jobs. In the 1890s, the family moved to Davis, perhaps because Bettie's father found work in the coal and coke mining, timber and leather tanning industries that were thriving on the mountaintop, valleys and deep canyons. Davis and its neighbor, Thomas, were company towns, largely dependent on the siblings of Senator Henry Gassaway Davis, who founded the West Virginia Central & Pittsburg Railway that connected with the B&O at Bloomington and reached Thomas in 1884, and West Virginia Pulp and Paper Company. At the end of the 19th century, Davis Coal & Coke was one of the largest mining companies in the world. West Virginia Pulp and Paper's wood yards in the area were vast enterprises.

It was in Davis that Bettie met George Bronson Newhouse (1877–1944), a young man from Moorefield who was living in Davis for perhaps the same reason as Bettie's father – good paying employment. They were married in Keyser on April 2, 1902, and established a residence here. They had one child, Helen, born in 1903. Mr. Newhouse became a sales agent for the New York Life and Metropolitan Insurance companies.

Mrs. Newhouse was known as a devout member of Trinity Lutheran. Her husband also joined the congregation. Sadly, Mrs. Newhouse was stricken with tuberculosis. In those days, there was no effective way to treat this dread disease; doctors believed that the best that could be done was to hospitalize TB patients in a high, cold place. As a result, West Virginia established its first tuberculosis sanitarium at Hopemont, Preston County, in 1911. It was there that Bettie was admitted as a patient in early April, 1914, for rest and to avoid infection of her family. After a stay of three months or so, all hope was lost for her survival; she returned to Keyser and died a few days later, on July 27, 1914. Her funeral was conducted by Rev. Harry Baughman.

Her husband continued to attend services at Trinity. He married Virginia Lillian Timbrook, a Romney girl; they had two children – George Jr. and Mary Frances. The family moved to Cumberland in the 1920s. Mr. Newhouse died in Cumberland in November, 1944.

Mr. Charles P. Pifer & Mrs. Emma Elizabeth Pifer

This article and the one to follow chronicle two brothers, Charles and William Pifer. Charles and his family were here for only a short time; William came and remained here for the remainder of his life. They were joined by a third brother, Clinton, in 1906.

They were children of a distinguished family of the Shenandoah Valley – Randolph Lee Pifer and his wife Mary (Cooper) Pifer. Capt. Pifer was an officer of the 51st Virginia Militia, a farmer, and for a time, a postmaster. Another relative, Augustus Pifer, was a personal bodyguard of Gen. R. E. Lee. A fourth son, Ernest Pifer, served in Cuba as a Corporal in the U.S. Army Cavalry. The family lived several miles west of Stephens City in an area known as Mountain Falls, located on a tributary of Cedar Creek. Even today, Route 600, which intersects with U.S. 48, is still known as Pifer Road. Lutheran ties ran deep in the Pifer and Cooper families.

Charles Preston Pifer, Randolph and Mary's first child, was born in 1870 at Edinburg, in nearby Shenandoah County. Within a year or two, the Pifer family was back at the home place at Mountain Falls, where his siblings were born. In 1893, Charles Preston married **Emma Elizabeth Crisman**, the child of Jacob and Nancy (Larrick) Crisman, who lived in nearby Kernstown. Emma's father, Pvt. Jacob Crisman, achieved a degree of fame by his after-the-war testimony that he was personally responsible for the capture of the flamboyant Union cavalry leader Sir Percy Wyndham on June 6, 1862 at the battle near Port Republic, during which Gen. Turner Ashby was killed. Also a Lutheran family, Jacob and Nancy Crisman are buried at the Mount Hebron Cemetery in Winchester.

Charles farmed the land and, for a short time, tried his hand at operating a small general store. In c.1901, Charles, his family and his unmarried brother William, moved to Keyser.

Charles and Emma Pifer had nine children, two of whom were born in Mineral County: Preston Pifer, in September 1903, just a month after the formation of Trinity Lutheran, and Luther Crisman Pifer in 1906. The family then moved back to a farm near Kernstown. Mr. Pifer operated a grocery store and was Postmaster of Bartonsville, Virginia. During the difficult time of the late 1920s, the family moved to Berkeley County, West Virginia, where he did carpentry work and three of their children found work in a hosiery mill. Mr. Pifer died in Martinsburg in 1947; his wife Emma died in 1957.

Mr. William C. Pifer

The lives of at least three generations of local residents were touched in many ways by charter member, **William Custis Pifer.**

Younger than his brother Charles, also a charter member, and older than his brother Clinton, who also became a faithful member of Trinity church, W. C. Pifer was born near Stephens City in 1878. He came to Keyser very early in the 20th century and immediately launched his multi-faceted career. For more than fifty years, he operated a music store and was Keyser's link to sheet music, instruments, records, early radios and machines like the Victrola. After learning about emerging developments that ultimately led to television, he delighted in telling stories about the possibility of sending movies over the radio waves. Surely, had it been invented during those days, his iPhone would have been among the first in town and his constant barrage of advertisements in the local newspaper would have been touting the wonderment of it all.

W. C. PIFER
First National Bank Building

Representative of the
GULBRANSEN
Player-Piano

Easy to Play

He married Maude Chrisman, a local Keyser girl, in 1907. Maude died in 1923, and Mr. Pifer then married a widowed member of the congregation, Mrs. Sarah Ellen (Cleveland) Bosley, in 1940. A native of Oakland, she had moved to Keyser in 1920 with her husband Dr. Joseph Scott Bosley and their son, John. They became members of the congregation in 1922, beginning a three-generation relationship of the Bosley family with Trinity Lutheran. Dr. Bosley, who died in 1932, was a pharmacist at the Romig Drug Company.

W. C. Pifer served the community in elected positions as councilman and mayor for several terms. He was the first manager of the State of West Virginia's alcoholic beverage store in Keyser, a position subject to the political winds in Charleston.

His outside interests were numerous. He won prizes at the area's annual poultry festival for his displays of Rose Comb Brown Leghorns, raised in the yard while the family was living on Willow Avenue. He was one of Keyser's early owners of a motorcycle. The local newspaper reported that one of his hunting days resulted in bagging fifteen squirrels. In 1915, he killed the first wild turkey of the season, a "gobbler with 8 inch beard."

In August 1927, the newspaper printed a story related by Mr. Pifer: "There are mountaineers living in Hampshire County who have never heard a radio, according to W, C. Pifer, a local business man, who has returned after spending a week in camp at Ice Mountain, that county. Pifer took his radio set with him and invited mountaineer neighbors in on the night of the Dempsey-Sharkey fight and many of them had their first experience with the radio. The women seemed much more curious than the men, he said."

W. C. and Maude Pifer had six children: Robert Arnold Pifer (1909-1948); Isabelle Pifer (1912-1997) married John Smith Herrick; Kenneth Chrisman Pifer (1912-1994) married Martha Bruce Dellinger, a Westernport girl, and then married Edna Warweg; Geraldine Allene Pifer, RN (1914-1991) married John K. Reimer; William Randolph Pifer (1915-1973) married a Keyser lass, Jean Jeffries (1916-2009); Marjorie Louise Pifer (1920-1979) married Sol Pottish (1910-2007).

W. C. & Sarah Pifer (c. 1943)

Until his death at the age of eighty-three on September 1, 1961, Mr. Pifer was steadfast in his faith and devotion to Trinity Lutheran, and still selling a piano or two from his home.

A third Pifer brother, Clinton Luther Pifer (1882-1943), came to Keyser in 1906 with his wife Nannie (Ewing) Pifer (1885-1957), whom he married in March of that year. Like his brothers, Clinton and his wife were dedicated members of Trinity Lutheran. Several of their children and grandchildren were baptized and/or married in the church. Many will remember their daughter Margaret "Peg" (Pifer) Hollen and her husband Ken, stalwarts of the community for many, many years.

Mrs. Margaret C. Shaffer

Oh, there's much to say about the Joseph Shaffer family, so let's begin with Mrs. Shaffer. Brought into this life on April 23, 1870, **Margaret Catherine (Geldbaugh) Shaffer** was the youngest of the three "Geldbaugh Sisters" gifted to Trinity Lutheran by Jacob and Christine (Nightingale) Geldbaugh. The sisters were schooled in faith at Newburg's Holy Trinity Lutheran, of which their parents were charter members.

"Maggie" Geldbaugh married Josiah (Joseph) Shaffer on April 14, 1891. Almost immediately, they set up housekeeping in Keyser. They rented a house on Spring Street and began their family of two boys, Chester (1892-1973) and Winifred (1895-1965) and two girls, Nyta (1899-1945) and Margaret (1904-1997). Mr. Shaffer worked as a carpenter and car-builder for the B&O. They moved around the corner to 159 W. Piedmont Street, a home they eventually purchased.

Mr. Shaffer came from a Methodist background, so it is likely they joined one of the local Methodist congregations until Trinity Lutheran was organized in 1903. Mrs. Shaffer was a charter member; Mr. Shaffer transferred his membership, and all, including the children, were deeply committed Lutherans for the remainder of their lives.

Regrettably, neither of the parents enjoyed long lives. Mrs. Margaret Shaffer died of cancer at age fifty-three on August 16, 1923; Mr. Shaffer passed on October 26, 1925. Mrs. Shaffer's obituary and report of her funeral speak to the depth of love and respect that her fellow parishioners and neighbors felt for her. On August 16, 1923, her obituary began:

> After a lingering illness lasting about one year, during which time loving hands and anxious hearts were busy, Mrs. Margaret Shaffer, wife of Joseph H. Shaffer, died this morning at 9:30. Her friends have been very anxious concerning her for weeks, and for more than a week, traffic had been cut off from the block in which she lived.

About her funeral, the newspaper reported:

> One of the largest funerals ever held in Keyser was Saturday at 2:30 from the Trinity Lutheran Church, Rev. J. W. Drawbaugh officiating, where the last rites were given over the remains of Margaret Shaffer, wife of Joseph Shaffer. She was a charter member of the church and actively engaged in all church work, having served as President of the Ladies' Aid Society and being Alto Soloist in the choir for years. The floral tributes were profuse and beautiful. The honorary pall bearers were composed of the Church Council, being J. C. Kephart, George M. Loy, Raymond Davis, Dock Athey, W. E. Coffman, and William Wolfe. The active pall bearers were six of her nephews, Lawrence, Emmett and Warren Kolkhorst and Ray, Luther and Walter Kephart. Interment was made in Queen's Point Cemetery.

Just over two years later, Mr. Shaffer died of a heart attack. Those same six nephews carried his remains to the grave, as they had done for their Aunt Maggie; Jacob Avers and James M. Clem joined the list of honorary pall bearers.

Their first child, Chester Ward Shaffer, and Emily Virginia Cook were married in 1914 at Trinity Lutheran by Rev. Harry Baughman. Chester worked for the B&O in Cumberland, where they were members of St. Paul's Lutheran Church. They had three children: Mary Margaret (Mrs. Vernon Higgs), Nyta Virginia (Mrs. Phillip Keller) and Betty Louise (Mrs. Wallace Ullery).

Winifred McClellan "Dyke" Shaffer was one of Keyser's all-time great athletes. One of the original members of the famed Collegians in 1913, he was a standout guard of the team for fifteen years and competed with several of the earliest stars of the national basketball leagues while playing for the Collegians and the Akron Professionals in the Central Professional League. For many years, he was an outstanding outfielder for the local B&O baseball teams that won two system-wide championships in 1917 and 1928. He first married Eva Christian, a nurse at the Hoffman hospital, in 1925; she died prematurely in 1932. They had one son during their relatively short marriage, Frederick Lee "Fritz" Shaffer (1927-2011). He married a Burlington girl, Pauline Bane, and became a professor of Electrical Engineering at Cal Poly, San Luis Obispo, California. "Dyke" eventually remarried, to Miss Elizabeth Finnell (1910-1975), a local girl, in 1944. He died on December 9, 1965. "Dyke" Shaffer is remembered as an outstanding athlete, a gregarious man, a true friend to young and old, as a faithful, loyal and supportive member of Trinity Lutheran, and even as an outstanding card player.

There's an interesting side story here, and it relates to Richard A. "Dyke" Raese, a name synonymous with the modern history of West Virginia University. The tenth of eleven children (born 1909) in the Davis, West Virginia, family of Minnie and John Raese, he worked in his family's general merchandise business and in 1932 earned a degree at WVU. Family lore has it that he chose his nickname as a child because he wished to emulate a favorite player on the semi-pro basketball team known as the Keyser Collegians; thus he assumed the name from Dyke Shaffer and was never called "Dick." For a time after college graduation, Raese coached at his home high school in Davis and then became a highly successful coach at WVU, business leader and generous patron of the university.

Nyta Catherine Christian (Shaffer) Greenwade was a renowned vocalist, as was her husband, John Perry Greenwade (1894-1961). Their 1922 marriage was announced in the local newspapers:

> The wedding of Miss Nyta Kathryn Shaffer and John Perry Greenwade was solemnized Tuesday afternoon at 2:30 o'clock, at Trinity Lutheran church. An orchestra consisting of Mrs. Clem E. Montgomery, pianist, and Warren, Emmett and Lawrence Kolkhorst, with string instruments played a prelude. Mrs. Joseph Nowatski sang "O Promise Me" and Rev. J. W. Drawbaugh "O Perfect Love." The ushers were Paul J. Davis and Barclay Inskeep, and the best man was Edward Gerstell. The Maid of Honor was Miss Grace Avers of Cumberland, and the bridesmaids, Misses Nina Lee Harrison and Margaret Shaffer. The flower girls were Margaret Newhauser and Mary Shaffer. The bride is a daughter of Mr. and Mrs. Joseph Shaffer and is a graduate of Keyser High School and the former Preparatory School. She is a teacher in the third grade of the public school and will continue her work in that capacity.

Perry worked as a clerk in his father's mercantile store for awhile, then became a fire insurance salesman and worked at Kelly-Springfield Tire Co. The couple lived on Overton Place and provided a home there for her brother "Dyke" and his young son after his first wife died.

Lutheran League Quartette – Nyta (Shaffer) Greenwade at right

Mrs. Greenwade directed the choir at Trinity and was a member of the nationally famous Legionettes Quartette, which began as a church organization and was officially named the Lutheran League Quartette of West Virginia. They appeared at many national conventions and sang with Rudy Vallee, Morton Downey and many others. So well known was Mrs. Greenwade that the Governor of West Virginia designated her to be the state representative to lay the wreath on the tomb of the Unknown Soldier at Arlington in 1937. After her death in 1945, her husband established the Nyta Greenwade Scholarship, the first scholarship fund ever to have been given to Potomac State College. Mr. Greenwade migrated back to Keyser Presbyterian, the home church of his mother.

Margaret Shaffer wed William Allan Smith (1900-1969), the son of a coal operator and merchant in Blaine; they were married in 1929 by Rev. Vorberg. The couple lived in Kitzmiller, where they had a son, Michael, and where Allan was engaged in the coal business. They later moved to Cumberland, where Allan worked for the Kenneweg Wholesale Co. They were active members of St. John's Lutheran Church. Following her husband's death, she moved to the Washington area to be near her son and his family.

Mrs. Virginia H. Shafferman

Records of the Evangelical Reformed Church at Nordhorn, Germany, document the January 31, 1850 birth of Hendrikjen "Jennie" Heetlage, who was to become **Mrs. Virginia H. "Jennie" Shafferman.** Her parents, Lambert and Gese (Hüesman) Heetlage had been married in this same church on January 4, 1845 and lived in the small nearby town of Bakelde. They had three children. The first two were born in Germany: Geerd "George" Heetlage, born in 1847, and the aforementioned Hendrikjen "Jennie" Heetlage in 1850.

The Heetlage family emigrated from Bremen to Baltimore aboard the ship Hahnemann in October, 1851, at the urging of Mr. Heetlage's sister and brother-in-law, Mr. and Mrs. Henry Shrader, who had come to America a few years earlier and were living in Tucker County. The Heetlage family settled in a remote area near the Shrader farm. Their third child, John Henry, was born in May 1853. Lambert Heetlage, Jennie's father, farmed the land and is known to have worked at a lumber mill near Terra Alta in 1854-1855 but then disappears from the records.

Jennie's mother Gese, often known as "Tracy", then married Joseph Kephart. Their only child was John Conrad Kephart, a charter member of Trinity Lutheran. His birth, in 1858, is recorded in the official birth registry of Tucker County upon a report by John Conrad's half-brother, George Heetlage. Young John Conrad was left fatherless at a very early age when Joseph Kephart died in 1861. Jennie's mother had lost two husbands and was once again faced with the extreme difficulty of being alone with her children in a very remote area. Sometime during the 1860s, she made the decision to move her family to nearby Newburg, a thriving community where relatives and friends from the "old country" were living.

On September 24, 1871, Jennie Heetlage married Francis "Frank" Shafferman (1839-1883) in Newburg. An immigrant from Germany, he had served in the 17th Regiment, West Virginia Infantry, during the last year of the Civil War. He was a charter member of Holy Trinity Lutheran Church, Newburg, when it was organized in 1870. Mr. Shafferman worked for the B&O railroad.

Mrs. Shafferman's mother, Gese "Tracy" (Hüesman) Heetlage-Kephart, was living with the Shafferman family in Newburg at the time of Census of 1880; no records to document her later life and death have been discovered.

The Shaffermans had five children, two of whom died in infancy. All were born in Preston County.

Charlotte Elizabeth "Miss Lottie" Shafferman (1874-1954), who never married, continued to live in the family home at 46 Spring Street until her death.

John Henry Shafferman (1878-1898) worked as a fireman on the B&O for a short time before succumbing to typhoid fever.

Rose Christine Shafferman (1882-1942) married Edward Bolen (1882-1951) in 1907. He came to Keyser from Front Royal and worked as a welder at the B&O. They lived in the Shafferman home on Spring Street, raising their daughter Virginia and caring for Mrs. Shafferman until her death, The Bolens, Mrs. Shafferman and Miss Lottie were vigorous and faithful members of the congregation throughout their lives. The Shafferman family attended a local Methodist church until Trinity Lutheran Church was formed in 1903.

The timing of the family move from Preston County is a bit uncertain. Daughter Rose Bolen recalled that she was six years of age when her family came to Keyser (c.1888). Everything seems to agree with that recollection. Except... There are gravestones at Queen's Meadow Point Cemetery for Francis Shafferman (1839 – Sept. 24, 1883) and the two infant daughters, Tracey (1872-1872) and Annie (1877-1877). It is proven that the deaths of the two infants occurred in Preston County, well before the move to Keyser. No official record of Mr. Shafferman's death has been found. It is highly likely that the three markers are "memorials" rather than markers of actual graves. Assuming that the surviving family erected these memorials, the date of Mr. Shafferman's death is probably accurate.

Regardless of the exact date of their migration from Newburg to Keyser, Mrs. Shafferman must have thought about the family difficulties during her own childhood when her father and step-father died untimely deaths. Move to Keyser? Her brother and step-brother were already living there. Many Newburg friends were also moving there, following the fortunes of the railroad. It was the logical place to move. Even then, her only known source of income was a meager pension she received from her husband's military service. It's likely she took in transient railroaders who needed a place to sleep and perhaps a meal or two until they were back on the road again, crewing a train to Brunswick, Grafton or Fairmont. There was a ready market for this service; Keyser had no "railroad hotel" akin to the large facilities in Grafton and Cumberland.

Mrs. Jennie Shafferman, a victim of the dreadful influenza epidemic, died at her home on February 19, 1920. Her funeral was conducted by Rev. W. V. Garrett. Her obituary noted that she "was buried at Queen's Point cemetery, beside the body of her son Henry, who died several years ago." This adds further credence to the notion that her husband and two infant daughters are not actually interred there.

No trace of Mrs. Shafferman's brother George has been found after 1880. Mrs. Shafferman's brother John Henry was enumerated in 1880 while living in a Keyser rooming house with his half-brother Conrad Headlough, the latter obviously being John Conrad Kephart! Both were working for the B&O Railroad. John Henry Headlough married Miss Nancy Paulina Ice at Keyser on September 26, 1883. The couple moved to Cumberland where he continued to work for the railroad. Upon his death in 1918, newspaper accounts noted that Mr. and Mrs. Bolen and Ruth, Walter, and Luther Kephart attended the funeral service.

Mr. John T. Sincell & Mrs. Valetta Irene Sincell

John Thomas Sincell was born September 8, 1866, in Frederick County, Maryland. During the 1870s, his parents, Charles and Leah (Richardson) Sincell moved the family to Oakland, where his father continued to work as a blacksmith. Young John was selling insurance before coming to Keyser in 1902. **Valetta Irene (Brown) Sincell** was born in the District of Columbia on February 14, 1881; her parents were Wilson E. Brown, a carpenter, and his wife Martha. John and Valetta were married on June 24, 1903.

In Keyser, Mr. Sincell immediately built a solid reputation throughout the region as a trusted businessman and owner of a general store. He was way ahead of his time in merchandising skills, advertising, and customer service.

For two decades, the Sincells were deeply committed members of Trinity Lutheran. Mr. Sincell was Trinity's first Sunday School Superintendent. They transferred their memberships to Keyser Presbyterian in 1923 and remained members of that congregation until Mr. Sincell's death on March, 19, 1937. The funeral was conducted by their neighbor Dr. John Wood, the beloved Presbyterian minister and father of the noted author Sarah Catherine (Wood) Marshall. After Mr. Sincell's death, Mrs. Sincell moved to Oakland and became a member of St. Mark's Lutheran. Mrs. Valetta Sincell died on March 29, 1961, in Pittsburgh. They had no children.

The lives of Mr. and Mrs. Sincell were well-summarized by Harold C. Effland, editor of the *Mineral Daily News Tribune*, in his "News and Views" column of April 7, 1961:

> One of Keyser's most prominent citizens of yesteryear passed away last week in a Methodist Home for the Aged at Mt. Lebanon (Pittsburgh). Reference is made to Mrs. Valetta I. Sincell, 80-year-old widow of the late John T. Sincell, who died in 1937. Mrs. Sincell left here shortly after her husband's death in 1937 and resided in Oakland and Pittsburgh. She had been in the Methodist Home for three years.

Her husband was president of Sincell Company, Inc., here until the charter was surrendered in 1908. The business continued as The Sincell Company which carried the trademark, "Family Outfitters." James H. Swadley Sr., who once worked for the Sincells, told us this week that the store was first started in the old First National Building, located where the National Bank of Keyser now stands. That building burned, but before that The Sincell Company had moved to the building at Armstrong and Davis Sts., now occupied by Wolf Furniture Company. The business had its opening there in October 1, 1907, and continued until it was liquidated in March of 1932 [a casualty of the Great Depression]. After that Mr. Sincell served as Justice of the Peace until his death.

We don't remember, of course, but we have been told that the store was known as one of the finest between Washington and Cincinnati. It was equipped with New-Way fixtures, best of its kind, and everything, except the shoe and corset departments, was under glass. We were told it resembled a French Shop. Besides Mr. Swadley, we were able to learn of at least three other local persons still living who were employed here. One is Mrs. Rilla Wildemann, now employed at Elyse's Dress Shop on Main Street here. The others are Louise Kephart and Jennie Wageley Swadley, both of here. Mrs. Sincell was a Brown from Washington, D.C., who met Mr. Sincell during the summer season at Oakland. Incidentally, the Sincells built the home on Overton Place now owned by the Fred Hamills. Mrs. Sincell was buried Monday in Oakland. She is survived by one sister and a number of nieces and nephews in Oakland.

The history of the building on Armstrong Street that housed the Sincell Company illustrates the evolution of a durable property in downtown Keyser. When first constructed by F. M. Reynolds, it was half the size of the still-existing structure. Three stories high, Sincell occupied the eastern and rear portions of the ground floor and part of the two upper floors; the Keyser branch of the U.S. Post Office was located on the west side, adjacent to the corner of Armstrong and Davis streets. Sincell himself referred to the location of his store as the Post Office Building. Judge Reynolds then built an "L" form addition on Armstrong Street and the east (Sincell) side of the building to add retail spaces on Armstrong Street and stockroom space on the ground floor and apartments on the upper floors next to the earlier building. By the mid-1920's, when the Post Office moved to a new adjacent location, the structure was thence called the "Sincell Building".

After the Sincell Company shut it doors, a variety of businesses, offices and apartment dwellers occupied the building.

Following protracted legal proceedings that were resolved in late 1938, the building was acquired by Atty. George F. Arnold and S. P. Amtower from the estate of Judge F. M. Reynolds. Within a few months, the building was then leased to the Great Atlantic & Pacific Tea Company. The A&P immediately began major modifications to the building and opened a new store there. The A. & P. store on Main Street, operated by Paul D. Peters, closed immediately; the A. & P. store in the K. of P. building, operated by Joe Weaver, continued to operate for only a short while.

Records of the transactions also confirm the presence of a two-story building at the rear of the Sincell building that was the home of the Keyser Post Office from 1926 to 1935. An alleyway, in back of the Sincell building and the adjacent Goldsworthy's barber shop, provided access to the rear of the Reynolds (Corwin) Hotel. In 1935 the Post Office would again move to its first federally-owned facility at the corner of Davis and Piedmont streets, built on land that had been the site of the Ritzell family residence for many years.

The year of 1939 was one of great improvements in downtown Keyser. The *Mineral Daily News-Tribune* of August 29, 1939, reported:

> The Sidewalk Supervisors of Keyser are getting worried. They are supervising their last big project with the erection of the marquee in front of the new theatre today. When that is finished their work will be over and no other job looms in sight. For the first time in several months they will be without something to do and they are frantically looking for some new construction they can supervise.
>
> They are looking back over the past few months at a job well done. It has been filled with all kinds of construction and they have learned much as they have stood with a knowing air, conversing with their brethren on technical questions that only a few weeks before had not even entered their minds. Keyser's construction boom has helped them a lot and now we have several citizens who are authorities on all phases of the building game.
>
> It all started when local merchants started improving the fronts of their buildings. The erection of new glass fronts drew many spectators who admired the cohesive qualities of the sticky black stuff that was used.
>
> Then came the WPA sidewalk project. The proper formula for mixing cement was absorbed and it was probably the first time that many of our townspeople learned that the WPA workers really worked.
>
> The remodeling of the Sincell building for the A. & P. Super Market drew large crowds of Supervisors and because it was convenient much more time could be spent seeing that the job was done right. The new American Super Market on Main Street also has had its quota of Supervisors who now and then invade the second floor for inspection of Henry's bowling and billiard parlor. By the way, we understand that a few of the most accomplished Supervisors will be admitted to witness the actual laying of the alleys.
>
> And now it's all about over. The only thing to do is to hope for another project of some sort because it would be a shame to see such an organization as the Sidewalk Supervisors of Keyser become extinct.

Mr. Harry A. Sliger & Mrs. Bertha Sliger

Truly a Lutheran family. **Harry Arlington Sliger** and **Bertha Caudy (Arnold) Sliger** were born of Lutheran parents. Mr. Sliger's ancestors were charter members of Mt. Zion Lutheran Church in Preston County. Bertha's mother, Mrs. Jennie Arnold, was a charter member of Trinity Lutheran.

He was born in Piedmont on June 18, 1876 to Thornton and Elizabeth (Murphy) Sliger; she was born in Keyser on January 30, 1884 to John Wesley and Jennie (Young) Arnold. Prior to their marriage, Harry was employed at the paper mill and worked part-time in a local barbershop. As the romance between Harry and Bertha was becoming more intense and she was only sixteen years of age, the Arnolds decided to send her to Winchester to live with relatives and go to school. Mr. Sliger wrote to the young lady and told her that if she didn't come back home he was coming to Winchester and would bring her home! Of course, her parents wouldn't let her come home until she finished school for the year. He went to Winchester on the train and brought her home. He walked into the Arnold home with Bertha and told Mr. Arnold that he had brought Bertie home and he intended to marry her. They were married in the Grace M. E. Church on April 28, 1901.

COURTESY OF NANCY LEE COFFMAN HOWARD

Shortly after their marriage, the couple settled in Keyser and Mr. Sliger opened his own barbershop in September, 1901. Four years later, he moved his business from Center Street to Main Street; fifteen years later, the shop was moved to Armstrong Street. Mr. Sliger retired in 1960, having operated his business for over fifty-eight years. Along the way, the family moved from Sharpless Street to a new home at 37 N. Water Street, built by fellow Lutheran charter member Henry W. Baker and very near the home of Mrs. Sliger's parents.

Mr. and Mrs. Sliger were active members of Trinity, serving the congregation in many ways. Among their countless contributions to Trinity, Bertha taught the Cradle Roll Sunday School class for many years and was an active member of the Ladies' Aid Society; Harry was a member of Church Council for many years.. They were also very involved in numerous acts of service to the community and enjoyed a busy social life with scores of friends. Like her mother, Mrs. Sliger was proud of her heritage and a member of the United Daughters of the Confederacy.

They were blessed with of four children, one of whom, Elizabeth Virginia Sliger (1903-1904), died as a two-month old infant. Their other three children were exemplary citizens and faithful Lutherans throughout their lives.

Richard Arlington Sliger (1902-1991) learned his father's skills as a barber at an early age. Then, after more than a decade of barbering together, he moved to Frederick in 1932 to operate a barbershop in the Francis Scott Key Hotel. The following year, he married a local Frederick girl, Miss Blanche Crum (1902-1980). After the hotel shop closed, he took on the position of clerk in the county Treasurer's office. He continued to barber on a part-time basis for several years. Following the death of his first wife, he married Blanche's younger sister, Isabel Crum (1911-2006). He was a long-time member of Frederick's Evangelical Lutheran Church. Richard and Blanche Sliger had one son, Richard, Jr. (1940-2011).

Arnold Thornton "Pooge" Sliger (1904-1970) worked at a number of jobs before becoming a regional representative for the Lutheran Brotherhood Insurance Society and owner and operator of the Sliger Insurance Agency. In conjunction with his brother, he purchased and operated a confectionary store on W. Piedmont Street in 1927. The Collegiate Sweet Shop operated until 1931, when it was sold to Dr. Eugene Clevenger. For several years during the Great Depression, Mr. Sliger worked for the Federal Works Administration. He exhibited his great sense of humor when telling an amusing story about those days to someone at the Keyser *Mineral Daily News* in 1934, who repeated it to readers of the long-running and highly popular *Colyum* of important and not-so-important local tidbits. "Arnold "Pooge" Sliger, in town for a brief visit from the Reedsville Homestead Project, tells that all the reading he did this summer did him some good. "Pooge" confined most of his literature to magazines of the rough paper type telling of thrilling adventures in the air and armed conflict. These war stories had "Pooge" so well trained that when he was put in charge of a gang to dynamite tree stumps and rocks a few weeks ago, he was setting off the blasts with the ability of a veteran. So used was he to the barrages and cannonading in his stories that he didn't even blink an eye when a stick of dynamite went off about ten yards from him." He was a charter member of the Keyser Kiwanis club. "Pooge" was a devoted Lutheran and sang in the choirs all of his life.

Mary Evelyn Sliger (1916-1997) was a woman of amazing talent. A musical prodigy, she was teaching piano lessons while still a teenager. She was the organist at Trinity Lutheran for more than six decades, enabling the church to be widely recognized for its outstanding musical talent and programming. Many youngsters were introduced to good music as members of the Junior and Cherub choirs, among her most cherished achievements. She married Robert Thornhill Coffman (1915-1964), who became a renowned physician and surgeon, practicing in Keyser at Potomac Valley Hospital. Dr. and Mrs. Coffman had two daughters, Nancy Lee and Barbara.

As the years came and went, and other charter members of Trinity Lutheran passed on to their reward, Harry and Bertha Sliger became the last remaining of the original group of forty. Mr. Sliger died on March 24, 1966, just a month shy of their 65th wedding anniversary. Mrs. Sliger, the youngest charter member, died eight months later on November 25, 1966.

Many remember the beautiful stained glass window beside the choir loft in the old church that was presented by the Sligers and Mrs. Arnold in remembrance of departed family members including baby Elizabeth and Mrs. Sliger's sister, Laura.

Mr. Benjamin Souder

Benjamin and Sarah (Wilson) Souder

Benjamin Souder was born on June 30, 1853 at Bergton, Rockingham County. The photograph and paragraph that follows were published in *Biography and Genealogy of Some of the Anthony Souder and Margarite Maurer Family* (1997), written by Warren J. Souder:

Josiah Souter [Benjamin Souder's father] owned a large farm of the most desirable land in the Bergton valley. During the Civil War, Josiah was "deferred" from the Confederate Army because he was a blacksmith who was to shoe the soldiers' horses when they were at his forge. He placed shoes on the horses of both armies. Confederate soldiers camped at his farm and destroyed the flax crop by using it for bedding. Horses were in demand by both of the armies, north and south, as well as the irregulars who ravaged the area. Josiah would often hide his horses on the mountain top where there was an apple, peach, etc. orchard called the High Hot. For the farm there were about ten horses. Several times during the year, three to four wagons were loaded with produce and taken to Broadway where there was a rail road station and the farm products were traded for other needed products. Josiah was a Justice of the Peace and with other justices he held court and heard many trials. He was one of the founders of Phanuel's Evangelical Lutheran Church.

Benjamin Souder was one of fifteen children. In the midst of the Civil War and its aftermath, Benjamin went to school and ultimately became a teacher in the local public school for several years. In 1877, he married Margaret Wilson (1856-1944), whose family lived on the other side of the ridge along the South Fork, near Milam, where Hardy, Pendleton and Rockingham counties come together. They began their family of nine children, six of whom lived to adulthood, while living on the Souder family farm. They moved to Missouri for a time in the 1880s, and then came to the very small settlement of Schell, near Elk Garden, in 1890. He operated a small dry-goods store and was postmaster there for more than a decade. Their youngest daughter Bessie (Mrs. Frank Greenwade) was born there.

The family then moved to Keyser and established a residence on Argyle Street. Within a decade, Mrs. Souder inherited some of the family land in the South Fork Valley. In 1911, Ben and Margaret moved there. Mr. Souder operated the farm and, like his father had done a half-century before, trucked meat and produce for sale in Keyser and other communities. An announcement in the *News-Tribune* in November, 1914 advised residents that Mr. Souder was due to arrive with "a two-horse wagon load of porkers."

Their son, Charles Webster Souder, established his family residence in Keyser, so Ben and his wife had a place to stay when they came to town. They maintained their membership at Trinity Lutheran and often attended services. They had many friends here, who usually called him "Uncle Ben."

Benjamin Souder died at the farm near Milam, in Pendleton County, on March 12, 1929, when he suffered a stroke of paralysis and never recovered. His body was brought to his son's home on Allegheny Street. Former pastor Rev. C. P. Bastian, with whom the Souder's had a close personal relationship, and the current pastor, Dr. Robert T. Vorberg, conducted the funeral service. Pallbearers were selected from Mr. Souder's Sunday School Class: Perry Greenwade, Byron Kesner, Robert Fisher, Luther A. Kephart, Walter G. Kephart and Warren Kolkhorst. Honorary pallbearers were: George Loy, Richard Sliger, T. H. Frankhouser, and J. C. Kephart. The choir of the Lutheran Church sang his favorite hymn, "Abide with Me," followed by "Let Me Not Come With Empty Hands," sung by Trinity's renowned quartet of Mrs. Anna Montgomery, Mrs. Marie Farley, Mrs. Virginia Kolkhorst and Mrs. Nyta Greenwade

Heading south on Rt. 259 from Baker and past Lost River, Mathias and the WV-VA state line, there is a turn-off marked by the sign pointing to Bergton and Criders. Bergton Road passes through a gap and into a hidden valley beyond, surely "the most desirable land in the Bergton valley." There stands the Martin Luther Evangelical Lutheran Church, home of a small rural congregation that remains as an outpost of vitality in the religious life of the area. Phanuel's Evangelical Lutheran Church, where the Souder family worshipped, was located on a knoll near the present building and graveyard.

In the Bergton Valley, SAU-der is the preferred pronunciation of the family name.

Mr. Parker M. Spangler & Mrs. Laura Bertha Spangler

Parker M. Spangler, consistently identified as P. M. Spangler, was born in Westernport on April 24, 1863. His parents, George W. and Catherine (Koontz) Spangler were Marylanders – he from Williamsport and she from Baltimore. George Spangler, an Elder of Mt. Calvary Lutheran, was a tailor. Later in his life he became a coal merchant amid the rapidly growing mining industry of the North Potomac and George's Creek valleys. **Laura Bertha (Bomberger) Spangler** was born in Williamsport. Her father, Emanuel Bomberger, was a master cabinetmaker at the M.P. Möller Pipe Organ Company, Hagerstown, until his death in 1904. Both families had strong ties to Lutheran churches in Williamsport and Hagerstown. It is logical to assume that both of these families might have had a hand in the donation of a small Moller organ to the new Trinity Lutheran Church of which their son and daughter were charter members.

P. M. Spangler and Miss Bertha Bomberger were married on July 10, 1889, at the Bomberger residence in Williamsport. Over the next two decades they lived in Westernport, Frostburg and McCoole, where they purchased a home in 1899. For several years Mr. Spangler was railway express agent for the Western Maryland Railway in Keyser. His father, the coal trader, died in 1898, and it appears that his son Parker acquired and continued to practice his father's penchants for investments and trading. He was a vocal advocate for a Keyser-McCoole highway bridge as early as 1903 and was one of the original directors of the Keyser Board of Trade in 1907. Meanwhile, the Spanglers never took their eyes away from the Hagerstown area. By 1910, he was operating a dry goods store in Waynesboro, Pennsylvania. In 1912, he opened a 5 and 10 cents store on Green Street in Piedmont. Newspaper accounts of 1913-15 note that the family was living in Piedmont while spending the summers at Pen-Mar, a resort community along the Western Maryland Railway, north of Hagerstown and astride the Maryland-Pennsylvania border. The Spanglers bought land at Pen Mar in 1914 and built a home there, which they called "Oakleigh Cottage". Mr. Spangler told the editor of the Keyser newspaper that he and his wife would retain their real estate in the area because they were confident in the future of the community. By 1920, he was working in a machine shop; in 1930, as a carpenter. He also operated a grocery store. Beginning in 1931, Mr. Spangler, with Mrs. Spangler's help, shepherded the Pen Mar amusement park through the difficult years of the Great Depression and the onset of World War II.

But let us return to their important roles in the formation of Trinity Lutheran Church, especially Mrs. Spangler. She, along with Miss Martha Watson and Miss Annie Carl, worked diligently at the groundwork that led to the formation of the congregation. She was a stalwart member of the Ladies' Aid Society that provided assistance in a multiplicity of ways: before the formal organization in 1903, during the campaign to acquire land and build a sanctuary, and for many years thereafter. Mrs. Spangler and Miss Watson co-authored the brief history of the congregation that was distributed in 1936. Mr. Spangler was a Deacon, member of Trinity's first Church Council and superintendent of the Sunday School. Their membership at Trinity continued, but for many of those years their involvement was from afar – Pen Mar.

P. M. and Bertha Spangler had three children: George Russell Spangler (1892-1964), Ellen Catherine Spangler (1893-1893) and Elsa Hoffman Spangler (1894-1978). All were born in Keyser.

Bertha Spangler died on August 29, 1942; P. M. Spangler died just over a year later, on November 26, 1943.

If one searches the Internet closely, you may find a photograph of Mr. Spangler sitting on the edge of the magnificent carousel at Pen-Mar Park during the mid-1930s.

Mrs. Diana Wagoner

Mrs. Diana (Troutman) Wagoner was born at Wellersburg on February 26, 1852, and grew up on a remote farm between Wellersburg and Mt. Savage. Her father, William Troutman, came from an Evangelical Reformed background; her mother, Louise (Lepley) Troutman's family background was Lutheran.

Her husband, Marcus Wagoner (1842-1927), was the son of Michael Wagoner and Julia Ann Rice. The Wagoner ancestors were among the earliest settlers of the Patterson Creek valley, including Capt. Wagoner, a local resident, who was at Fort Ashby during the French and Indian War. Several generations of the family accumulated many valuable farms in the district.

Diana Troutman and Marcus Wagoner were married on Christmas Day, 1874. They had four children: Ada, Bertha, Russell, and Lilly.

In 1902, the Wagoner's sold their farm and moved to Keyser, where Mr. Wagoner worked as a highly skilled carpenter. In 1907, they contracted Mr. D. B. Biser to build them a new home at the corner of Orchard Street and Fort Avenue, where they lived for the remainder of their lives. Those visiting this home, even today, see examples of fine workmanship in the style of the Arts and Crafts movement that must have come from the able hands of Mr. Wagoner.

The Wagoner family was generous in support for the work of Trinity Lutheran, from the early days of the Ladies' Aid Society to a bequest that enabled the construction of the addition to the parish house in 1978. Their children lived interesting and productive lives.

Miss Ada Louisa Wagoner (1877-1962) taught school in Mineral County and was a first grade teacher in Keyser for several years before going to Washington, D. C. in 1916, where she taught in a school for special needs children until she retired. She moved to St. Petersburg, Florida in 1950, where she died in 1962. She never married.

Mrs. Bertha (Wagoner) Hugill (1881-1978) was a school teacher in West Virginia and Pennsylvania. At one time, she was an accountant with the Baltimore & Ohio Railroad. She married John Hugill (1874-1923), a Clarksburg native, at a quiet ceremony in Oakland in 1913. Mr. Hugill was working as a machinist in Beaver Falls, Pennsylvania, when he died at age forty-six of chronic myocarditis. Mrs. Hugill went back to teaching, lived in many locations, including Los Angeles, from where she returned to Fairmont-Clarksburg in 1947. Her last home was in Aurora. She died in the hospital at Hopemont. She outlived her husband by fifty-five years. During their relatively short marriage, they had no children.

Russell Gilmore Wagoner (1883-1959) married a Cumberland girl, Miss Lillie Davis (1885-1964). After railroad employment in Keyser and Massachusetts, they settled in the Pittsburgh area where he was employed for many years by the Koppers Coal Company. In retirement, they moved to St. Petersburg. Their daughter Louise married Hugh Brankstone.

Miss Lilly Bernice Wagoner (1885-1974) never married. After high school graduation she attended the preparatory school to learn the office skills that served her well throughout her life as a stenographer at the woolen mill and various positions with the West Virginia State Roads Commission. She was a student of history and charter member of the Potomac Valley Chapter DAR, She lived at 66 Fort Avenue, adjacent to the Wagoner family home, built for her by her father.

Diana Wagoner died in Keyser on May 20, 1934. The Wagoner home had been sold to Ernest A. See, a lawyer and future long-time circuit court judge, and his wife Lillian. Mrs. See was a treasured member of the Trinity Lutheran family; Judge E. A. See, a faithful member of the Church of the Brethren, often attended services with Mrs. See.

Mr. Augustus S. Wolf & Mrs. Christina Jane Wolf

Augustus Shuey Wolf was born on April 4, 1852, in Boalsburg, Pennsylvania, less than five miles from the site of Penn State University, which was chartered when "Gus" was but three years of age. His family, nurtured by parents Emanuel and Leah (Shuey) Wolf, were members of Boalsburg's Zion Lutheran Church. Surely influenced by his father's work as a tinsmith, Gus learned the craft of metalworking to become a blacksmith. In the late 1870s, he came to Keyser and was readily employed. He eventually formed a partnership, Moomau, Wolf & Co., with Jacob Moomau, a wagon-maker. After Mr. Moomau's death, Mr. Wolf bought-out another local blacksmith shop, owned by Harry Kercheval, and became the sole owner of the business.

Christina Jane (Head) Wolf was a child of Lt. Col. William T. Head (1826-1883), 17th Regiment WV Infantry, and Malinda Reed (1830-1910), a girl from Cameron, Marshall County, where Christina was born on May 9, 1861. The Heads were among the very earliest settlers of the Patterson Creek valley, owning large tracts of land near the junctions of Mikes Run, Staggs Run and Patterson Creek. Known early-on as Sheetz's Mill, it became known as Headsville. The Headsville Post Office was chartered in 1868. At the time of its closure in 1951, the post office had occupied the same building for longer than any such establishment in the United States. Col. Head brought his family to Keyser in the 1870s.

Augustus Wolf and Christina Head were married on November 25, 1880. They had seven children: Ella Pearl, Ida McCarty, Gertrude, Leah Frances, Georgia Reed, Thomas Emanuel, and Myra Elizabeth.

As one learns about the lives of the Wolf family, several impressions are inescapable: this was a very close-knit, caring, hard-working and conservative family, strongly tied to Water Street.

They lived on N. Water Street before purchasing a home "across the tracks" on Eden Street, now known as Welch Street, near its intersection with Water Street, where Mr. Wolf did his blacksmithing. In 1912, the family moved to 66 S. Water Street, a home purchased from W. W. Kesner.

Throughout their lives, the children and their families remained close to the home-place. In hard times, they were welcomed into the home to live. When they were able to have their own residences, they chose to live on Water Street, close to the home-place. The three orphaned children of their daughter Gertrude were raised by Gus and Christina.

Their social engagements revolved around Trinity Lutheran; Mr. Wolf was a founding Elder of the congregation and Mrs. Wolf served as the presiding officer of the Ladies' Aid Society, which was frequently entertained at the Wolf home.

Mr. Wolf shod horses, made tools and other implements, sold bicycles, and did metal repairs of all sorts. There was a constant flow of business from the City of Keyser. Hard work? In July, 1913, in the midst of a terrible heat-wave, the *Keyser Tribune* reported: "Mr. A. S. Wolf was overcome by heat on Saturday last, while at work shoeing a mule. He was found unconscious lying under the mule and was at once taken home. We are glad to state that he is now much better."

Conservative? The family lifestyle certainly supports this conclusion, but there is an amusing newspaper story that amplifies the notion. In 1914, Mr. Wolf joined nearly fifty of Keyser's leading citizens in protest:

> *To the Honorable Mayor and Members of the Council, Keyser, W. Va. – Believing the dances known as the Tango, Hesitation Waltz, Turkey Trot and other fancy dances now being taught to be immoral, indecent, vulgar, and unbecoming and knowing that the ban has been placed on the dances at Charleston, our state capitol, We the undersigned citizens do hereby petition your Honorable Body, to use your power in prohibiting these dances.*

Augustus Wolf's earthly life expired at home on May 8, 1921. The flower bearers at his funeral were members of Trinity's Church Council: Byron Kesner, J. E. Geldbaugh, Jacob Avers, Edward Bolen, George M. Loy, Robert Lee Fisher, Sr., Joseph Shaffer and John T. Sincell. Rev. J. W. Drawbaugh officiated.

Mrs. Christina (Head) Wolf passed on November 15, 1936. Officiated by Rev. Felix Robinson, participants in her services included the West Virginia Legionettes quartette, John Sincell, George Loy, Harry Sliger, W. E. Coffman, Jack Lotspeich, and Marshall, Harry and Ray Virts.

Their first child, Miss Ella Wolf (1881-1947) worked in the nearby woolen mill for many years. A semi-invalid for several years, she died of injuries received from a fall. She never married.

Ida Wolf (1883-1946) married Joseph W. Fromhart, a railroader. They lived in Newburg for a while but settled in Keyser for the remainder of their lives. They had one son, Richard, who was also a railroader.

Gertrude Wolf (1886-1919) married Patrick Whitehouse, who worked at the local pottery, B&O and woolen mill. They had three children, Wilbur Augustus, Christine (Mrs. Rufino Prieto) and Francis Elizabeth (Mrs. Andrew Murray), who were orphaned when both parents died of influenza during the epidemic of 1918-1919.

At camp on the North River (c. 1933)
(Front) Dr. Harry Kight, Bud & Martha Lee Kight
(Back) Miss Ella Wolf, Mrs. Christina (Head) Wolf

Leah Wolf (1888-1978) married Charles Bower. Before her marriage, she also worked at the woolen mill. They had three children: Arlington, who died in infancy; Beverly, who died of meningitis as a young child, and Barbara Lee (Mrs. Aubrey Johnson), a Navy telegrapher during World War II, who died in Richmond on August 11, 2019.

Georgia Wolf (1897-1983) married Roland Ravenscroft. They had two children: Elyse Jane (Mrs. Charles Peoples), and Patricia Louise (Mrs. William Toth).

Thomas Wolf (1899-1959) died an accidental death in Pittsburgh. He was a bugler for the 13th Cavalry during World War I.

Myra Elizabeth Wolf (1902-1976) married Harry T. Kight (1899-1952), a prominent Keyser pharmacist who purchased the Keyser Pharmacy from Henry Grusendorf in 1927. Myra and Harry Kight had two children: Harry "Bud" Kight and Martha Lee Kight (Mrs. Charles Blackburn).

The North River "camp" acquired by Dr. Kight became a favorite destination for family members. His granddaughter, Mrs. Charlene (Blackburn) Liller recalls the family lore that Dr. Kight would close the pharmacy in late evening on summer nights, drive to the cottage on North River, and return the next morning to reopen the store. Mrs. Kight and her family maintained the family tradition of deep involvement in all aspects of congressional life at Trinity Lutheran.

Coda

When the membership rolls were opened, numerous family members of the forty began their official relationships with the congregation. Other families and individuals joined them. By 1906 the communing membership had nearly doubled. And they kept coming.

Among them were many who were exceptionally important to the success of Trinity Lutheran Church. Mere mention of just a few of the family names brings back the recollections: Athey, Boor, Bosley, Chapman, Coffman, Davis, Fisher, Greenwade, Heare, Kesner, Knott, Loy, Newhauser, Ravenscroft, Scheer, Staggs, Steiding, Tasker, Virts, Watson, Wiley and so many more. A more complete list of congregational members of the mid-1920s may be found in Appendix III.

Chapter 5 – The Shepherds

Strong preachers and teachers who excelled at fostering congregational fellowship and community outreach...

WILLIAM C. NEY (1903–1906)

The Rev. William Cramp Ney was born on January 8, 1879, in Harrisburg, PA, one of eight children of Solomon and Laura (Cramp) Ney. He began his college studies in Gettysburg in 1898. As an exceptional divinity student at the Theological Seminary, William C. Ney was asked to begin his pastoral work in Keyser. He arrived in Keyser in early June and conducted the first service on June 14, 1903 in the name of the General Synod of the Lutheran Church. A few weeks after the Charter was approved on August 16, Brother Ney returned to Gettysburg to continue his studies, coming to Keyser periodically to carry on his work here. Following his ordination by the Maryland Lutheran Synod, Rev. Ney was called as the first full-time pastor of Trinity Memorial Lutheran Church on June 1, 1905.

COURTESY OF TRINITY LUTHERAN CHURCH

Rev. Ney shepherded the congregation through a period of very rapid growth in membership, the acquisition of property and the construction of the church sanctuary on Davis Street. Trinity was truly blessed by the presence of this exceptional missionary.

He accepted a calling to Holy Trinity, Elkins, in November 1906. On June 12, 1907, in Keyser, he married Miss Elsie West Baker, the daughter of Henry and Jane Baker, charter members of Trinity Lutheran. The ceremony was performed by Rev. W. A. Wade, a seminary classmate of Rev. Ney. Rev. Ney was then called to St. Paul's Lutheran in Newport, PA in 1910. His wife Elsie passed away in 1918, leaving two children, Florence Elizabeth Ney (Singe) (1908-2004) and William Luther Ney (1911-1993).

After ten years of service in Newport, Rev. Ney accepted a call as missionary pastor of Temple Lutheran, Brookline, PA. In 1921, he married Mrs. May K. (Lower) Charlton (1874-1946). He remained at Temple Lutheran until his retirement in 1951. Rev. Ney returned to Keyser on several occasions to participate in anniversary celebrations and other special events. He was the guest preacher on August 16, 1953, the observance of Trinity Lutheran's 50th anniversary.

Rev. William C. Ney died in 1967 while living at the Masonic Home in Elizabethtown, Lancaster County, PA. His lifespan of eight-eight years, six months and one day has not been exceeded by any of the subsequent pastors of Trinity Lutheran.

McCall Piatt Bastian (1907-1912)

The Rev. Dr. McCall Piatt Bastian, better known locally as Rev. C. P. Bastian, was born in Lycoming County, at White Deer Valley in Central Pennsylvania, on February 8, 1864. He attended Susquehanna Missionary Institute, graduated Gettysburg College in 1894. From 1894 until 1900 he served as principal of the Muncy Normal School and for a year he was affiliated with the Emporium public schools. He then returned to Gettysburg to prepare for the ministry and graduated Gettysburg Theological Seminary, where one would expect he met Trinity's first pastor, William Ney.

Rev. Bastian was ordained and called by a Lutheran congregation in Littlestown in 1903. Four years later, he was called by Trinity Lutheran and installed as its minister on April 14, 1907.

He was a very popular and able pastor. His speaking skills were exceptional, as were his abilities to engender fellowship among members of the congregation and reach out into the community with his amiable personality and wit. He spoke at events throughout the community; his special services held at Trinity for local social and service organizations and trade unions were well attended. It was during his pastorate that a club house was built behind the church (c.1911) to provide rooms for Sunday School classes, meetings, dinners and other social events. The congregation doubled in size during his five years at Trinity Lutheran.

To the deep regret of his parishioners, he tendered his resignation here, effective March 1, 1912. It was the desire of his entire membership to have him continue his pastorate here, but they consented to release him that he might have the privileges of a larger field and enlarged opportunities. He then immediately accepted the call to become pastor of Christ Lutheran church in Charleroi. After serving that congregation for seven years, he accepted a call to Holy Trinity Lutheran in Berlin, in nearby Somerset County. There he remained for twenty-three years, during which he served terms as president and secretary of the Central Pennsylvania Lutheran Synod. Dr. Bastian received the degree of Doctor of Divinity from Susquehanna University. He retired from active ministry in 1942.

He was first married to the former Clemmie Follmer. They had three children; the youngest, their daughter Kathryn Virginia Bastian was born in Keyser on September 3, 1907. Following Clemmie's death on Dec. 27, 1927, Rev. Bastian married Mrs. Blanche Harnish.

Even after leaving Trinity, he maintained his deep and loving relationships with many in Keyser.

Following his retirement, Dr. Bastian and his second wife resided in Altoona, where he died at his home on January 18, 1946.

Harry F. Baughman (1913–1918)

The Rev. Dr. Harry F. Baughman was Trinity Lutheran's third Pastor. He came to Keyser directly after his June graduation from Gettysburg Theological Seminary.

On October 27, 1913, the *Evening Times* newspaper reported:

> The members of the Lutheran church gave a reception to their pastor, Rev. H. F. Baughman, at the church on Friday night. A large number availed themselves of the opportunity to meet Rev. Baughman. Mr. and Mrs. John Sincell, Mr. and Mrs. Chas. Broome, Mr. Geo. Loy, Rev. Baughman, Mr. and Mrs. Sliger were in the receiving line. Mrs. Aleta Snyder and Mrs. Claude Clevenger pointed out the way to the refreshment room, which was in charge of Mrs. Joe Shaffer and Mrs. Gus Wolf, who were assisted by a number of the young ladies of the church. Rev. Baughman is a young man, and is taking a special interest in the children and the Boy Scout movement. The excellent church orchestra furnished delightful music during the evening.

COURTESY OF TRINITY LUTHERAN CHURCH

Rev. Baughman was beloved by the congregation and the community. He organized the Christian Endeavor Society, which was well attended by the young people. He organized an orchestra that performed before and after services. Directed by Lawrence Kolkhorst, members included Warren, Emmett and Anna Kolkhorst, Virginia Knott, R. A. Stoutamyer, and Walter Kephart. He served as Secretary (1915-1917) and President (1917-1918) of the Lutheran Synod of West Virginia.

Harry Fridley Baughman was born in Everett, Bedford County, Pennsylvania, on January 23, 1892. After coming to Keyser, he met a lovely young lady, Miss Joretha Ambrose Liller, whom he married on October 17, 1916. Harry's father, a Lutheran minister himself, united the couple in marriage. Harry and Joretha had one son, Peter Fridley Baughman.

After leaving Keyser, he served as pastor of St. Stephen's Lutheran Church, Pittsburgh, and Trinity Lutheran Church, Germantown, PA. During his pastorate in Germantown, he was awarded the honorary degree of Doctor of Divinity by Gettysburg College in 1931. He joined the seminary faculty as a professor of homiletics (the art of preaching) in 1941 and was named its president in 1951.

Rev. Baughman was a gifted and prolific preacher, a talent that came to light very early in his life. Later in her life, his sister Mary told the following story:

> It was the custom for every child in the Sunday School to be given a little Christmas box of hard candy, the kind of box with a handle, and an orange. An orange was very, very special then. We'd all be dressed fit to kill to say our speeches or sing our songs. The year that my younger brother Harry was four, he stood up to give his speech and then wouldn't come down when he had finished, saying "I still have to say Mary's speech." After delivering my speech he still wouldn't quit. After he had recited "Mary had a little lamb" and a couple of other pieces, he was finally lured down. Apparently the quite positive congregational reaction weighed more heavily in the lad's mind than our father's admonitions, for the boy grew up to become the Rev. Harry F. Baughman, president of the Lutheran Seminary at Gettysburg.

When Rev. Harry F. Baughman arrived in Keyser in 1913, he encountered a crisis in the world of sports. The renowned basketball team at Keyser Preparatory School (now Potomac State College) had been disbanded when Prof. Joseph Stayman, president of the school, learned that some team members had engaged in "activities unbecoming to college students" following a game in Garrett County. Garrett was a 'wet' county and Mineral was 'dry'. You get the point...

Paul J. Davis, who later became President of the Keyser National Bank, set out to help organize an independent team with the college players and some new talent. Learning that Rev. Baughman had been the star of the Gettysburg team, he was quickly added to the roster. Clem Montgomery, Perry Greenwade and Dyke Shaffer were among other Trinity members who played for the new independent team, the Keyser Collegians.

Keyser Collegians (c. 1915–1916)
Front, l–r: Rev. Harry F. Baughman, Paul J. Davis, Mutt Lowden
Standing, l–r: John Carter, Clem Montgomery, Herbert Moore, Perry Greenwade, Dyke Shaffer

But there arose an unusual dilemma. It seems that some members of his congregation felt that basketball was an inappropriate avocation for a minister, especially since players wore shorts during the games. The astute Rev. Baughman proposed a compromise that was acceptable to his parishioners. He wore trousers during 'home' games, and reverted to shorts for 'away' games! He was obviously wearing his 'home' uniform when this team photo was taken. Decades later, Davis told sportswriter J. Suter Kegg that Baughman was the "best shooter" he had ever seen.

At the conclusion of the team's first season, the *Mineral Daily News* published the following article on April 6, 1914:

> The Keyser Collegians closed their basketball season in a whirlwind manner Friday night by defeating the champion Coney aggregation to the tune of 38-13. The game was by far the most exciting ever played here and was played before the largest crowd that has ever witnessed a game in Keyser. The Armory was filled to capacity. Regardless of the fact that the Collegians were late in getting started [and ineligible to win the championship], the season has been a very successful one. The only game lost was the one played against Fairmont, and this would have no doubt been won had the Collegians had the regular team on the floor.
>
> The individuals of the Collegian team are to be praised upon the "big league style" in which they played throughout the season. Baughman, at center, played his position like a "star". He was one of the mainstays of the team-work and in the majority of games caged between fifteen and twenty field goals. Greenwade played a good game at both guard and forward, being able to fill both positions like an "old timer." Capt. Davis is to be complimented on his consistent playing and manner in which he captained the team, secured game, etc.

William "Willie" Boor, another member of Trinity, played for the Collegians in the 1920s.

W. V. Garrett (1919-1920)

The Rev. Dr. Wouter Van Garrett was born in Hanover, Pennsylvania, on November 27, 1891. His father was a cigar maker. The presence of the Garrett family in York County is well documented to the mid-1700s as is the family association with St. David's Lutheran Church.

As a youngster, he was a student at the Gettysburg Academy boarding school. He then enrolled at the Millersville Normal School (now Millersville University) and became a public school teacher. In

1912, he accepted a $200 scholarship from the synod and enrolled at Gettysburg College; he received his B.A. degree in 1916. While a student at Gettysburg Seminary he served as a supply pastor at the North River church at Rio, in Hampshire County. He accepted a call to Trinity Lutheran in March, 1919, and began his full-time pastorate immediately following completion of his studies and graduation.

Perhaps the congregation saw in Garrett a parallel with the backgrounds of Ney and Baughman. But that outcome was not realized during his brief stay in Keyser. A week after his marriage in August, 1920, he resigned his pastorate at Trinity on September 1, 1920, and moved back to Pennsylvania to be with his wife and both of their families. There he realized his full potential as a pastor. He served as the pastor of Trinity Lutheran, Steelton, and Immanuel Lutheran, Norwood, before being called by Evangelical Lutheran, Frederick, Maryland in 1944, where he remained for ten years. During his pastorate in Frederick, his congregation gained a large number of new members. He then became the pastor of the Lutheran congregation in Sea Isle, New Jersey, for three years, and retired in 1957.

Dr. Garrett was awarded a honorary Doctor of Divinity degree from Gettysburg in 1945 and served as president of the Maryland Lutheran Synod. He was musically talented and a prolific author, writing many articles for various denominational publications as well as secular papers and magazines.

Dr. Garrett and his wife had one child, Robert L. Garrett. Wouter Van Garrett died on April 8, 1962, at the age of seventy, in Harrisburg.

J. W. Drawbaugh (1921-1925)

The Rev. Jacob Wilbur Drawbaugh was born on October 15, 1896, at Steelton, home of the Pennsylvania Steel Company, near Harrisburg. All six of his siblings were girls. He was Baptized and Confirmed in faith at St. John's Lutheran Church, Steelton. He enrolled at Gettysburg College in 1914, sang in the Glee Club, played varsity football, and received a B.A. degree in 1918. It wasn't announced until after his graduation that he had married Amelia Marie Perry (1897-1967). When he was home on Christmas vacation, he and Miss Perry went off for a day's visit to relatives, so they said, but instead journeyed to Baltimore where they were married on December 27, 1916 – six months before she graduated Central High School, Harrisburg.

He went to work for Harrisburg Boiler and Manufacturing. After a few short months, he returned to Gettysburg with Marie to prepare for the Lutheran ministry. She enrolled as a student at Gettysburg College and later became a leader in the women's alumni society of the college.

While still in his final year of seminary studies, he was identified as a candidate for the open position at Trinity Lutheran. After hearing him preach a sermon in Keyser in early January, 1921, the congregation responded favorably. He was invited back for a second time. Immediately following that service, the congregation formally voted to extend a calling to Rev. Drawbaugh. Upon graduation in May, the young family of father, mother and their first child, Marna Jane (1919-2005), moved to Keyser and he began his ministry. The formal service of Installation was held on December 4, 1921.

THE SPECTRUM – GETTYSBURG COLLEGE

Rev. Drawbaugh immediately enmeshed himself in the life of the congregation and the community and perhaps was a bit more evangelistic in style than his predecessors. He encouraged organizations within the congregation to further promote fellowship among members, adults and children alike. He took up leadership of the community Boy Scout troop, engaged local veterans organizations, social and service clubs, and added his vocal talent to the musical scene.

Then, on May 15, 1922, the *Mineral Daily News* reported the following:

"Rev. Drawbaugh Suffers Breakdown – The congregation of Trinity Lutheran Church received a shock at the morning services yesterday when the Rev. J. W. Drawbaugh suffered a breakdown shortly after he began his sermon. Rev. Drawbaugh was obviously nervous when he arose to deliver his text, and after a few words sank into his seat at the pulpit, in a semiconscious state.

Dr. A. A. Scherr was worshiping in the congregation and rendered medical aid to the stricken pastor, after which he ordered Rev. Drawbaugh to be removed to his home. Rev. Drawbaugh was taken to the Scherr residence where after a restful night he was reported as doing nicely. Overwork is given as the reason for the breakdown."

Rev. Drawbaugh sought treatment in Baltimore and at the Jefferson Hospital in Philadelphia; he returned to Keyser in mid-June. During the service on June 25, he suffered a relapse. The family then went to Crystal Springs, Pennsylvania, for two months of rest to hasten his recuperation. Upon his return, he reduced his activities somewhat but continued to serve the congregation in an exemplary manner. Marie gave birth to two children during their time in Keyser – Charles Perry (1921–1997) and Alice Idella (1923–1998). He served as vice-president of the West Virginia Synod and the executive committee of Loysville Orphans Home.

His friendly and accommodating style is well-illustrated by an amusing story in the local newspaper, published on June 20, 1925:

> "On Tuesday afternoon, two people walked leisurely into the department store of the Sincell Company, looked about and then stepped into the elevator and ascended to the second floor. Presently the Rev. J. W. Drawbaugh of the Lutheran Church entered the store and with J. H. Swadley [who worked for Sincell] went to the second floor. In a few minutes Mausby L. Rogers and Mrs. Myrtle Connell Inskeep were united in marriage. It was two o'clock in the afternoon, and so quietly was the whole thing pulled off that even the clerks and proprietor did not know of the wedding taking place in the store until today. Both the bride and the groom have lived in Keyser for several years and are well known. The groom was a soldier in the late war and saw service in France and was in some hot battles, but stayed with them, facing fire and shell, until the end. The News published many interesting letters from him, written while at the front."

Three months later, on September 20, 1925, Rev. Drawbaugh announced that he had accepted a call to St. Luke's Lutheran, Baltimore, and that he would deliver his farewell sermon on October 11, at the evening service. Rev. Drawbaugh and his family made many warm friends in Keyser. The parishioners didn't want him to leave and the council actually refused to accept his resignation. Rev. Drawbaugh felt it was his duty to accept the Baltimore calling. Notably, he returned on numerous occasions to participate in weddings, funerals, evangelical events, and to enjoy fishing in camps along Patterson Creek and the South Branch. Their fourth child, Jacob Wilbur, Jr. (1928–2000), was born in Baltimore. Wilbur and Marie were divorced in 1944 and he remarried that same year.

Rev. J. W. Drawbaugh retired after forty-five years in the ministry. He died on May 16, 1968 while living on his farm near Cockeysville.

Robert T. Vorberg (1926–1933)

The Rev. Robert Traugott Vorberg was born in Milwaukee on April 19, 1868. His father, George Albert Gottlief Vorberg was a Lutheran minister. Recent communications from a great-grandson of Rev. Robert T. Vorberg note that the Vorberg family was originally from Sweden and that there are four-hundred years of Lutheran ministers in the family, including one who was Chaplain to King Gustavus of Sweden during the 1600s.

Rev. Vorberg was an 1889 graduate of Wagoner College, located in Rochester at the time, and the conservative Philadelphia Seminary in 1892. He was ordained by the Lutheran Church Missouri Synod in 1893. His first call was to Zion's Lutheran, Newark, New Jersey. In 1895 he was called by Trinity Lutheran, Floradale, Ontario, Canada, where he served from 1895 to 1901. He then returned to New York, where he served several upstate congregations until his call to First Evangelical (German) Lutheran in Nashville, Tennessee, c.1910. His penultimate calling was to St. Luke's Lutheran, Marietta, Ohio, c.1918, where he remained until he came to Keyser in late 1925 and was formally installed as pastor of Trinity Lutheran in April 1926. Highly experienced, he was the first pastor of Trinity Lutheran who was not a recent seminarian.

Considering his background, it is not surprising that he was seen as a conservative minister and individual. And yet, he was highly ecumenical in his outreach. Shortly before his death he hosted a special service at Trinity for the Odd Fellows and Rebekah Lodges.

Vestments for the pastor and choir and candles on the altar became standard practice for worship. He introduced the ritual Blessing of the Palms. During his pastorate, the parsonage at 47 South Main Street was purchased.

He married Salome Amalia Ungerer in 1893. They had seven children: Magdalene Emily, Emily Henriette, Edith Salome, Martin Philip, Robert George Gustav, Salome Edith Sarah and Ruth Elizabeth.

Confirmation Class of 1931
(front) Elizabeth Loy, Gertrude Pennell, Rev. Robert Vorberg, Mary Evelyn Sliger, Christine Whitehouse
(back) Robert Lee Fisher, Abram T. Goldsworthy, Jack Bosley, James W. Goldsworthy,
William Cook, Charles Chapman, Joseph Scherr

Although he had been in poor health for a year or two, Dr. Vorberg's sudden death came as a shock to the community. A group of women of the church were meeting with Mrs. Vorberg at the new parsonage. After helping his wife wipe the dishes, he retired to his room, telling her he would call if he needed her. During the meeting Mrs. Vorberg thought she heard him call and went to his room to find him dying. Robert T. Vorberg left this life on July 7, 1933, a victim of heart failure, at the age of sixty-five.

FELIX G. ROBINSON (1934–1937)

A native of nearby Oakland, Felix G. Robinson was born July 24, 1898, a son of Dr. John and Martha (Hinebaugh) Robinson. He was a veteran of World War I. He graduated Gettysburg College and Seminary and was ordained in October, 1925. He served Emanuel Lutheran in the Bronx and St. John's-by-the-Sea Lutheran on Long Island for several years before being called by Trinity Lutheran in Keyser. He also worked at the Westminster Choir School, Princeton, N.J. and the Arthurdale Community Church.

In addition to being a highly skilled musician himself, Rev. Robinson was highly supportive of the music program at Trinity Lutheran. His enthusiasm spread throughout the community and beyond. He developed and directed the annual Mountain Choir festival at Mt. Lake Park amphitheater for several years, which attracted much attention and had such guest stars as Reinald Werrenrath and

Eleanor Steber of the Metropolitan Opera. Mrs. Eleanor Roosevelt was interested in his choral work while at Arthurdale. He directed the Oakland Centennial in 1949 and the Friendsville Bicentennial in 1966, writing the music for each celebration.

COURTESY OF TRINITY LUTHERAN CHURCH

Along his path of life, he left the ministry and became a member of St. Peter's Catholic Church, Oakland. He composed, wrote, and lectured on church liturgy and music. He died suddenly on Monday evening, September 11, 1967, at his home, "Mendeli", in Oakland. He was 69 years of age.

And now, here's a fascinating story of Rev. Robinson's ministerial career before he came to Keyser in March, 1934, published in *The Gettysburg Times* on September 4, 1933:

Friends Stand By Minister:
Rev. Felix G. Robinson Retained By Congregation; Use Private Home.

The Rev. Felix G. Robinson, formerly of Gettysburg and a graduate of Gettysburg College and seminary, appears to have a complete victory in his difference with one of the wealthy members of his congregation at Long Beach, L.I., according to an article appearing in the current edition of *Time* magazine. The article, under a heading, "Unchurch" follows:

"Four years ago, the Riverside Drive home of Mrs. Paul Condit-Smith, sister of the late General Leonard Wood, was dismantled, loaded on barges and taken to Long Beach, L.I. There it was remodeled to become St. John's Lutheran Church-by-the-Sea. Last week it became the property of a Long Beach businessman named Charles W. Ackerman. He was scarcely pleased to have it.

Businessman Ackerman's troubles with St. John's Church-by-the-Sea were of long standing. Last winter, as chairman of the church council, he squabbled over policies with the pastor, the Rev. Felix G. Robinson. One day, Pastor Robinson angrily struck businessman Ackerman, who retaliated. Businessman Ackerman held a $10,000 bond as guarantee of a mortgage on the church. To protect his investment, he bid on the church at a foreclosure sale. Last week he presented his fellow Lutherans with an ultimatum: they could oust Pastor Robinson and buy businessman Ackerman's church, or they could get out.

The congregation promptly got out, taking their pastor with them and setting up a church of their own in a private house. Businessman Ackerman ruefully surveyed his Church-by-the-Sea, wandering what one can do with an unchurched church.

The Later Years

Here we conclude the biographical sketches of Trinity's earliest pastors. In the interest of thoroughness, the following information about its later pastors has been gleaned from church records and other sources.

C. K. Spiggle (1937–1949)

The Rev. Charles Krauth Spiggle served for eleven years as pastor of Casebeer Lutheran in nearby Somerset County, one of Pennsylvania's largest country parishes. He resigned at the very end of 1936 and moved to Cumberland to become the regional representative of the Lutheran Brotherhood. He first came to Trinity as a frequent supply minister following the departure of Rev. Robinson and accepted the calling to become Trinity's pastor in June, 1937. A conservative in practice, he was a very vigorous man. He supplied the church at Westernport while they were without a pastor. During his pastorate at Trinity, the magnificent M.P. Möller pipe organ was acquired and Mary Evelyn (Sliger) Coffman began her sixty-year tenure as the primary organist. Rev. Spiggle served the congregation until his death at the age of sixty-five on July 5, 1949.

L. E. Bouknight (1949–1952)

The Rev. Louis Elbert Bouknight was Trinity's only pastor called from the South Virginia Synod. He was a graduate of the Lutheran Theological Seminary in Columbia, South Carolina and came to Keyser after an eight-year pastorate at Bethany Lutheran Church, near Lexington. He put emphasis on thoroughness in catechetical instruction, in finance, and in conservative Lutheran practice. He was the first pastor to wear a cassock and stole in the Trinity pulpit. He demanded thorough instruction before reception of new members. Planning for a Parish House began during his tenure. He died on January 28, 1968, Waynesboro, Virginia, at the age of sixty-eight.

Donald D. Anderson (1952–1963)

The Rev. Dr. Donald David Anderson was a native of Morgantown. The early summer of 1952 was a busy time for him: accepting the calling to Trinity Lutheran and beginning his pastorate here, graduating Gettysburg Seminary, and marrying his wife Lorna. He excelled in all aspects of ministry. He was an effective preacher and teacher, greatly strengthened the programs for children and helped to make Camp Luther a "must do" experience. His friendly demeanor and leadership skills were admired by all. During his eleven-year stewardship, the Parish House was built and completed in 1953 at a cost of $46,000. These years also saw great improvement in the church building and parsonage. The new Common Service Book (the "Red Book") was adopted. For the first time, Trinity had a paid secretary. He left Trinity to become Assistant to the President of the Western Pennsylvania – West Virginia Synod; he was elected as Secretary of the Synod in 1966. He received his doctorate degree from Thiel

College in 1970. He died on January 28, 2013, at the age of eighty-seven. At the time of his death, one of his daughters wrote: *"His 29 years in an elected position in the Lutheran church may very well have set a record. Upon his retirement, he began serving as a part-time interim at his home congregation of St. John's Lutheran Church of Highland [near] Pittsburgh where he had been a member for 25 years. As other pastors came and went, Pastor Anderson remained on staff, and what began as a "temporary" call lasted another 25 years! Someone wrote once that when you were with Don Anderson you felt that you were the only person in the world."*

This was the Rev. Anderson we knew and loved.

Rev. R. J. Westerberg (1963–1965)

The Rev. Robert J. Westerberg was a graduate of Gustavus Adolphus College and the Augustana Lutheran Theological Seminary. The Augustana Synod became a member of the Lutheran Church in America through merger. Prior to his Keyser tenure, he ministered to churches in Bruno, Minnesota, and Harcourt, Iowa. It was during his time here that the church built a new parsonage, costing $29,000. He led thorough catechetical instruction and Bibles were purchased for every confirmand for the first time. He left Keyser and was eventually called to a pastorate in Pennsylvania. He died on January 26, 2002, at Marlborough, Massachusetts.

Gerald Huhn (1966–1970)

The Rev. Gerald Huhn came to Trinity Lutheran Church from his graduation at Gettysburg Seminary and was formally installed on July 17, 1966. While he was pastor here, it was decided to build a new church. The groundbreaking was held August 3, 1969; the cornerstone was placed on October 12 and the dedication of the new building was held on June 14, 1970. Rev. Huhn was very interested in contemporary worship and ministry to the youth. He left Trinity on July 31, 1970, to accept a call to Holy Trinity Lutheran Church, Hershey, Pennsylvania.

Donald W. Moore (1971–1981)

The Rev. Donald Woodrow Moore was born August 6, 1913, at Hagerstown and was a graduate of Shepherdstown High School, Shepherd College and the Lutheran Theological Seminary, Mt. Airy (Philadelphia), Pennsylvania. He served long tenures at three congregations in Pennsylvania and became the Dean of the Pittsburgh District of the Western Pennsylvania – West Virginia Synod. Nearing retirement age, he and his wife Lillie chose to come to Keyser to be closer to Shepherdstown. Rev. Moore assumed the pastorate at Trinity on July 15, 1971. They fell in love with Trinity Lutheran and Keyser, and the congregation and community fell in love with them. He retired on January 1, 1981; they purchased a home in Keyser and remained here. Rev. Moore died in Keyser on April 11, 1991; Bishop Alexander Black and Rev. Bradley Will led the funeral service at 2:00 pm on Sunday, April 14. In her later years and following the 2010 death of their son Don, Mrs. Moore moved to Chambersburg to be near their daughter Anne (Moore) Cowley. Lilly (Rockenbaugh) Moore died on February 22, 2012, at age 97. Rev. Moore and his wife were lovely and faithful children of God.

Jack R. Stennett (1981-1988)

The Rev. Jack R. Stennett came to Trinity Lutheran from Grace Lutheran Church, St. Albans, West Virginia. He received degrees from Indiana University of Pennsylvania and Shippensburg State College. While at the Gettysburg Seminary he served a one year internship at Greencastle and did a meaningful summer of work at Woodville State Hospital at Pittsburgh. It was during his tenure at Trinity that a shared ministry with Mt. Calvary, Westernport, began. He resigned during the summer of 1988 to accept a call at Zion Lutheran , Danville, Ohio.

Bradley J. Will (1989-1994)

The Rev. Bradley Will, a native of Mesa, Arizona, was a 1985 graduate of Luther College and a recent graduate of Wartburg Theological Seminary, both in Iowa, when he accepted the call to Trinity Lutheran. He was an effective minister and quite involved in community activities. He left Trinity to accept a calling to Bethlehem Lutheran, Traverse City, Michigan.

Matthew Riegel (1994-2000)

The Rev. Matthew Riegel, a native of Birdsboro, Pennsylvania, joined the roster of Trinity Lutheran pastors who were recent graduates of Gettysburg Seminary. He served an internship at Bedford's Trinity Lutheran Church, where he was ordained, before coming to Keyser to begin his ministry in the late summer of 1994. He was called as the Chaplain of the Lutheran Campus Ministry at West Virginia University, effective August 1, 2000. He was elected Bishop of the West Virginia – Western Maryland Synod of the Evangelical Lutheran Church in America and began his service in that office on September 26, 2015.

Sally Bartling (2001-)

The Rev. Sally Bartling, while employed in the private sector, was called by the Lord to enter the ministry. She studied at the seminary at Gettysburg, near where she was living. Upon her graduation, she was called by the joint ministries of Trinity Lutheran and Mt. Calvary Lutheran and has served both congregations with distinction. Pastor Bartling is also actively engaged in campus ministry at Potomac State College.

William Wayne Wolfe

No discussion of the pastors of Trinity Lutheran can be considered complete without mention of William Wayne Wolfe. For several decades, including his later years, he often served as a layman supply pastor in Trinity's pulpit. Other area congregations, including Janes A.M.E. Church, just a few steps from his home on Church Street, called upon Mr. Wolfe to preach from time to time.

William W. "Willie" Wolfe was born in Cumberland in 1900, the son of Charles Clinton Wolfe, a railroad conductor, and Katie Leone (Clevenger) Wolfe. After her husband's untimely death in 1902 at age thirty, Katie and her son moved to Keyser, where her widowed mother and several of her siblings resided. (Her brother Claude was married to Kate (Avers) Clevenger, a charter member of Trinity.)

Mr. Wolfe graduated Keyser High School in 1918 with another son of Trinity Lutheran, Clifton

L. Avers. He was president of his senior class at KHS and great buddy of another classmate and well-known Keyserite, Ervin 'Ikey' Dayton. Following a very short stint at the B&O, Mr. Wolfe was employed by the Postal Service where he worked as a clerk and letter carrier from January, 1919, until retirement. Never married, he demonstrated his love for others by rearing Robert W. Smith.

Mr. Wolfe was an extraordinarily dedicated member of Trinity throughout his life. Taking his motivation from his mother, the Word and Trinity's early pastors, he studied the Bible and lived as a Christian. He was teaching the men's Bible Class before age of twenty and served as superintendent of the Sunday School (1921-1935). He served the Lutheran Synod of West Virginia as the first president of the statewide Luther League (1927-1929). Elected at a meeting at Grace Lutheran, Fairmont, in 1927, he led the first three annual conventions Parkersburg, Grafton and Charleston.

Mr. Wolfe was an exceptional student of history. He was an avid reader and had a talent for extracting nuggets of the past from his conversations with others. His small house was filled with documents and artifacts from nearby discoveries and distant exotic locales. As Keyser approached its 100th anniversary in 1974, Mr. Wolfe was officially appointed as the Centennial Historian. He wrote and published *A History of Keyser from 1737 to 1913,* a book that is still treasured by local historians. It is remarkable that he was able to accomplish so much research and accurately interpret his findings, decades before modern technology made many primary source documents readily available to the general public.

Few, if any, have had a more durable and meaningful impact on Trinity Lutheran and our community than Mr. William Wayne "Willie" Wolfe. He died on April 4, 1979.

Coda

Several other members of the Lutheran clergy had important roles during the early years of Trinity.

The Rev. Dr. Aaron Stewart Hartman (1845-1928) was elected to the Board of Home Missions of the General Synod. In 1890 he became General Secretary of this board, an office he held until 1916. It was his responsiveness as General Secretary that led to the assignment of divinity student William Ney and the formation of Trinity Memorial Lutheran Church in 1903. After the organization of the United Lutheran Church in America, he was chosen Educational Secretary of the Board of Home Missions and Church Extension and retained this position with the Board of American Missions until the time of his death.

The Rev. Dr. Charles S. Trump (1856-1919), the senior Lutheran pastor in the region in 1903, was born in Carroll County, Maryland. He engaged in an academic course of studies at the Western Maryland College before graduating Gettysburg Seminary and becoming the pastor of the Lutheran Church in Harpers Ferry. During that time, he also taught in the local public school. After two years, he was called to the old stone church in Centerville, Pennsylvania. In 1888, he resigned that pastorate to accept a call from St. John's Church at Martinsburg. Here he labored faithfully until his untimely death in 1919. His assistance was instrumental in the founding of Trinity Lutheran Church.

The Rev. Dr. Luther Ambrose Mann (1834-1908), pastor of St. John's Lutheran Church in Cumberland, was a strong supporter of Trinity during its earliest days. Born in Loudoun County, he attended school in Winchester, graduated Roanoke College and entered the pastorate at the beginning of the Civil War, during which he and his wife cared for sick and wounded soldiers.

The Rev. Wilbur C. Mann (1880-1959) was the son of Rev. L. A. Mann. He graduated Roanoke College in 1903 with an A.B. degree and then studied under the personal tutelage of his father. It was during this period that he served Trinity Lutheran as a supply minister during times when William Ney was unavailable because of his studies in Gettysburg. Rev. Mann was ordained in 1907 and became pastor of the church in Donora, Pennsylvania. He also served St. James Lutheran, Emsworth. He was a gifted preacher and organizer.

The Rev. Dr. Peter Bergstresser was a periodic supply minister during the period 1903-1905. A graduate of the seminary in Gettysburg, he was ordained in 1855 and was a noted Biblical scholar in the Lutheran world. He died in 1905, a week before his eightieth birthday, at Wilkinsburg, Pennsylvania, where he retired in 1903.

The Rev. Dr. John William McCauley (1878-1968) came to St. Paul's Lutheran, Cumberland, after completing his seminary studies and served until late 1910 when he accepted a call to the Church of the Incarnation, Baltimore. He then returned to Salem, Virginia, where he was born, to minister to congregations there. Two of his siblings were also Lutheran ministers.

The Rev. Luther F. Miller graduated Gettysburg Theological Seminary and was ordained and called to Mt. Calvary Lutheran, Westernport, in 1898. He remained there until mid-1904. In the *History of the Evangelical Lutheran Synod of Maryland* (Wentz – 1920) it is noted, "During the next year or so he toured in Europe and especially made a pilgrimage to the Luther country. On January 1, 1906, he became pastor of Bethany Evangelical Lutheran Church of Baltimore." He served there until 1923. By 1925 he was serving Bethel Lutheran, Manassas, Virginia. He retired from full-time ministry in 1937 and returned to the Hagerstown area, where he died in 1955.

Chapter 6 – The Music

*The Lutheran Church
seems to be filled with music...*

Music and a traditional liturgical setting have always played central roles in worship and outreach. Trinity was widely recognized as the musical center of the community. On June 15, 1914, the *Mineral Daily* commented: "The Lutheran Church seems to be filled with music."

Nearly a century later, in his sermon on the celebration of sixty years of ministry on May 20, 2012, Rev. Dr. Donald D. Anderson remembered his days at Trinity Lutheran:

109

I began my ministry at Trinity Lutheran Church in Keyser on June 1, 1952. Trinity was a wonderful, musical and loving congregation that taught me so much about being a pastor. Talk about music – Trinity had it all: a pipe organ and four organists; an adult choir of twenty-four, eighteen of those with voice training; a youth choir that sang regularly with eighteen to twenty-four youth from ages five to fourteen and a Sunday School orchestra. I had no thoughts of doing anything else in my ministry other than to serve this congregation.

Yes, for those in Keyser who wanted to experience great church music, Trinity Lutheran Church was the place to be. Vocalists and instrumentalists were highly talented. Parishioners and visitors sang from the pews and heard their voices blend with the best. And all who came experienced the beautiful musical illumination of worship. Thankfully, the tradition of excellent music is still alive at Trinity, where the musicians and the Holy Spirit lift high the assembled voices.

What follows are vignettes of musical events that provide a glimpse into the depth and breadth of the musical program and many of its talented artists. Presented chronologically, most are captured directly from newspaper articles of the day.

1910–1919

On December 22, 1911, the *Keyser Tribune* noted the upcoming Christmas services at Trinity.

Christmas at Lutheran Church – The Christmas sermon will be preached Sunday morning at 11 o'clock. Special music will be rendered by the choir. The Christmas service, "The Angelic Choirs'" will be given by the Sunday School and Choir combined on Christmas eve (Sunday) at 7:30 o'clock. An early service will be held at 6:30 o'clock Christmas morning. Everybody is most cordially invited to all these services.

On June 16, 1913, the *Mineral Daily News* informed its readers that Children's Day was celebrated at the local Lutheran Church:

Children's Day was observed in Trinity Lutheran Church yesterday with appropriate services. The church was beautifully decorated with potted flowers, roses and daisies. Two canaries added life to the service with their singing. The Sunday School choir, under the direction of Mr. D. T. Greenwade, rendered several selections very creditably. Solos by Miss Viola Wildemann and Miss Anna Kolkhorst and a duet by Misses Wildemann and Nyta Shaffer were the special features of the program by the adult department of the Sunday School. The musical part of the program was exceptionally fine and was greatly appreciated by the splendid audience.

The infant department was trained by Mrs. C. C. Clevenger and Mrs. H. A. Sliger, and rendered their part of the program in a very creditable manner. The program by the infant department included songs, recitations, and exercises by the little ones. The offering at this service is devoted to the cause of the Lutheran Orphanage at Loysville, Pa.

The schedule of Holy Week services in 1916 was published in the *Mineral Daily News* on April 18.

There will be special services at the Lutheran Church each evening this week in observance of the most solemn season of the Church year, Holy Week. Themes appropriate to the season will be presented. The subjects announced are: Tuesday, "The Forsaken Christ."; Wednesday, "The Denied Christ."; Thursday, "The Wounded Christ."; Friday, "The Crucified Christ."

There will be special music by the choir each evening. On Monday evening Mr. Greenwade and Mrs. Shaffer will sing, "The Love That Won."

The public are cordially invited to attend these services. The purpose is to commemorate the Passion of our Lord and to better prepare for the season of Easter.

At the Holy Week service in the Lutheran church tonight the choir will render the scared composition, "Ashamed of Jesus" specially arranged by Benjamin.

The theme will be "The Forsaken Christ." This is the season when the church calls to the followers of Christ to meditate upon His sufferings and death. It is the most sacred season of the church year, when the Passion of the Savior is commemorated. The services of the Holy Week are designed to draw us nearer to the Christ who died for us. The chief thought is the central theme of the Gospel, and great blessing is derived from thus commemorating the time of the crucifixion. Everyone is cordially invited to partake in these services.

1920–1929

On January 29, 1920, The *Mineral Daily* informed its readers:

Not very frequently do the church people have anything out of the ordinary, but the Lutherans made Sunday a very interesting occasion at both morning and evening services by the rendering of special music by young people, turning the day over to them. Twenty five boys and girls marched into the sanctuary singing. A junior sextet, consisting of Georgia Arnold, Ethel Dayton, Elizabeth Gull, Wealthy Gank, Ruth Tasker and Ada Lee Matlick sang. The duet by Irene Davis and Elizabeth Loy was very sweet and well rendered. These children are about four years of age. There were boy ushers.

At the evening service the Sunday School orchestra furnished the music. Frank Hott rendered a cornet solo, Lawrence Kolkhorst played a violin solo and D. T. Greenwade and Miss Nyta Shaffer sang a duet. Perry Greenwade, soloist, Mrs. Clem Montgomery and Lawrence Kolkhorst in a vocal duet also took part. Rev. W. V. Garrett gave a four minute talk. The church was crowded.

The orchestra was organized during the pastorate of Rev. Harry Baughman; Lawrence Kolkhorst was the director and his talented brothers and sister were mainstays of the ensemble that was a significant element of the musical program at Trinity Lutheran for four decades.

On June 22, 1922, McElwee's Band drew a huge crowd at an open-air concert in front of the church. Later that year, the Christmas Cantata "The Christ Child" was so popular and meaningful that it was repeated in January of 1923 in response to many requests. The choir put forth a great deal of effort to prepare this masterpiece in song.

In December 1923 the *Mineral Daily News* published this announcement: "Lutheran Church Choir to Give Christmas Cantata – A Christmas Cantata will be given at Trinity Lutheran Church, Sunday evening, December 23rd, at 7:30 P.M., by the mixed choir. This cantata, "The Light Eternal," will be the most beautiful of any rendered by this choir with musical accompaniment of string instruments."

By 1925, the Young Peoples Choir had grown to thirty members.

The choir appeared in vestments for the first time on Easter Sunday, March 31, 1929. Later that year, a special invitation was published in the *Mineral Daily and Keyser Tribune*:

> The Lutheran Church is making great preparations for its annual Christmas celebration which will be on three evenings. On Sunday evening at seven-thirty the Young Peoples Vester Choir will render a Cantata entitled "Bells of Christmas." This is unusually good and much enthusiasm and interest is being displayed in the rehearsals. Monday evening will be given to the little tots as at that time the Primary Department will have its entertainment, for which the little folks are practicing every afternoon. On Tuesday evening, Christmas Eve, just at midnight, there will be a Candle Light Procession by twenty members of the vested choir. This is a special service and will be very brief, but very impressive. The public is invited to attend all of these services.

1930–1939

The excellence of Trinity's musicians was widely recognized. Invited to lead the Ascension Day service held by the Knights Templar of Cumberland, the Men's Choir, composed of twenty-five young men, led the large audience in singing "Come thou Almighty King" and "Nearer My God to Thee" during an elaborate pageant. The choir sang an anthem, "The Heaven's Proclaim Him," and Mr. J. Perry Greenwade sang two solos. Mrs. Nyta Greenwade played the organ and directed.

An evening of special music was announced for June 19, 1934.

> There will be a special treat in store for the music lovers of Keyser this evening at the Trinity Lutheran Church at 8 P. M., when a musical, sponsored by the Young Women's Missionary Society, will be held. An orchestra under the direction of Emmett Kolkhorst will render several numbers, including two novelties. Rev. and Mrs. Felix Robinson, who are very talented artists, will be on the program which includes some of the best talent of this city. After the program, a social period will follow and refreshments will be served. A silver offering will be accepted at the door.
>
> The program will include the following numbers: Orchestra, Piano Solo – Elizabeth Loy, Tenor Solo – Felix Robinson, Orchestra, Ladies Quartette, Reading – Mary Frances Coffman, Orchestra, Baritone Solo – J. Perry Greenwade, Piano Duet – Turnley Sisters, Piano Solo – Mary Evelyn Sliger, and Orchestra.

On July 27, 1935, the *Mineral Daily News and Keyser Tribune* alerted its readers: "Lutheran Choir on the Air – The Trinity Lutheran Choir will broadcast over station WTBO in Cumberland Sunday afternoon from 5 to 5:30 o'clock. The choir is under the direction of Rev. Felix Robinson. Tune your radios in and hear the choir."

For many years, Mrs. Nyta Greenwade directed a talented and highly dedicated Junior Choir. In 1936, the overall attendance rate was 95 percent! Several members were recognized for having two years of perfect attendance: Fred and Irving Athey, Barbara Bowers, Donald and Joe Heare, Martin Kesner. Each received a silver cross, in recognition of their loyalty. Fay Rembold received a bronze cross for one year of perfect attendance.

Two years later, the Junior Choir numbered nearly thirty members: Fred Athey, Irving Athey, Barbara Bowers, Barbara Davis, Joyce Dayton, Cecilia Ann Gray, Helen Gray, Jackie Grubbs, Don Heare, Joe Heare, Rena Heare, Martha Lee Kight, Beverly Kolkhorst, Sarah Loy, Georgianna Mills, Betty Moomau, Billy Rogers, Fritz Shaffer, Connie Lou Shinn, Martha Springer, Shirley Virts, Martin Watson, Susanna Watson, Betty Weese, Shelia Wildemann and Ruth Wright.

The second annual Mid-Winter Choir Festival was held at Trinity on February 23, 1936, under the direction of Pastor Felix Robinson and Nyta Greenwade, organist. The *Cumberland Sunday Times* noted:

> Rev. Robinson pointed out that the purpose of the festival was to present all classes of church music and to deepen the appreciation and raising the standard of church music. The members of the adult choir were: Bassos: A. W. Heare, Roy Peterson, R. L. Fisher, John Athey, J. Perry Greenwade, Robert Lee Fisher, W. E. Coffman, William Knott, Emmett Kolkhorst; tenors: Abram Goldsworthy, Warren Kolkhorst, William Coffman, Jack Bosley, H. A. Sliger, W. H. Hoffman, Carlisle Fisher, Charles Chapman, John Stanhagen, Bernard Tasker; altos: Virginia Kolkhorst, Anna Montgomery, Mary Evelyn Sliger, Romaine Rohrbaugh, Martha Lee Tasker, Mary Frances Coffman; sopranos: Evelyn Shinn, Lucille Robinson, Elsie Kolkhorst, Marie Farley, Eleanor Kesner, Evelyn Rohe, Dorothy Michaels, Ruth Virts. The American Legion quartette sang and orchestral music provided under the direction of Lawrence Kolkhorst. The Junior Choir of twenty-five voices was well received.

On March 24, 1937, the *Mineral Daily News Tribune* announced the following:

> The Senior Choir of Trinity Lutheran Church is practicing on the Easter Cantata, 'The Resurrection Hope' which will be given Easter Sunday night at 7:30 P.M. The choir, under the direction of Mr. Roy Peterson, has been working faithfully on interpretations and expression of this cantata. Solos of the cantata will be sung by Emmett Kolkhorst, Warren Kolkhorst, Marie Farley, Evelyn Pownell, and Roy Peterson. The members of the choir are: Sopranos – Evelyn Sliger, Marie Farley, Myra Kight, Evelyn Pownell, Louise Gull, Elizabeth Stoutamyer; Altos – Virginia Kolkhorst, Mary Frances Coffman, Romaine Rohrbach; Tenors – William Coffman, Warren Kolkhorst, Arnold Sliger, W. H. Huffman, Jack Bosley; Basses – Roy Peterson, W. E. Coffman, William Knott, G. M. Loy, R. L. Fisher, Fred Frasher, Emmett Kolkhorst, J. A. Athey. Mary Evelyn Sliger is organist.

March 12, 1939, was a memorable day in the musical history of Trinity Lutheran – the dedication of the masterfully crafted M.P. Möller pipe organ (Opus 6737):

> The new Moller organ which has been recently installed in Trinity Lutheran church was dedicated at a special service on Sunday morning at ten-thirty o'clock.
>
> In the afternoon at four-thirty, Miss Katherine Moore, head of the music department of Potomac State School, assisted by Miss Mary Evelyn Sliger, gave a recital. Miss Moore was at the organ and Miss Sliger at the piano.
>
> The first part of the program included all types of music that showed the organ to the best advantage. Miss Moore played the following selections: The Lost Cord, by Sullivan; The Nightingale and the Rose, by Saint-Saens; Aragonaise, by Massenet; Liebestraume, by Liszt; Quartette from Rigolletto, by Verdi, and Vesper Hymns with chimes.

The group of organ and piano numbers included: Goin' Home, by Dvorak; The Swan, by Saint-Saens, and The Adoration, by Borowski.

On May 17, 1939, the *Mineral Daily News Tribune* reported this social event:

> Lutheran Senior Choir Honors Miss Sliger – Mr. and Mrs. J. Perry Greenwade entertained the members of the senior choir of Trinity Lutheran Church last evening at their home on South Main Street. Following the regular church choir practice, the guests were invited to the dining room where delightful refreshments were served. A color scheme of pink and white was used. Miss Mary Evelyn Sliger, whose marriage to Mr. Robert T. Coffman is a June event, was presented a lovely gift by the choir.
>
> Members of the choir are: Mr. and Mrs. J. Perry Greenwade, Mr. and Mrs. W. H. Kolkhorst, Mr. and Mrs. Emmett Kolkhorst, Mrs. H. T. Kight, Mrs. C. W. Farley, Mrs. R. A. Stoutamyer, Mrs. Evelyn Shinn, Mrs. Parker Pownall, Miss Louise Gull, Robert Scherr, W. H. Hoffman, G. N. Loy, William Knott, R. L. Fisher, W. E. Coffman, Robert Lee Fisher, Jack Bosley, J. A. Athey, and Miss Mary Evelyn Sliger, organist. Rev. and Mrs. C. K. Spiggle were invited guests.

Post-1940

The cantata, in four parts, was presented at the Trinity Lutheran Church Sunday afternoon. Featured soloists were Mrs. Carlyle Kauffman, Mrs. Clifford Gainer, Mrs. Evelyn Shinn, William Loy, Billy Rogers and Robert Lee Fisher. (1947)

Trinity Evangelical Lutheran Church

North Davis Street — Keyser, W. Va.

REV. LOUIS E. BOUKNIGHT, Pastor

Evening Vespers 4 P. M.
SUNDAY, DECEMBER 17, 1950

Senior Choir Presents

"The Babe Of Bethlehem"

By HARVEY B. GAUL

Director—Leonard G. Withers
Organist—Mary Evelyn Coffman

"Shepherd's Pipes" .... Harris
Prelude—"Yuletide Echoes" .... Hodson
Processional Hymn No. 21 .... "Come Hither Ye Faithful"
Scripture Lesson.
Offering and Prayer.
Offertory—"Cantique de Noel" .... Adam (Arr. by Noble)

"The Babe Of Bethlehem"

I. PRELUDE—THE FIELDS OF GALILEE
   Opening Chorus—"The Prophecy"

   O Lord arise, and help us for Thy Name's Sake.
   O Lord arise and deliver us for Thy Name's Sake.
   (From the Litany)
   Behold, the days come, saith the Lord, that I will raise unto David a righteous Branch. And a King shall reign and prosper and shall execute judgment and justice upon the earth.
   (From Isaiah and St. Matthew)
   SOLOIST—CLARA KAUFFMAN

II. THE TIME OF ANNUNCIATION
    The angel Gabriel was sent from God unto a city named Nazareth to a virgin espoused to a man named Joseph, of the house of David. (From St. Luke)
    SOLOIST—ANNA MONTGOMERY

    CHORUS OF ANGELS
    Holy, Holy, Holy, Lord God of Hosts. (From Sanctus)
    WOMEN'S CHORUS
    Hail thou that art highly favored. The Lord is with thee. Blessed art thou among women.
    (From St. Luke)
    SOLOIST—WILLIAM LOY

    SONG OF MARY (From the Magnificat)
    SOLOIST—BEVERLY BOWNE

III. THE SHEPHERDS IN THE FIELDS (Old English Carol)
     CHORUS
     SOLOISTS
     Robert L. Fisher, Jr.   Marie Farley
     Robert T. Coffman   William Loy

IV. THE MARCH OF THE WISE MEN (From The Hymnal)
    MEN'S CHORUS

V. AT THE LOWLY MANGER (Old English Carol)
   CHORUS
   SOLOIST—EVELYN T. SHINN

VI. Closing Chorus: COME YE LOFTY, COME YE LOWLY
    (Old English Carol)
    Blessed be the Lord God of Israel. For He hath visited and redeemed His people. And hath raised up a mighty salvation for us in the house of His Servant David. (From the Benedictus)

Benediction.
Recessional Hymn No. 34 .... "Joy To The World"
Postlude—"Hallelujah" .... Handel

MINERAL DAILY NEWS-TRIBUNE — KEYSER

The choir of Trinity Lutheran Church presented a cantata, "The Babe of Bethlehem" at the 4 o'clock vesper service yesterday afternoon. All seats in the church auditorium were filled and some listeners were forced to stand along the walls. The choir was under the direction of Leonard Withers, head of the Potomac State School music department. Mrs. Robert T. Coffman was accompanist and Mrs. Clara Kauffman, Mrs. Anna Montgomery, William Loy, Miss Beverly Bowne, Robert L. Fisher, Jr., Robert T. Coffman, Mrs. Marie Farley and Mrs. Evelyn T. Shinn were soloists. (1950)

Trinity Evangelical Lutheran Church
North Davis Street — Keyser, W. Va.
REV. L. E. BOUKNIGHT, Pastor

EVENING VESPERS 4 P. M.
Sunday, May 7, 1950

SENIOR CHOIR
Presents

Spring Musicale

Prelude—Fifth Nocturne .... Leybach
    The Shepherd and The Mocking Bird .... Berwald
    Dedication Festival .... Stults
Processional Hymn No. 276 .. Love Divine, all love excelling
Scripture Lesson .... Psalm 98
    At The Name of Jesus .... Marryott
    O Jesus, Thou Art Standing .... Stoughton
        Clara Spotts Kauffman, Soloist
Solo, Hear Me Lord .... Youse
        Evelyn T. Shinn
Russian Easter Carol Of The Trees .. Arr. Gaul
    Clara Spotts Kauffman, Soloist
Trio, I Heard a Forest Praying .. Peter De Rose
    Marie Farley, Anna Montgomery
    Virginia Kolkhorst
Hark! Hark, My Soul .... Shelley
    William Rogers, Clara Kauffman,
    Anna Montgomery, Soloists
Offering and Prayer
Offertory—Kamennoi Ostrow .... Rubenstein
    Solo, When Children Pray .... Fenner
        William Loy
    Out Of The Depths .... Fichton
        Marie Farley, Soloist
    The Lord's Prayer .... Malotte
Benediction
Recessional Hymn No. 574 .... Now The Day Is Over
Postlude—Fanfare .... Ascher

Director—Leonard G. Withers
Organist—Ruth Goldsworthy

COURTESY OF PATRICIA ATHEY ROGERS

    Earlier in the year, a Spring Musicale was presented that featured soloists Clara Spotts Kauffman, Evelyn Shinn, William Rogers, Anna Montgomery, William Loy, and Marie Farley. The three living members of the celebrated Ladies Quartette sang a trio. Organist was Ruth Goldsworthy. (1950)

    The Junior Choir at Trinity Lutheran Church presented a two-part cantata, "The Chorus In the Skies," yesterday morning during the regular service. Mrs. Robert T. Coffman was director. The cantata opened with the chorus singing "O Little Town of Bethlehem." followed by "While Shepherds Watched Their Flocks by Night," featuring the choir and a trio composed of Harold Matlick, Lowell Whipp and Lois Ann Whipp. The selection, "There is Room in My Heart For Thee," was presented by the choir and Denny Avers and Jeffrey Montgomery as soloists. The girls' chorus then sang 'It Came Upon the Midnight Clear," with a duet by Billy Athey and Kenneth Kolkhorst. The boys' chorus and choir combined sang "Oh, Come, All Ye Faithful." Nancy Coffman and Janice Fisher were soloists for "Silent Night," while the choir closed the service with "Joy to the World," "As With Gladness Men or Old" and "Oh, Come, All Ye Faithful." In addition to the soloists, other members of the choir included Sally Maiden, Sandra Staggs, Dinah Sue Wells, Melinda Watson, Marcella Ryan, Darlene Bill, Rosalind Engle, Connie Ryan, Karen Ryan, Dolores Fitzgerald, Andrea Murray, Mary Chapman, Mary Ann Fallon, Henry Hess, Richard Hess, Jimmy Gift and Tommy Feaster. (1954)

The community Christmas program will be held Sunday at 4 p.m. Directed by Leonard G. Withers, the Potomac State Singers, the choir of Trinity Lutheran Church and other vocalists from the city will combine their voices for the presentation. Soloists will be Cmdr. William Loy, Clara Spotts, and Frances Hartman. Accompanists will be Mrs. Robert T. Coffman, the organist at Trinity Lutheran and Frances Sarullo. (1962)

Those Who Led

Trinity Lutheran has been blessed to have musicians of excellence in its midst from its very beginning. The earliest directors of the choir at Trinity Lutheran were **D. T. Greenwade** and **Lawrence Kolkhorst**.

Virginia (Knott) Kolkhorst was a multi-talented musician – an instrumentalist mainstay of the church orchestra and a primary voice in the choir for 50+ years. She married another accomplished musician, Warren Kolkhorst, on April 7, 1921, in Oakland. It appears it all happened very quietly; their friends didn't learn of the marriage until early the following year!

Newspaper articles reveal that Mrs. Kolkhorst was directing the choir from time to time during the mid-late 1920s. When her brother-in-law Lawrence Kolkhorst moved to Cumberland in the mid-1930s, Mrs. Kolkhorst stepped forward to take the reins of the vital task of maintaining the excellence of Trinity's musical programming. She remained in the position until Leonard Withers became music director in 1947.

It will come as no surprise to learn that **Rev. Felix Robinson** directed the choir for special programs at the church – large cantatas and the like – and at regional choir festivals.

Nyta Catherine Christian (Shaffer) Greenwade was a renowned vocalist, as was her husband, John Perry Greenwade (1894–1961). Their 1922 church wedding was performed by Rev. J. W. Drawbaugh. Perry worked as a clerk in his father's mercantile store for awhile, then became a fire insurance salesman and worked at Kelly-Springfield Tire Co.

At Trinity, her musical talent emerged at an early age as a member of the Junior Choir. She excelled as a vocal soloist, accompanist and as a member of Lutheran League Quartette that ultimately became famous as West Virginia's Legionettes Quartette. When the group performed as a trio, Mrs. Greenwade was the accompanist. She was the organist at Trinity for many years.

Mrs. Greenwade taught music in the local elementary school and later moved on to Bruce High School, where she was supervisor of music for the last two years of her life. She was the organist and directed choirs at Trinity for many years.

After Mary Evelyn Sliger became the organist, Mrs. Greenwade remained as director of music at Trinity Lutheran until her death in 1945.

As one looks back on the countless blessings of Mrs. Greenwade's presence in our midst, one rises above the many. Loved by the children of the congregation, her cherub and junior choirs provided a steady stream of musical talent and appreciation that has survived her worldly presence among us. She was admired and beloved by all.

Mary Evelyn (Sliger) Coffman was a woman of amazing talent. A musical prodigy, she was teaching piano lessons while still a teenager.

She married Robert Thornhill Coffman (1915-1964), who became a renowned physician and surgeon, practicing in Keyser at Potomac Valley Hospital. Dr. and Mrs. Coffman had two daughters, Nancy Lee and Barbara. She was the organist at Trinity Lutheran for more than six decades.

(1st row) Marjo Anderson, Jeff Chidester, Jenny Chidester, Ann Ebert, Karen Heare
(2nd) Carol Athey, Missy Ebert, Brad Neville, Chris Chidester, Donna Riggleman, Duke Ebert
(3rd) Terry Lancaster, Mark Neville, Don Heare, Charlene Blackburn, Craig & Cynthia Goldsworthy
(4th) Barbara Coffman, Chris Neville, Diane Theis, David Blackburn, Don Athey

Many youngsters were introduced to good music as members of the Junior and Cherub choirs she nurtured – cherished among Mrs. Coffman's many achievements.

She became the first Director of Alumni Affairs at Potomac State College in 1961 and remained in that position for twenty-five years. In 1990, Mrs. Coffman received the Potomac State College Distinguished Service Award, in recognition of her truly outstanding service to the college and to the community at large. She touched the lives of so many.

Her gifts of talent and enormous amounts of time are among the greatest blessings bestowed upon Trinity Lutheran Church.

Leonard Grenfell Withers, son of a Baptist minister, was a graduate of the Cincinnati Conservatory of Music.

The June 7, 1939, issue of *The Cumberland News* announced the following:

> Potomac State President E. E. Church today announced that Professor Leonard Withers will replace Miss Katherine A. Moore as head of the department of music at the school. Miss Moore and President Church will be married in Fairmont June 15. Prof. Withers comes here from Parkersburg where he was director of music in the senior high school.

Mr. Withers became a primary contributor to music and the arts in Keyser, teaching instrumental music (piano was his forté), organizing and directing the Potomac Singers at the college and participating in many musical events throughout the community. His work was interrupted by World War II in mid-1942 when he enlisted in the U.S. Army. He served in North Africa and France.

Returning to Keyser, a hint of his growing relationship with Trinity Lutheran was published in the *Cumberland Evening Times* on October 1, 1946:

> A reception honoring members of the Potomac State faculty was held Saturday evening by Dr. and Mrs. E. E. Church at their Fort Avenue home. During the evening, Mrs. Church and Leonard Withers, who has returned as head of the music department after having served in the armed forces, played several two piano selections. A trio consisting of Mrs. Clem Montgomery, Mrs. C. W. Farley, and Mrs. W. H. Kolkhorst entertained with vocal selections.

Anna Montgomery, Marie Farley, and Virginia Kolkhorst were members of the Lutheran choir and the famed American Legion Ladies Quartette. Mr. Withers was approached by Mrs. Montgomery and Mrs. Evelyn Shinn about becoming the director of the Lutheran choir. He agreed to give it a try and remained in the position for nearly a quarter century.

Mr. Withers was a leader in the work of the Tri-State Community Concerts Association and Highland Arts Unlimited. His mentorship continued the tradition of great music at Trinity Lutheran and led many of his protégés to a lifetime of enjoyment of music and the arts. Later in his life, he and his sister Anne (1900-1999) moved to a retirement community in Harrisonburg, VA, where he died in 2000.

Following Mr. Withers' retirement, musical directors **Ruth Goldsworthy** and **Richard Ridder** have served with distinction.

The Quartette

Marie Farley, Anna Montgomery, Virginia Kolkhorst, Nyta Greenwade (1934)

Just how popular was the ladies quartette? Judge for yourself by reading the article that appeared in the *Mineral Daily News* on September 28, 1935:

> Championship Legion Auxiliary Quartette Is Given Gala Reception On Return Home – Keyser's West Virginia Legionettes, victorious in the contest for American Legion Auxiliary quartettes at the national convention in St. Louis, were given a royal welcome home last might. The four ladies, Mesdames C. W. Farley, C E. Montgomery, W. H. Kolkhorst and J. Perry Greenwade, were met at the Baltimore and Ohio railroad station by several hundred persons.
>
> Representatives of the Auxiliary and the Legion helped them off the train as the crack Drum and Bugle Corps of the local Post played. After preliminary greetings the four singers were paraded through the city behind the corps.
>
> At the Legion Memorial Home on Armstrong Street extended [the Alkire mansion], a gala reception awaited them. Hundreds of well wishers offered personal congratulations on the honors the ladies had achieved for themselves and brought to Keyser.
>
> A program, arranged for the evening, showed in some measure the appreciation the Legion Post and Auxiliary and the citizens of Keyser have for the singers. Paul C. Rouzer, Mineral County Superintendent of Schools, extended greetings to the ladies and offered congratulations. Other representative citizens of Keyser who extended the greetings of the city and the congratulations of various civic and social groups were Mayor C. L. Everhart, Assistant County Superintendent of Schools J. C. Sanders, Reverend L. St. Clair Allen, pastor of the First M. E. Church, Reverend Harry S. Coffey, pastor of' Grace M. E. Church, South, and Newton B. Carskadon.
>
> Reverend Felix Robinson, pastor of Trinity Lutheran Church, and Mrs. Robinson sang a duet. J. Perry Greenwade and Miss Lydia Mae Nowatskl also rendered vocal solos. The quartette then sang for the gathering a medley of numbers that was appreciated to the fullest extent. This was followed by gifts from well wishers. Each lady was presented with a dozen red rosebuds by Mrs. M. T. Virts on behalf of the Legion Auxiliary. C. S Briley, commander

of the local Legion Post, and Mrs. H. K. Briley, president of the Auxiliary Unit, presented them each with a bottle of perfume. Mrs. Greenwade then told the audience the experiences of the quartette on their trip and entertained them with the story of how they won the contest over thirty other quartettes from all parts of the nation. Delicious refreshments were served to climax an exceptionally successful evening.

Their fame spread well beyond Keyser. In 1934 the *Mineral Daily News* reported from Cumberland:

> Felix Robinson, pastor of Trinity Lutheran Church, of Keyser, W. Va., delivered a stirring address at the Ascension Day Service of Antioch Commandery, No. 6, Knights Templar, at the Masonic Temple here last night. His talk was especially appropriate to the day and to present-day conditions. The assemblage sang "Near my God to Thee" as the Knights Templar ascension scene was displayed.
>
> The Ladies Quartet, of Marie Farley, Anna Montgomery, Virginia Kolkhorst and Nyta Greenwade, sang "Were You There When They Crucified My Lord." J. Perry Greenwade, with Mrs. Greenwade, accompanist, sang "Is Not His Word Like a Fire?" from Elijah, and the Ladies Quartette rendered "The Lord's Prayer." Following the address of the Rev. Robinson, the ladies quartette sang "Now the Day is Over" and the Ascension Day service was closed with benediction by the Rev. Robinson. After the service, the quartette and Mr. Greenwade sang a number of selections, responding several times to the instant applause of the assemblage.
>
> The members of the ladies quartette, whose selections were all sung unaccompanied, were presented with corsage bouquets of roses with which they further adorned their costumes of pink and white.

Here's another article from the March 2, 1936 issue of the *Mineral Daily News and Keyser Tribune*:

> The famous American Legionette Quartette – Mesdames Montgomery, Farley, Kolkhorst and Greenwade – returned last night from Covington, Va., where they filled a number of engagements during the week end. They were accompanied by Miss Helen Dean, and during their stay there they were guests of Rev. and Mrs. Harry S. Coffey. [Rev. Coffey was a former pastor of Keyser's Grace M.E. Church.]
>
> Friday evening they were guests of Captain Thomas at the CCC camp at 6:30 and sang, and Friday night at 7:45 o'clock gave a concert at the Kiwanis dinner. Saturday afternoon they were guests of honor at a reception given by the American Legion Auxiliary and Saturday evening sang at the Westvaco Club House. Sunday morning the Quartette sang at the 11:00 o'clock worship service in Cranberry Methodist church with a congregation of more than 850. In the afternoon they presented a concert to which more than 1,000 attended,

They shared their extraordinary talents at innumerable events throughout the region, swelling the attendance at community musical events, weddings and anniversaries, civic clubs, and even PTA meetings. Public figures and their constituents enjoyed their performances. The quartette appeared at the inauguration of West Virginia Governor Homer A. Holt in 1937 and at the 1939 West Virginia convention of the Lions Club when Harley O. Staggers was elected to the position of District Governor. During the 1937 visit to Charleston for the January inaugural, the hotel where they were staying caught fire. The exposure to cold and smoke aggravated a cold that Mrs. Greenwade had when she left home and caused pneumonia to develop. She remained hospitalized in Charleston for several days before returning home with Mrs. Montgomery who remained with stayed with her.

During World War II, their patriotism was front-and-center. A 1942 article in the *Mineral Daily News-Tribune* illustrates their involvement on the home front:

> The Civilian Defense Corps parade at 7:15 tonight and the graduation at 8:00 are two occasions which many Keyser citizens have been looking forward to for a long time. The Tri-Towns Municipal Band will lead the procession. All Office of Civil Defense volunteers who have completed their required training will be presented with their certificates and arm bands at the graduation exercises to be held in the auditorium. E. E. Church, president of Potomac State College, will make the principal address of the evening. The American Legion Quartette, Keyser's pride and joy, will further delight the audience with some of their special renditions. The high school auditorium seats over 1000 people and a capacity audience of Keyser citizens are expected to be present.

If you wanted to draw a big crowd, you invited the quartette to sing! Their celebrity was astonishing and remains unsurpassed in the history of Keyser.

Coda

So how did the famed West Virginia Legionettes become guests at the White House?

Having won national fame, the quartette sang at the commencement exercises of Moorefield High School in the spring of 1941. Mrs. Eleanor Roosevelt was the guest speaker. Greatly impressed by the talent of the singers, she spoke of inviting them to tea. Shortly thereafter, a telegram from the White House formally extended Mrs. Roosevelt's invitation. Following their visit to the White House for tea with the First Lady, the quartette sang at the commencement exercises of Southeastern University of Washington, at which West Virginia Congressman Jennings Randolph was the featured speaker.

And what about the name(s) of the quartette?

They started out as a church organization and were officially named the Lutheran League Quartette of the State of West Virginia. By virtue of the fact that the husbands of all four women were members of the American Legion, the group became active in the affairs of the American Legion Auxiliary. As the West Virginia Legionettes, they entered the national competition for quartettes, singing at national meetings of the American Legion throughout the United States, and were awarded first place on four different occasions: St. Louis; 1935; Cleveland, 1936; Chicago, 1937; and New York, 1939. They were not eligible for the competition in 1938 because of having been the winners for three consecutive years.

Chapter 7 – Chronicles

Ties that bind us together...

OH, THEY CAME – TO WORSHIP AND TO SERVE. Trinity Lutheran became the focal point in their journeys of faith.

Trinity Lutheran flourished in membership, ministry and outreach during the two decades that followed its founding, and beyond. Herein is a chronicle of just a few of the events that more fully paint pictures of events that characterize the vibrancy of the congregation.

Among the sparse early records that have been found is a listing of congregation members who received the Sacrament of Holy Communion during the mid-1920s. For some individuals, the dates of important events in their affiliation with Trinity Lutheran were recorded – when and how they became members (accessioned), by Baptism, Confirmation, or Letter of Transfer. For some, the records indicate when and how they left Trinity, by death, resignation, or Letter of Transfer. Although the compiler of these records is not identified, he was surely Rev. J. W. Drawbaugh, who was the pastor during the time that many of the recorded events took place, or Rev. Robert Vorberg, using information compiled by Drawbaugh.

A complete transcription of these invaluable and fascinating records may be found in Appendix III.

The Trinity Lutheran sanctuary and the club house that was used for Sunday School classes, meetings and social events were busy places. Sundays at Trinity Lutheran often included three well-attended services – morning, mid-day and Vespers – each with a unique sermon. Mid-week services were also held from time to time, on remembrance days such as Ascension Day, during the seasons of Advent and Lent, and throughout Holy Week. Meetings of the Ladies' Aid Society, missionary societies, Bible study groups, youth organizations, choirs practicing and orchestra rehearsals. Services that included Communion, less frequent than the more recent practice of weekly celebration of the Sacrament, filled the church. Crowds overflowed the facilities when non-Lutheran townspeople came for the renowned musical and social events.

During a special sequence of sermons at evening services in 1911 that he called "The Home Series", Rev. C. P. Bastian offered discourses on The Husband, The Wife, The Father, The Mother, The Children. The general public was invited and the services were well attended.

A special "Go to Church Sunday" was observed by several Keyser congregations on Sunday, February 7, 1915. Pastor Baughman presided over the Sunday School at 9:45 A.M., Morning Service at 11:00 A.M. and Evening Worship at 6:45 P.M. At the mid-day service, Rev. Baughman spoke about "Why Be a Church Member." His theme for Evening Worship was "The Life of The Christian." The orchestra was present to provide music at all three services. Attendance and membership continued to grow.

The Ladies' Aid Society thrived in its role as a focal point of congregational life. In the midst of a sustained heat wave during the summer of 1914, many parishioners (not just the ladies, mind you) took advantage of the opportunity to attend a meeting of the Ladies' Aid Society in the coolness of Maplewood Farm, at Claysville, where Miss Martha Watson was residing: Mesdames Charles Broome, J. T. Sincell, Jacob Avers, Joseph Shaffer, Anna Kolkhorst, Claude Clevenger, Eva Bisset, Gertie Whitehouse, Gus Wolf, Russell Wagoner, Bennie Wells, Charles Hodges, Bertie Sliger; Misses Belle MacDonald, Annie Kolkhorst, Minnie Bright, Nita and Margaret Shaffer, Christine, Katherine and Elizabeth Clevenger, Louise and Bernice Wagoner, Viola Wildemann, Madge Amtower, Francis Whitehouse; Rev. Baughman; Messrs H. A. Sliger, Lee Kesner, C. G. Scribner, Richard and Arnold Sliger, Wilbur Whitehouse and Wylie Lauck.

In 1916, the ladies of the community who were actively engaged in the Women's Suffrage movement, the New Era Circle, held meetings at the Lutheran Club House. On one occasion they were entertained by Mrs. Blanche Harrison and Mrs. Effie Baker Welch. A reception was held at Mrs. Welch's home, after which the guests and members of the circle assembled at the Club House of the Lutheran Church for a chicken dinner, followed by ice cream, cake and mint and peanuts, served by the Suffragettes. The club room was tastefully decorated in yellow iris and butter cups. The favors were dainty boutonnières of a buttercup design, and the place cards were miniature U.S. maps.

On Tuesday evening, June 19, 1917, the Ladies' Aid Society held one of their many "lawn fetes" on the lawn back of the Church. Hand-churned ice cream, strawberries picked from the gardens of members, and freshly baked cake were served. The event was enjoyed by the congregation and the general public.

On another summer occasion, the Ladies' Aid Society held a huge picnic on the lawn of Mr. and Mrs. D. A. Kesner's farm on New Creek Drive. Well over one-hundred ladies, men and youngsters came to enjoy the food and fellowship while relaxing under the shade of the large trees.

November was the time for the annual Christmas Bazaar. The following is typical of the annual announcements that reached out to the entire community, even the children:

> The Ladies Aid Society of the Lutheran Church will hold a Bazaar in the Coffroth Building on Main Street, Tuesday and Wednesday.
>
> Aprons, fancy work and hand-made articles for Christmas presents will be for sale. A Fish Pond will be a special feature for the children.
>
> There will be a Tea Room where you can entertain your friends with a cup o' tea, cake, cookies, sandwiches and other good things.
>
> A Food Sale will be held in connection with the Bazaar and all kinds of food for sale such as cake, pies, salads, doughnuts, home-made bread rolls, and home-made candy
>
> The patronage of the public is solicited and it will pay any one to visit the Bazaar before doing their Christmas shopping elsewhere.

During World War I, a large American flag was presented to the congregation during a patriotic service for the enlisted and drafted men. Those honored were: Fred R. Koelz, Newman A. Smith, Glen O. Workman, Lloyd Douglass, B. Lowther, Harry and Ray Virts, Martin Watson and Perry Greenwade. The men's choir led the music at the 7:30pm service. During the war, many citizen of the community volunteered to package surgical dressings to be sent to field hospitals and medics of the American Expeditionary Force in France. To ensure the work was done properly, special procedures were required. Volunteers received their training in classes conducted at the Lutheran Club House. A public notice of thanks was extended to Rev. H. F. Baughman and members of the congregation for their kindness and the privilege of using the Lutheran facilities.

In November, 1918, the Seventh Annual Convention of the Synod of West Virginia met at Trinity Lutheran Church. Pastors and delegates were in attendance from all the General Synod Lutheran Churches of the State. The opening session was a service with Holy Communion and a sermon by the President of the Synod, open to all members of the congregation on Tuesday evening, November 5. This meeting of Synod was of special interest in that it was the last before the merger of three great bodies of the Lutheran Church – the General Synod, the General Council, and United Synod of the South – into the United Lutheran Church of America. The convention concluded with a worship and ordination service on Thursday evening. The ULCA merged into the Lutheran Church in America (LCA) in 1962; subsequently, the LCA was one of the formative bodies of the Evangelical Lutheran Church in America (ELCA) in 1988.

Anniversaries

The congregation has always enjoyed celebrating its past, present and future in connection with special anniversary events.

Trinity Lutheran Church commemorated its **10th Anniversary** during Thanksgiving week of 1913. On Thanksgiving evening, a program of special music was presented by the choir, orchestra, several soloists, a duet sung by Misses Nyta Shaffer and Viola Wildemann, and a men's quartette that last sang together during the earliest years of the congregation: J. Perry Greenwade, George Loy, William Ney, and George Newhouse. On Friday evening there was a gala social and reunion with former pastors William Ney and C. P. Bastian. Current pastor Rev. Harry Baughman officiated at Sunday services that included an array of musical offerings. Rev. Ney, the founding pastor, delivered the sermon at the morning service; Rev. Bastian, Ney's successor, spoke in the evening.

The Rev. Dr. William C. Ney returned again to deliver the sermon at the **12th Anniversary** celebration in November, 1915. The Rev. Dr. A. S. Hartman, D.D., secretary of the Board of Home Missions, came from Baltimore to preach the sermon at Vespers. In mid afternoon, all the Protestant ministers of Keyser gave short talks. Of course, there was music; many non-members attended and were warmly welcomed.

The **400th Anniversary of the Reformation** was observed in a community-wide meeting held at the Keyser High School auditorium in November, 1917. Special music was presented by the Lutheran choir and orchestra. A renowned Lutheran historian came from Gettysburg to speak at the large gathering. The previous week, members of Trinity attended a Reformation program in the Tri-Towns. Morning services were shortened so those going to Piedmont could catch Train No. 11; they returned to Keyser later in the afternoon on Train No. 46. .

On June 2, 1918, the congregation celebrated the **5th Anniversary of Dr. Baughman's pastorate**. The *Mineral Daily News* had informed its readers:

Tomorrow will mark the fifth anniversary of the present pastorate of Trinity Lutheran Church. On the first Sunday in June 1913, the present pastor took up the active work. A casual survey of the church statistics show that during these five years about 130 members have been received in to the church, nearly ten thousand dollars contributed by the congregation for all purposes and about $1500 for benevolence. The debt then rested on the church has practically all been removed and a parsonage purchased. This anniversary will be marked with appropriate services tomorrow morning at 11 o'clock. Special music will be rendered by the choir.

As an interesting aside – On the same front page as the above notice was an announcement that involved a son of Trinity Lutheran Church, Raymond W. Virts (1896–1975) – a reminder that World War I was still ongoing:

Keyser Lad On Torpedoed Transport Lincoln – Ray Virts, Son of Mr. and Mrs. W. H. Virts, on Sixth Trip Has Thrilling Experience.

WASHINGTON, May 31 – The American transport President Lincoln, bound for the United States, was sunk at ten o'clock this morning by a German submarine.

Though details are lacking it is assumed from the fact that the transport was returning to the United States and that few if any troops were on board. Meagre reports so far received mention no casualties. Official announcement of the sinking was made about four o'clock this afternoon by Secretary of the Navy Daniels as follows: "The Navy Department has received a dispatch from Vice-Admiral Sims stating that the U. S. S. President Lincoln was torpedoed at ten-forty o'clock this morning and sunk an hour later. The vessel was returning from Europe. No further particulars have been received."

The Vessel, registering 18,072 tons, was formerly of the Hamburg-American line and with all other German merchant ships in American waters at the time that were seized by the government when the United States entered the war. This loss is the second instance of an American transport to fall victim to the German U-Boats.

To commemorate the **25th Anniversary**, a special service was held on August 26, 1928. Plans for the **30th Anniversary** were interrupted by the death of Rev. Vorberg on July 7, 1933.

On March 4, 1943, during the World War II, members of the Ladies' Aid Society observed the **40th Anniversary** of that organization. Mrs. Herndon Athey hosted the event at her home on Overton Place. Present were the two original members of the Society still living – Miss Martha Watson and Mrs. Leona (Wolfe) Schoppert. Mrs. Shoppert was a resident of Piedmont and member of Mt. Calvary Lutheran.

Trinity Evangelical Lutheran Church of Keyser celebrated its **50th Anniversary** of the organization of the congregation on Sunday, August 16, 1953.

The *Cumberland Evening Times* published a summary of the events the following day:

> Rev. William C. Ney, Brookline, Pa., delivered the anniversary sermon. The Keyser church was Rev. Mr. Ney's first pastorate. He spoke on "Let Us Go Up and Possess It".
>
> The church choir presented a program which included "The Lord Brings Back His Own" and "The Holy City." Four charter members, Mr. and Mrs. H. A. Sliger, W. C. Pifer and Mrs. Nanny Gull, were honored at the service.
>
> The King's Daughters Bible Class, under the leadership of Mrs. R. T. [Mary Evelyn] Coffman, honored Rev. Mr. Ney and the charter members at a reception at the church. Officers of the class served refreshments. Included were Mrs. Walter [Mary] Kephart, president; Mrs. J. A. [Jane] Athey, vice president; Mrs. F. O. [Edith] Workman, secretary-treasurer and Mrs. E. A. [Ernestine] See, teacher. Others assisting were Mrs. Charles [Martha Lee] Blackburn, Mrs. Walter [Anna] Mott, Mrs. Frederick [Barbara] Athey, Miss Maureen Fitzgerald, Miss Donna Rae McKee, Miss Nancy Lee Coffman and Miss Sally Bruner
>
> Rev. and Mrs. Donald D. Anderson, pastor, and Rev. Mr. Ney received the guests. Music was furnished during the reception by the Sunday School orchestra, under the direction of Mrs. James W. [Ruth] Goldsworthy.

On August 16, 1963, Trinity Evangelical Lutheran Church observed the **60th Anniversary** of its founding with a dinner in the parish house. Mrs. Sarah Avers and Mrs. Louise Leatherman were co-chairmen. Toastmaster William W. Wolfe presented a brief history of the church and honored Harry A. Sliger and his wife Bertha (Arnold) Sliger as the only living charter members.

(Front) Mary Evelyn Coffman, Mr. and Mrs. Harry Sliger, Elizabeth Soutamyer, Louise Leatherman
(Back) Arnold Sliger, Carl Avers, Myra Kight, Walter Kephart

With Mr. and Mrs. Sliger in this photograph are seven children of charter members: Mrs. Mary Evelyn (Sliger) Coffman and her brother Arnold Sliger, Mrs. Elizabeth (Gull) Stoutamyer and her sister Mrs. Louise (Gull) Leatherman, Carl Avers, Mrs. Myra (Wolf) Kight, and Walter Kephart.

At the time marking the 60th Anniversary, Trinity Lutheran was without a full-time pastor. Rev. Donald D. Anderson had resigned, effective June 16, 1963, to become the Assistant to the President (Bishop) of the Western Pennsylvania – West Virginia Synod. The new pastor, Rev. Robert J. Westerberg, began serving the Keyser parish on November 4 and was formally installed as Trinity's pastor on December 15, 1963. The most frequent supply minister during the interim was church member William W. Wolfe.

The **70th Anniversary** was marked with a congregational banquet at the Vo-Tech Center, New Creek Drive, on Saturday Evening, October 6, 1973. Dr. James Courtier was chairman of the Anniversary Committee responsible for planning. Following the dinner, Kenneth Matlick, vice president of the congregation, introduced the toastmaster for the evening, James Terry, who was a member of the Church Council of Trinity and the Executive Board of the Western Pennsylvania – West Virginia Synod. The Rev. Dr. Donald D. Anderson, a former Pastor of Trinity, now serving as Secretary of the W. Pa. – W. Va. Synod, made appropriate remarks concerning the history of the local Church. Rev. Ward Harvey, Pastor of First United Methodist Church, greeted those present on behalf of the local Ministerial Association. The present pastor of the congregation, Rev. Donald W Moore, introduced the main speaker for the occasion, the Rev Hartland H Gifford, editor for adult resources in the office of the Division of Parish Services of the Lutheran Church in America, Philadelphia. He addressed the gathering on the subject "Why the Church?" At the Anniversary Communion Service on Sunday, Oct. 7, Rev. Anderson preached on the subject "Seventy Years is a Beginning..." Following the Service, the congregation gathered in the Parish House for renewing old friendships and refreshments at a hospitality hour.

A celebration of the **90th Anniversary** was held on September 26, 1993. Richard Ridder worked with the Worship Committee to formulate plans for the day and prepare the choir. The guest preacher for the day was the Rev. Dr. Lowell Almen, Secretary of the Evangelical Lutheran Church in America. Former pastor Rev. Donald D. Anderson and Bishop Alexander Black, Bishop of the West Virginia – Western Maryland Synod, were welcomed by Trinity's pastor Rev. Bradley Will at a reception following the service. Sarah Circle president Debbie Heare gave a pot of flowers to anniversary organizer Evelyn Manns. Mrs. Ila Machamer was honored for being the oldest member of the congregation and Mrs. Nellie Wells was recognized for being the member with the longest continuous membership.

The **100th Anniversary** featured a magnificent cantata based on Martin Luther's "A Mighty Fortress," performed by the combined choirs of Trinity and Mt. Calvary, under the direction of Mr. Richard Ridder. The *Mineral Daily News Tribune and Echo* said afterwards that the magnificent event "no doubt caused the angels to dance."

GREAT FELLOWSHIP

From its earliest days, the Lutherans in Keyser have enjoyed a life of great fellowship that was centered on their church. The congregation, the Ladies' Aid Society, Sunday School classes, Luther League and other church organizations sponsored scores of social events, attended by many. Personal announcements published in the local newspapers frequently mentioned non-church social gatherings among members of the congregation. It is clear that these Lutherans were a loving, close-knit, but welcoming, flock of believers.

A brief announcement in the September 8, 1911, issue of the *Keyser Tribune* noted the beginning of a wonderful congregational tradition, the annual Sunday School picnic:

> Labor Day was almost as quiet as Sunday in Keyser. The banks and nearly all of the stores were closed, the post offices observed holiday hours. The Baracca class, of the Lutheran Church, had a picnic at Mill Meadow.

The youth were fully engaged. The Junior League of the Lutheran Church held a Weenie and Marshmallow Roast at the home of Mrs. J. Perry Greenwade. Games and music were the features of entertainment and the twenty young people present spent a most delightful evening. On another occasion, the Junior Luther League held a Halloween Party on Friday evening at the church. Forty young people were present. In 1926, the *Mineral Daily News* informed its readers:

> The Lutheran Young Peoples Choir gave a surprise party at the home of Mrs. Greenwade, who was very agreeably surprised. The chief attraction of the evening was a mock wedding. The bride was very beautifully arrayed in a green dress with a white lace curtain for the veil. The evening was delightfully spent in dancing and games. At a late hour delicious refreshments were served. Those present were Misses Viola Cook, Helen Tasker, Salome and Ruth Vorberg, Eloise Scherr, Madge Ravenscroft, Hazel Hesen, Virginia and Frances Doak, Mrs. Greenwade, Mrs.

Wells and Mrs. Drawbaugh, Messrs Charles Randalls, John Stanhagen, Ray Bell, Fred Purgitt, Stanley Spotts, Henry Cornelius, William Cather, Mr. Drawbaugh and Mr. Greenwade.

Back to the picnics. The Lutheran Sunday School celebrated Labor Day 1913, by holding their annual picnic in Mill Meadow:

> At 8 o'clock a.m., the teams, which had been hired for the day, were at the church and ready to convey the scholars and their provisions to the picnic grounds. Weather conditions were promising and the prospects for a very pleasant day were fine. The children of the primary and intermediate departments of the Sunday School were the first on the grounds and proceeded at once to amuse themselves with the delights of nature and with children's games. By half past ten all the members of the school were on the ground and enjoying themselves in various ways. Swings were put up and made secure for children. Lemonade was prepared for the refreshment of all by the ladies, and the frequent visits made to the barrel were proof of its excellent quality. Probably the most enjoyable feature of all was the dinner; the families all came bountifully provided with the necessary lunches of chicken, sandwiches, eggs, olives, salad, fruit and cake. The young men amused themselves in the afternoon with a game of baseball to the great delight of the loyal rooters. The older men amused themselves by pitching horse shoes, at which pastime Messrs Kephart, Wolf and Kesner claimed the honors. After a supper, as lavish as the dinner, the members of the school were conveyed to the city by the teams, everybody expressing themselves as having had an enjoyable day.

By 1915, the annual picnic had grown to even greater proportions and was, in every sense of the word, a success.

> At 10:30 "Cy" Scribner's auto truck began to convey the picnickers to the chosen spot, a grove on the farm of Mr. H. B. Smith near Hoover's Hollow. There the energetic committee had made complete preparation for the amusement of the young people and the comfort of all. Swings, merry-go-round and straw bed were busy all day. Baseball and horse shoes claimed the attention of many of the young people, while McIlwee's band cleared the ears of all who were present, thus adding a great deal to what was a most enjoyable day. A game of ball between the band and the Sunday School caused a great deal of interest. The feature of the game would have been Dr. Ford's steal of several base had it not been that Joe Shaffer announced dinner just as the Ford approached the base and instead of stopping the "Little old Ford, it rambled right along" toward the dinner table, but unfortunately struck a stake and skidded on its hood for ten yards. The dinner provided by the ladies was remarkable for its excellent quality and great quantity. It is needless to say that everyone had a good time, the children came home tired but happy and all voted it the best picnic ever enjoyed by the Sunday School. The thanks of the school were tendered to Professor McIlwee whose band regaled the company with choice music, to Mr. Smith, whose grove was used and to Mr. Keenan for the use of the water wagon.

The picnics were inclusive of non-Lutherans, without reservation. In advance of the just-described 1915 event, an invitation was published in the Keyser newspapers:

*Don't you know that the Lutheran Sunday School is going to
hold its annual picnic next Monday?
Don't you know the public is invited?
Don't you know Prof. McIlwee's Concert Band will furnish music?
Don't you know the M. E. Southern Base Ball Team will cross bats with the Lutherans, and, the
young ladies, will challenge the winner?
Don't you know that "Cy" is going to haul the people to and from the grounds
and the Lutherans will pay the freight?
Don't you know there will be a Funny-go-round, three swings
and a straw bed for the little folks, and
Harry Nicholas will defend his honor for keeping the Pig in the Pen, and
Davis, Kesner, Wolfe and Kephart, will fight it out pitching horse shoes,
while the ladies root for their favorites?
So bring your baskets full of good things to eat, and don't forget that
this is YOUR picnic and we don't care how much you take of it.
So remember Labor Day, Monday next.*

In 1928, the 18th annual picnic of Trinity Lutheran Sunday School, held at Patterson's Beach, Burlington, was one of the best outings enjoyed by the Sunday School. An unusually large number of the members and their friends were present, and in the morning many took part in various athletic contests. In the afternoon, swimming contests and a baseball game between the single and married men amused the crowd, after which the prizes donated by the merchants were given to the winners. Music for the event was provided by the Kolkhorst Concert Band. The contests and the winners were:

- 50-yard dash for girls – Won by Ruth Vorberg. Prize donated by Scott Bosley.
- Sack Race for boys – Won by Joseph Scherr. Prize donated by A. P. Brown & Bro.
- Sack Race for girls – Won by Madge Miers. Prize donated by Stauring Jewelry Co.
- Sack race for men – Won by Richard Fromhart. Prize donated by McCoole's Store.
- 75-yard dash for boys – Won by William Coffman. Prize donated by Trenton's Market.
- Three-legged race for boys – Won by Romaine Kephart and Robert Coffman. Prize donated by Keyser Pharmacy.
- Three-legged race for men – Won by Richard Fromhart and William Coffman. Prize donated by Kaplon's Men's Shop.
- Baseball Throw – Won by Irene Davis. Prize donated by Keystone Store.
- Egg Carrying Contest – Won by Mrs. Clara McVaney. Prize donated by Keyser Bakery.
- Cracker Eating Contest – Won by "Chicken" Avers. Prize donated by A. & P. Tea Co. (D. P. Peters).
- Bean Guessing Contest – Won by Carlisle Kauffman. Prize donated by Sliger Bros.
- Horseshoe Contest (Doubles) – Won by W. B. Kesner and Richard Sliger. Prizes donated by Workman's Market and J. H, Dean.

- Horseshoe Contest (Singles) – Won by John Stanhagen. Prize donated by Sanitary Market.
- Oldest woman present – Mrs. J. C. Kephart. Prize donated by M. C. McKenzie.
- Oldest man present – J. C. Kephart. Prize donated by Coffman-Fisher Co.
- The youngest boy present – Won by Frederick Lee Shaffer. Prize donated by J. H. Roderick Dept. Store.
- The youngest girl present – Won by Sarah Catherine Loy. Prize donated by The Sincell Co.
- The largest family present – Won by J. C. Kephart family. Prize donated by Peoples Pharmacy.

One can only imaging how many crackers "Chicken" Avers consumed, but he was a lanky six foot two and likely weighed no more than 140 pounds – thin as a rail. We know that the youngest attendee, Freddie Shaffer, was only thirteen months old, and Mr. Kephart, the oldest, was nearing his seventieth birthday.

Joyfully, Trinity continues this wonderful tradition!

Sports

Sports, then as now, played a major role in the social lives of local residents, and church-sponsored teams were extremely popular. Trinity Lutheran was at the pinnacle of success in Church League basketball and baseball. New members, particularly young men, came to Trinity because they wanted to play for the best. We can credit the beginning of this savvy recruiting strategy to Rev. Harry Baughman.

Baughman himself was an outstanding basketball player and star of the famed Keyser Collegians. Several of his parishioners were also members of the Collegians team and also led the Lutherans to memorable Keyser Church League basketball championships.

In September, 1923, a newspaper headline declared:

Handsome Entertainment for Champions of Sunday School Baseball League at Church: Preceded by a Street Parade – Members of the Lutheran baseball team, Champions of 1923 of the Keyser Sunday School League, were given a banquet at the Lutheran Sunday School. Before the feast, an automobile parade was had around the streets of Keyser proclaiming the champion team. To use the words of the toastmaster, Rev. Drawbaugh, the banquet was a real "Dutch feed." Chicken, mashed potatoes, tomatoes, apple-sass, salad, ice cream, cake, coffee and cigars were served and partaken.

Those present besides the members of the Sunday School, as invited guests, were: Ernest A. See, President of the League; W. Elliott Nefflen, Secretary; G. Ed. Sirbaugh, Treasurer; W. E. Drake, Mgr. First M. E. team; W. Kagey, Mgr. U. B. team; L. Kidwell, Mgr. Catholic team; W. E. Wells, Mgr. M. E. South team; Malcolm Frye, Mgr. Presbyterian team.

The Lutheran team clinched the championship several weeks before the end of the season. The M.E. South team finished a distant second. On July 9 the Lutherans overwhelmed the United Brethren team by a score of 20-4; Clem Montgomery led the team that day with two home runs. Other names appearing in the Lutheran team box scores were Avers, Boor, Diehl, Kephart, Robison, Shaffer, Thrasher, and Yost.

DENNY AVERS

The 1923 Keyser Church League baseball championship trophy still rests in the archives of the church. Decades later, the talent had waned, but we still had lots of fun and were proud to represent the congregation.

Luther League

The Luther League, a primary predecessor to today's Youth Ministry program of the Evangelical Lutheran Church in America, was a focal point for youth and young adult activity. The earliest references to meetings and activities of the "Luther League" at Trinity Lutheran date to 1923, during the pastorate of Rev. J. W. Drawbaugh. The group met on Sunday evenings, before the Vespers.

In November, 1927, Luther Leaguers from numerous congregations in West Virginia and Western Maryland met at Grace Lutheran Church in Fairmont. With the full support of the synod, the West

Virginia State and Synodical Lutheran League was formally organized. The statewide representatives elected officers that included two members of Trinity – William W. Wolfe (President) and Vivian Bissett (Treasurer).

In June, 1928, the Luther League of West Virginia convention was held in Parkersburg. Mr. Wolfe was the presiding officer. Among others from Keyser who attended were Rev. Robert Vorberg, who was instrumental in the formation of the statewide body, William Coffman, Vivian Bissett, Louise Gull, Fannie Tasker and the Ladies Quartette of the Trinity Memorial Lutheran Church – composed of Mrs. Clem E. Montgomery, Mrs. Charles Farley, Mrs. Warren Kolkhorst and Mrs. J. Perry Greenwade. The quartette was especially invited to sing and furnished much of the music for the convention.

The 1929 convention was held in Grafton. We are fortunate to have a photographic record of that meeting

COURTESY OF DINAH COURRIER

Miss Bissett, Rev. Vorberg and Mr. Wolfe are standing on the far-right of the front row. The ladies of the Quartette are on the far-left side. Mr. Wolfe (President), Miss Bissett (State Corresponding Secretary) and Mrs. Greenwade (Junior State Secretary) were elected officers of the league.

At the 1930 convention in Charleston, Mr. Wolfe 'retired' from his position; Miss Bissett and Mrs. Greenwade were reelected to their offices. Plans were approved for the fourth convention to be held in Huntington the following year.

Generations of those growing up in Trinity have fond memories of being Luther Leaguers. Their enthusiasm, enjoyment, learning, and work on church and community projects were strong threads in the fabric of fellowship, spirituality and character that defines Trinity Lutheran Church and its family of believers.

Camp Luther

For more than seventy years, the youth of Trinity Lutheran have enjoyed a memorable and life-changing faith-based camping experience at the 4-H camp near Cowen, West Virginia. The days at Camp Luther have always been filled with swimming and games, treks in the woodland areas covered by blooming rhododendrons and mountain laurels, fishing in the Gauley River, good food, campfires, opportunities to interact and learn from outstanding clergy and lay leaders, sing and worship. Then, as now, campers have formed lifelong friendships as they walked this section of the path along their journey of faith.

The earliest local newspaper record of participation in the "Lutheran Youth Camp at Cowen, W. Va." was published in 1947. Campers from Trinity Lutheran that year included Harold Kephart, Phyllis Riggleman and Harry Stoutamyer; Miss Sue Theis was a counsellor. Transportation was provided by Mrs. Marie Farley and Mrs. Elizabeth Stoutamyer.

The earliest newspaper record of participation in "Camp Luther" was recorded in 1950. Miss Mary E. Knott, Miss Bobbie Jean Riggleman and Harry Stoutamyer were representatives from the parish. Their presence at the camp was awarded by the congregation in recognition of their exemplary attendance at Sunday School and church services.

By 1952, the list of campers had grown substantially: Nancy Coffman, Joe Hanna, Rick Kephart, Barbara Knott, Donna Rae McKee, Bobbie Jean Riggleman and Lois Whipp. Rev. Don Anderson was a camp counsellor. Mt. Calvary had an even larger group of campers: Margaret Alkire, Eddie Batie, C. A. Beck, Jr., Broadus Bowman, Patsy Cosgrove, William Hays, Judith Lupton, Delores McKenzie, Vivian Faye McKenzie, Alan Wilson and Joy Wilson. Rev. Bob Cassell and several others served on the camp staff.

The following year, the group had grown so much that an Osgood bus was hired to provide transportation! Rev. Anderson had moved up to become assistant camp director. Mrs. Lorna Anderson, Mrs. Edith Workman, Mrs. Donna Kephart, Miss Mary Elizabeth Knott and Miss Bobbie Jean

137

Riggleman were counsellors. The youth from the congregation who enjoyed the camp were: Byron Athey, Denny Avers, Bobby Bailey, Darlene Bill, Nancy Lee Coffman, Carol Cook, Julia Cook, Rosalind Engle, Janice Lee Fisher, Maureen Fitzgerald, Judy George, Lonnie George, Joe Hanna, Richard Hess, Donna Rae McKee, Rick Kephart, Mike Montgomery, Andrea Murray, Mary Riggleman, Connie Ryan, Delmer "Butch" Ryan and Lois Ann Whipp. Mrs. C. E. McDaniels was the camp nurse.

By 1955, Rev. Anderson was the camp director. Attendees included: Scott Bosley, Mary Chapman, Nancy Coffman, Mary Ann Fallon, Tom Feaster, Henry and Richard Hess, Donna Rae McKee, Mary Riggleman, Marcella Ryan, Melinda Watson, Dinah Wells, Lois Whipp and Lowell Whipp.

In 1964, Carole Athey, Joyce Buckalew, Mary Chapman, Duke and Missy Ebert, Donnie and Karen Heare, Gary Kephart and Terri Lancaster were among those who enjoyed two weeks at Camp Luther.

In 1977, Camp Luther was a one-week experience attended by Fred Athey, Bucky Cain, Debbie Chaney, Susan Chaney, Carl Corbin, Gary Corbin, Tammy Corbin, Jay Courrier, Jay Hanna, C. W. Morton, Suzanne Sites and Susan Smith. By 1982, the number of attendees from Trinity was back up to nineteen: Chris Biggs, Debra Chaney, Marty Chaney, Susan Chaney, Gary Corbin, Tami Corbin, Amy Courrier, Tona Courrier, Joel Harr, Kelly Knight, Adam Kuykendall, Crissy Perea, Matthew Sites, Suzanne Sites, Philip Sharps, Janis Stennett, Debby Walker, Kevin Wentworth and Kim Wentworth.

Over the years, the Camp Luther experience has evolved to keep pace with the interests and needs of the campers. It remains "the place to be" in mid-June of each year, including 2019!

Coda

The fine article that appeared in the *Mineral Daily News* of September 1, 1925, provided an apt description of Trinity Lutheran Church. Perhaps this might be the first published history of the congregation. Now, nearly a century later, as we read these words again, we realize they are timeless.

MINERAL DAILY NEWS

Lutheran Church Established In Keyser, 1903

The local Lutheran church is not nearly as old as some of the churches of the community. In fact, it is among the younger of Keyser's churches. However, there were a number of adherents to the Lutheran faith in our city for many years before they were organized into a congregation, and who largely identified themselves with the other congregations of the city. Occasionally a Lutheran pastor would come and hold a service for the people.

It was not until 1903 that the General Synod's Board of Home Missions and the Synod of Maryland, working co-jointly, sent a young seminarian, the Reverend W. C. Ney to Keyser and here in the Odd Fellows Hall, sometime during the month of June, was held the first of a series of Lutheran services which resulted in the establishment of a church. On Sunday, August 16, 1903, in Carskadon Hall, now Thompson Furniture Co., a congregation was organized under the name of "Trinity Memorial Evangelical Lutheran Church" and the first Holy Communion was administered. The Reverend Doctors L. A. Mann, Cumberland; Charles Trump, Martinsburg; and Luther F. Miller, Baltimore, assisted Pastor Ney on that day. Forty charter members were enrolled.

Another "big day" for this congregation was Sunday, October 14, 1906, when after several years of struggle, holding its meetings in halls and working under several disadvantages, the congregation which had now grown to 78 in number, had the great joy to have their newly built church consecrated. The Reverend Doctor Hartman of Baltimore preached and the President of the Synod of Maryland was present. Besides the church edifice, the following things were consecrated to holy uses: an altar, pulpit and lecture of oak, made and presented to the church by Mr. Henry Neuhauser and son, the silver alms basins presented by Mr. P. M. Spangler, the altar and pulpit vestments presented by the Ladies' Aid Society, and a pulpit bible presented by Mr. Conrad Fisher, in memory of his wife, Mrs. Elizabeth Fisher.

Soon after this, Pastor Ney left and Pastor C. P. Bastian assumed charge. He in turn was succeeded by Pastor Harry F. Baughman who resigned in 1919. Pastor W. V. Garrett became the next pastor in 1920 and after a short pastorate resigned the same year. The present minister, Pastor J. W. Drawbaugh, was called in 1921.

The church has grown steadily all these years and has played an active part in the Christian life of the community. It has been fortunate securing scholarly and well-trained pastors who have made themselves and likewise their church a force for civic, social and spiritual health in our city.

Not only does the local Lutheran church play an active part here, it is also active in Synodical affairs. When in 1911 the Synod of West Virginia was formed the local church was transferred from the Maryland Synod and became one of the charter members of the Synod of West Virginia. From among its pastors, Trinity church has given the Synod of West Virginia a President and a Vice-President.

Its present church edifice, while not so large nor costly as many of Keyser's churches, is very complete and churchly and for the time, serves very well the congregation's needs. The church has also purchased the parsonage adjoining the church and a lot adjacent to the parsonage with a view toward future expansion and rejoices that it is entirely free from debt or any encumbrances whatever.

Among the parochial activities of Trinity Evangelical parish are the Bible School with its corps of efficient teachers; the Ladies' Aid Society; the Luther League; the Woman's Missionary Society, which is very active; and the Light Brigade, which gives the children of the parish missionary instruction.

This church, while conservative in character, is always ready to unite with all the other churches of the city to help make Keyser the cleanest in morals, and most truly Christian of any in the State.

While much has been added to the history of Trinity Lutheran Church in the ensuing years, we rejoice that the character of the congregation has remained constant: steadfast in faith, conservative in its practices, reaching out in service to the community as disciples of our Lord and Savior and welcoming all who seek the presence of the Holy Spirit in their lives.

Chapter 8 – Epilogue

It's Christmas Eve. Midnight is approaching. Parishioners, relatives and friends have come to celebrate the Holy birth of Jesus.

Seen are many old friends, back in town for the holidays. But the congregation is hushed. We wait for the first sound of the organ, the reading of the Word of God, the beautifully combined voices of the choir, the anthem solo, the lighting of candles and singing *Silent Night*.

Then we hear it. Resonating the pipes of the organ is the quiet beginning of the *Yuletide Echoes*.

And all is well, as the Peace of the Holy Spirit comes to us once again.

In this, our home – the house of the Lord.

This is the legacy passed on to us by the founding saints and those who followed.

And now, whenever that is, we come, again and again, to this sacred place.

We come, seeking God's grace and forgiveness in the sacraments and the Word. The beautiful and timeless liturgy we know so well guides our worship and refreshes so many thoughts of the presence of a merciful and loving Father.

The faces and voices are different now. The world is different. But we are strengthened by the Word, the Sacraments, and those around us. May it ever be so.

And all is well, as the Peace of the Holy Spirit comes to us once again.

In this, our home – the house of the Lord.

This is now our legacy, to protect and to magnify, to pass on to others who will come.

– Denny Avers, 2019

Appendix I

THE ORIGIN
of
Trinity Memorial Lutheran Church

KEYSER, WEST VIRGINIA

Compiled by
Mrs. P. M. Spangler and Miss Martha Watson
February, 1936

WISHING to attend the regular Communion service, there being no Lutheran Church in Keyser up to the year nineteen hundred three, Miss Anna Carl, Miss Martha Watson and Mrs. P. M. Spangler decided to take an afternoon train to Westernport, Md., and to attend services at Calvary Lutheran Church. The Rev. Luther F. Miller was the pastor there.

During the trip to Westernport the ladies were discussing the inconvenience of traveling five miles to church service, as in those days it meant a tiresome drive by horse and buggy, or the use of unsuitable train schedules. As a part of this conversation, Mrs. Spangler asked the question, "Why do we not have a Lutheran church in Keyser?" Miss Carl replied, "Well, why not?" This little seed of thought, planted that afternoon grew until we now have Trinity Memorial Lutheran Church in Keyser.

By the time the services at Calvary Church were finished, the ladies had become so enthusiastic with their idea of a church in Keyser that they thought it wise to confer with Rev. Miller regarding the matter. Rev. Miller was a kindly, able and active pastor. His advice, information and help were freely given, and must certainly have contained plenty of the will to do or die, for the ladies turned their faces homeward imbued with the determination to work for a Lutheran Church in Keyser.

Beginning early in February, nineteen hundred three, Miss Anna Carl, Miss Martha Watson, Miss Margaret Koelz and Mrs. P. M. Spangler started out to canvass the town for members. They found a goodly number of adherents to the Lutheran denomination scattered over Keyser. Many of these people holding positions of high responsibility in the various Keyser churches. They were rendered valuable assistance by the following named gentlemen: Dr. John W. Hall, Mr. John T. Sincell, Mr. John G. Koelz and Mr. P. M. Spangler. These gentlemen canvassed the town with particular regard to the men to be found of the Lutheran faith.

After the canvass, the progress made seemed good enough to expand the work, Mrs. Spangler invited Rev. Miller to come to her home and organize an Aid Society. This was done on March fifth, nineteen hundred three. Those present at this meeting were Mrs. Henry Baker, Miss Anna Carl, Miss Lena Wolfe, Miss Martha Watson, Mr. and Mrs. P. M. Spangler and Rev. Miller. Mrs. Spangler was appointed president, Miss Carl secretary and treasurer, which position she held until her death, June tenth, nineteen hundred ten. New members were added to this society steadily until it numbered twenty-five persons. Diligence and perseverance marked the efforts of this group, as the following records show:

From June, 1903, to March 31, 1904, dues and entertainments held during that time brought in
.... $164.16
April 1, 1904 to March 31, 1905.................................... 358.21
April 1, 1905 to March 31, 1906.................................... 185.45
This making a total of $707.82 for three years work.

TRINITY MEMORIAL LUTHERAN CHURCH

As an aside notation, let one who as a child witnessed the above efforts speak.

Many hours were spent in baking pies, crullers, and making candy. The sale for these delicious edibles accounted for many of the dollars turned in by this society. Then there were oyster suppers given, during which much fun and music were furnished by the church quartette: Mr. D. T. Greenwade, Mr. George Loy, Mr. Isaac Neuhauser and Rev. Ney. A Lutheran supper was always well patronized. Good cooking and attractive menus, coupled with good fellowship appealed especially to the masculine population of Keyser. But, while we like to dwell in memories of the pleasures of these events, let us not forget to honor the toil of these Aid Society members and their helpers. We must admire their spirit and willingness to persevere in this foundation labor of the church.

On March ninth, nineteen hundred three, Rev. Dr. Stewart Hartman, Secretary of the Board of Home Missions, was written to, and work accomplished laid before him. He was invited to come and look over the field. This with a view of establishing a Lutheran Mission in Keyser. On May second, nineteen hundred three, Dr. Hartman came to Keyser. A committee of men met with him and went over the field. He was delighted with the situation. The Board granted Dr. Hartman authority to name Rev. William C. Ney, as a very promising young student minister, to take charge of the work for the summer. On June first, nineteen hundred three, Rev. Ney came to Keyser, making his home with Mr. and Mrs. P. M. Spangler. He entered the work at once, and was rewarded with splendid results. June fourteenth, nineteen hundred three, he conducted the first service in the name of the General Synod of the Lutheran Church. For his sermon he used the text from Numbers, 13th chapter, 30th verse, "Let us go up at once and possess it, for we are well able to overcome it." After three Sunday evening services held in the Odd Fellows Hall, the place of worship was changed to Carskadon's Hall, this being a more central location. Here on July fifth, nineteen hundred three, the first Sunday School service was held, and church service was continued.

About thirty persons attended the first Sunday School. Rev. Ney acted as Superintendent, Mr. Frederick Koelz as Secretary, Mrs. Claude Clevenger as Organist; the following as teachers: Miss Anna Carl, Miss Elsie Baker, Miss Maria Fry, and Mrs. P. M. Spangler, with eight little ones as the first Primary Class. Records show that in three years, or by nineteen hundred six, this little Primary group had grown to eighty members, with forty enrolled on the Cradle Roll. The Sunday School had also grown to be a body of young and adult people. The Lutherans at this time were developing a great spirit of unity and Christian fellowship that was to carry them on to greater heights for the glory of God.

Rev. Dr. Ney proved to be a good shepherd for this scattered flock. He was a friendly, affable man. His personality attracted men and women from all walks of life. He was an earnest minister, a cheerful companion.

MISS MARTHA WATSON

MRS. P. M. SPANGLER

With unspeakable joy and happiness, by the grace of God the Mission was given a great experience to enjoy. On August sixteenth, nineteen hundred three, the formal organization of Trinity Memorial Lutheran Church congregation of Keyser, W.Va., took place. The installation of its officers, the reception of its charter members, and the first celebration of Holy Communion. Officiating at this service were the saintly Dr. L. A. Mann, of Cumberland, Md., Rev. Charles Trump, D.D., of Martinsburg, W.Va., and Rev. Luther F. Miller, Westernport.

After the adoption of a constitution, these officers were installed into the duties of their respective offices:

    Dr. John W. Hall,   Mr. P. M: Spangler,
    Mr. John T. Sincell,   Mr. John G. Koelz,
    Mr. A. S. Wolfe,   Mr. William Boehmas, [sic]
        Elders.   Mr. Jacob Avers, Deacons.

        Miss Gay Greenwade, Church Organist
        Mr. Daniel T. Greenwade, Choir Director

Following the installation of officers, forty adherents to the Lutheran faith, some by letter of transfer, others by renewal of their profession of faith, were accorded the right hand of Christian fellowship in the name of the new congregation. The Charter membership Roll was as follows:

Mrs. John Arnold	Mr. and Mrs. J. C. Kephart
Mr. and Mrs. Jacob Avers	Mrs. Annie Kolkhorst
Mr. and Mrs. Henry Baker	Mr. Henry Lampers [sic]
Mr. and Mrs. Charles Balthus	Mr. C. T. Mandler
Mr. and Mrs. F. W. Boehmas [sic]	Dr. E. T. Martin
Miss Anna Carl	Mrs. F. Moffit
Mr. and Mrs. J. W. Clem	Mrs. George Newhouse
Mrs. Claude C. Clevenger	Mr. and Mrs. C. P. Pifer
Mrs. Harry Gull	Mr. W. C. Pifer
Dr. John W. Hall	Mr. Benjamin Souder
Mr. John G. Koelz	Mrs. Shafferman
Mrs. E. H. Gerstell	Mrs. Joseph Shaffer
Mrs. M. B. Wagner [sic]	Mr. and Mrs. John T. Sincell
Mr. and Mrs. A. S. Wolfe [sic]	Mr. and Mrs. H. A. Sliger

        Mr. and Mrs. Parker M. Spangler

During Rev. Mr. Ney's absence at school the winter of 1903-4, the congregation was served very ably and acceptably by Rev. Wilbur Mann, of Cumberland, Md., Dr. Peter Bergstresser, of Pittsburgh, Pa.

Once again a change was made in the place of worship, when the congregation moved to Johnson's Hall.

Shortly after this, events moved rapidly, each adding joy and enthusiasm to every one interested in the work.

PASTOR WILLIAM C. NEY

On June first, nineteen hundred five, Rev. Ney having finished his work at Gettysburg Seminary, was called as Pastor.

June twenty-second, nineteen hundred five, the lot upon which the church now stands, was purchased for the sum of one thousand two hundred fifty dollars, ($1,250.00). Five hundred dollars ($500.00) of the purchase price was paid by the Ladies' Aid Society. The seven hundred fifty dollar ($750.00) balance furnished something tangible to work for. Dollar by dollar, in numbers large and small, amounts were gathered, until on January fifteenth, nineteen hundred six, the final seventy dollars ($70.00) was paid. This represented up to that time the congregation's greatest material possession.

This Deed, made this twenty-third day of January, in the year one thousand nine hundred and six, by and between Harry G. Fisher, grantor, and John T. Sincell, George M. Loy and A. S. Wolf, trustees of The Trinity Memorial Evangelical Lutheran Church of Keyser, grantees. Witnesseth, That for and in consideration of Twelve hundred and fifty dollars, cash in hand, the receipt of which is hereby acknowledged, the said grantor doth grant unto the said grantees as trustees as aforesaid with covenants of general warranty the following described real estate in Keyser, Mineral County, State of West Virginia, to-wit: That certain lot and part of a lot on Davis Street of said town and known and numbered as hereinafter mentioned on the map of H. G. Davis and Co. Addition of said town of Keyser, that is to say lot number one hundred and sixteen (116) and eighteen foot frontage of lot number one hundred and fifteen (115), the full lot and part of a lot making a continuous frontage of forty-three (43) feet on said Davis Street and extending back one hundred and six feet and five inches to Apple Alley. This being the lot and a portion of part of a lot conveyed to the said Harry G. Fisher by J. O. Thompson and wife by deed hearing date the 15th day of May, 1905, and of record in the Office of the Clerk of the County Court of Mineral County, West Virginia, in Deed Book No. 27, page 326. To Have and To Hold unto the said grantees, their successors and assigns forever.

Witness the following signature and seal.
HARRY G. FISHER [SEAL]

State of West Virginia, Mineral County, to-wit:

I, H. L. Arnold, a Notary Public, in and for the County and State aforesaid, do hereby certify that Harry G. Fisher, whose name is signed to the foregoing writing hearing date the 23rd day of January, 1906, has this day acknowledged the same before me in my said county.
Given under my hand this 23rd day of January, 1906.
H. L. ARNOLD, Notary Public.

Mineral County, ss.

Be it remembered that on this 23rd day of January, 1906, at 9 o'clock A. M., the foregoing deed, with the certificate thereto annexed, was presented in the Office of the Clerk of the County Court and admitted to record.
J. V. BELL, Clerk.

State of West Virginia,
Mineral County, to-wit:
I, T. T. Huffman, Clerk of the County Court of said County of Mineral, the same being a Court of Record and having a seal, do hereby certify, that the above is a true and correct copy from Deed Book No. 27, at page 578, one of the public records kept in my office. And I do further certify that under the laws of the State of West Virginia, I am the legal custodian of said record.
In Testimony, thereof, I have hereunto set my hand and affixed the seal of the said County Court, at Keyser, West Virginia, this 17th day of April, 1936.
T. T. HUFFMAN, Clerk County Court.

PASTOR H. F. BAUGHMAN

Every effort was now made to erect a church building. In a little less than a year's time, on June seventeenth, nineteen hundred six, the congregation gathered about the foundation of this building and laid the corner stone in the name of The Triune God. Dr. Mann preached the sermon from the text recorded in Isaiah 28th chp., 16th verse, "Therefore thus saith the Lord God, Behold, I lay in Zion for a foundation a stone, a tried stone, a precious corner stone, a sure foundation: he that believeth shall not make haste."

The foundation of this building was under the supervision of Mr. John Streets, a negro stone mason. Mr. Streets was a local mechanic. He was highly pleased and felt honored to be allowed to lay this foundation. With great fervor he declared, "This is the first and only church I ever built, and I'm going to see that it's done right." To everyone engaged in this work, seemed to be given the strength and inspiration to do their utmost.

With faith and hope in God, the work was continued, until the time when another mile-stone was reached on our road of endeavor. On October fourteenth, nineteen hundred six, seventy-eight members of the congregation, instead of the initial forty, had the rare privilege of approaching the Holy of Holies, to present a building made by the hands of men unto the Father of all men. This building was dedicated in the name of the Father, and of the Son, and of the Holy Ghost. Here let us read as reported in October nineteenth, nineteen hundred six issue of The Keyser Tribune:

"The past Lord's Day was a joyous one for the Lutheran congregation of this town. It was on that day that the handsome church on Davis Street was dedicated. The ideal autumn weather contributed much toward making the feast of dedication a most happy occasion. Rev. Dr. Hartman, of Baltimore, Md., preached two very interesting and helpful sermons during the day, and made the solicitation for funds. The platform meeting held in the afternoon, in which four ministers from the town took part, was greatly enjoyed by a large audience. In consequence of the hearty response to the solicitations for funds, enough was quickly and easily raised, or pledged, to cover remaining indebtedness of the church. The church as it now stands cost five thousand dollars, and the lot one thousand two hundred fifty dollars. A total of six thousand two hundred fifty dollars."

In addition to the above quotations, let us quote from Rev. Ney's closing remarks made upon this occasion:

> May this hour laden with so great joy, mark one more mountain top experience in our life; so that as we go down into the valley of tomorrow it may be with a deeper love for God and Man, and a quickened zeal for better service unto both. As we move onward may we move up-ward to that blessed day when we shall no longer serve him in temples here below, but enter into a perfect service of Him in that temple whose builder and maker is God, Eternal in the Heavens.

The building stands strong and beautiful, and is a credit to Mr. Henry Baker, the architect and contractor under whose supervision it was built. Early in the Fall months, in time for winter comfort, Mr. P. M. Spangler and Mr. William Weagley installed a steam heating plant.

PASTOR R. T. VORBERG

PASTOR W. V. GARRETT

PASTOR FELIX ROBINSON

The first wedding solemnized in the church was our organist, Miss Gay Greenwade and Mr. Isaac Neuhauser, on June 19th, 1907. At a meeting of the West Virginia Synod in October, 1911, Trinity Memorial church of Keyser, W. Va., was transferred to that body. The first organ used by the congregation was presented by Mr. M. P. Moller, of Hagerstown, Md.

The memorial windows add much beauty to the church, and were presented by the following parties:

Mr. D. T. Greenwade, in memory of Clifton Greenwade, a son.
Mr. John T. Sincell, in memory of Charles Sincell, his father.
Mr. and Mrs. Henry Baker, in memory of John W. Baker, a son.
Mrs. John Arnold and Mrs. H. A. Sliger, in memory of their dead children.
Mrs. M. B. Wagner [sic], in memory of Wm. Troutman, her father.
Mrs. Shafferman, in memory of her husband and son.
Rev. Ney, in memory of his maternal grand-parents.
Sunday School Class No. 2, one window.
Sunday School Class, No. 3, one window.
The Baptismal Font was presented by the Cradle Roll.
The furniture which adorns the pulpit platform was presented in behalf of the family of Mr. Henry Neuhauser.
Silver collection plates were presented by Mr. and Mrs. P. M. Spangler.
Pulpit hangings were presented by the Ladies' Aid Society.
The hand work on the Veil for the Altar was done by Mrs. T. B. Fry.
Carpet and Choir chairs were presented by the Ladies' Aid Society.
Pulpit Bible was presented by Mr. Conrad Fisher in memory of his wife.
The first chairs used in the Primary Department were presented by Miss Catherine Neuhauser, she gave one dozen chairs.

On March 31, 1919, the property situated on the north side of the church was purchased by the congregation, for the sum of two thousand nine hundred dollars, ($2,900.00). This property was used as a parsonage for some time.

On October 23, 1926, an opportunity occurred to procure a good property on South Main Street. This being a larger home and in the best residential district, making a very suitable parsonage. The purchase price of this property was nine thousand two hundred fifty dollars ($9,250.00).

The following pastors have served the church:

> Rev. William C. Ney, June 1, 1903, to October, 1906.
> Rev. C. P. Bastian, March 3, 1907, to 1912.
> Rev. Harry Baughman, June 1, 1913, to November 10, 1918.
> Rev. W. V. Garrett, March 9, 1919, to September 1, 1920.
> Rev. J. W. Drawbaugh, April, 1921, to October, 1925.
> Rev. R. T. Vorberg, D.D., April, 1926 to July 8, 1933.
> Rev. Felix G. Robinson, March 2, 1934

Here we leave Trinity Memorial Lutheran Church counting its many Spiritual and Material blessings. That the future will bring joy to the hearts of those destined to carry on its work, we have no doubt. Those who have brought it this far will attest that any labor or sacrifice for its glory is not too much, nor to be ever regretted.

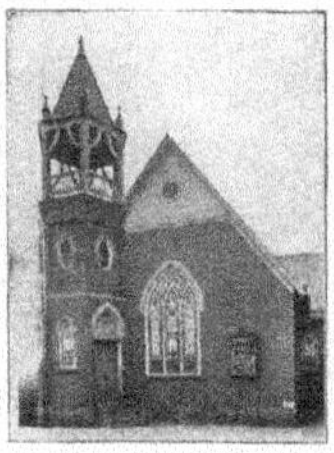

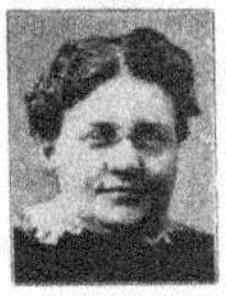

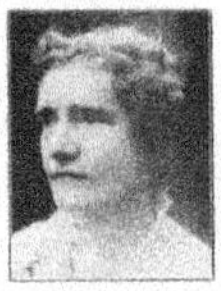

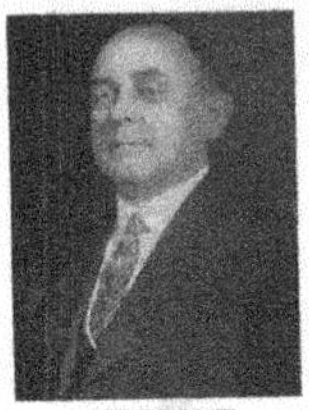

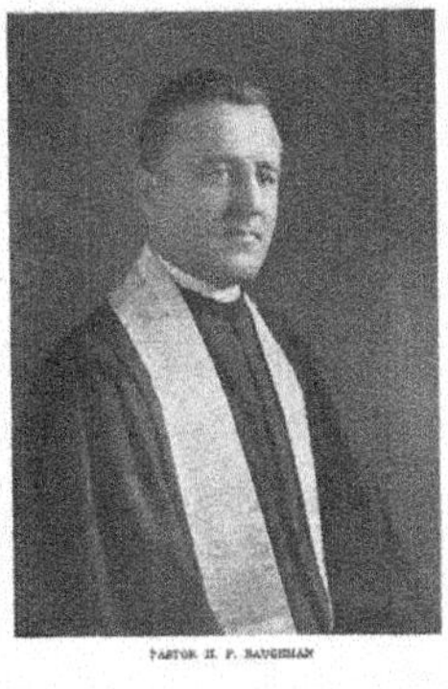

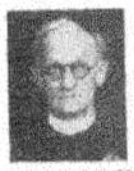

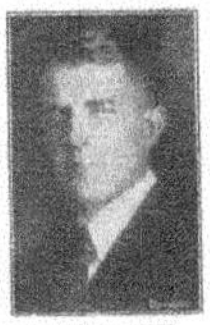

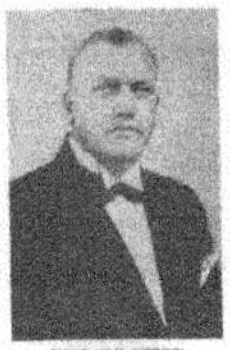

Appendix II

Seventieth Anniversary
1903 - 1973

Trinity Evangelical Lutheran Church
Keyser, West Virginia

The booklet distributed at the time of 1973 anniversary celebration included Part I – the text of the 1936 history pamphlet. The earlier document is fully transcribed in Appendix I and is not repeated here.

Part II

The Rev. William C. Ney, D. D.

The Rev. Ney came to Trinity Evangelical Church upon completion of his studies at Gettysburg Theological Seminary on June 1, 1903, and terminated his pastorate here in October 1906. The first church was built during his term as pastor at a cost of $1,250.00 for the lot and $5,000.00 for the building. There were seventy-eight members. The cornerstone was laid June 17, 1906, with Dr. Mann preaching the sermon. The church was dedicated October 14, 1906. Dr. Stewart Hartman preached the sermon.

Rev. Ney's first confirmation class consisted of two persons, Icy Avers and Gertrude Wolfe. Rosie and Charlotte Shafferman were the first members after the charter was opened.

The first wedding solemnized in Trinity was the marriage of Miss Gay Greenwade, church organist, to Mr. Isaac Neuhauser, on June 19, 1907.

Among the donations made by the general public to the building fund for the first Trinity Lutheran Church in 1905 and 1906 were the following:

Col. Thomas B. Davis	$200.00
Sen. Steven Elkins	20.00
Sen. Henry Gassaway Davis	20.00
John Streets[1]	15.00
Charlie Yee[2]	5.00

The Rev. C. P. Bastian, D.D.

Rev. Bastian came to Keyser as Pastor of Trinity Evangelical Church, March 3, 1907, and terminated his pastorate in 1912 when he accepted a call to a Pennsylvania Church. He was a very active pastor with an evangelistical style. He visited many homes of unchurched people and held noonday services at the Baltimore and Ohio Railroad Shops, where he came in contact with many men. He organized a young men's club, and with the help of these young men, he built a club house back of the church where many festivities were held. Many new members were added to the church as a result of his work. A prohibitioner, Rev. Bastian led an active fight against saloons and was a leader in obtaining a local option law against the sale of liquor.

---

[1] Mr. Streets, a Negro, later built the church's foundation.
[2] Mr. Yee, a Chinaman, owned a laundry in Keyser.

The Rev. Harry F. Baughman
D.D., LL.D., L.H.D.

Rev. Baughman came to Trinity Lutheran after his graduation from Gettysburg Seminary, June 1, 1913. He was a very gifted speaker of positive Lutheran theology. While here, he organized a men's choir and a church orchestra that played before and after services. He also organized the Christian Endeavor Society, which was well attended by the young people of the church. Rev. Baughman established early Easter morning services.

He was President of the West Virginia Synod, and later in his life became President of Gettysburg Seminary.

Because he was interested in athletics, he assembled a team called the "Keyser Collegians". Three of these players were members of Trinity. Through this activity, he acquired quite a following of young men in our community.

The orchestra he organized was composed of Director Lawrence Kolkhorst, Warren Kolkhorst, Emmett Kolkhorst, Anna Kolkhorst, Virginia Knott, R. A. Stoutamyer, and Walter Kephart -- all members of the church. Others who were musicians in the town were added to the orchestra: Bill Robey, Ira Ravenscraft, Cleytus Shaffenaker, Harry Rogers, and Mac Swadley. Rev. Baughman left Trinity on November 10, 1918.

The Rev. W. V. Garrett, D.D.

Rev. Garrett was only at Trinity for a brief pastorate, March 9, 1919, to September 1, 1920. There was no new activity while he was here.

The Rev. J. W. Drawbaugh

Rev. Drawbaugh came to Trinity April 19, 1921, and stayed until October 1925. While he was here, we adopted the Common Service Book. He established the midnight Christmas Service and organized the Sunday School. He also organized the Women's Missionary Society and the Light Brigade Junior Missionary Society as well as the Lutheran Brotherhood.

Rev. Drawbaugh was a gifted preacher as well as a fine singer.

The Rev. Robert Vorberg, D.D.

Rev. Vorberg came to Trinity Lutheran in April 1926. He died during his Service here, July 8, 1933.

He practiced positive Lutheran doctrine and was very conservative. He encouraged vestments for the pastor and the choir and was the first to use candles on the Altar. He also introduced the blessing of the Palm on Palm Sunday.

He was president of the Conference and reorganized the Luther League. While he was here the congregation purchased a new parsonage.

The Rev. F. G. Robinson

Rev. Felix Robinson came to Trinity Lutheran Church March 1, 1934, and was with us until January 31, 1937. He put much emphasis on development of music. He was also very active in adding many new members to the church, among which were many adult baptisms. Later in his career, he joined the Catholic Church.

Rev. Robinson took part in many musical affairs in Keyser, such as Community Concerts, etc.

The Rev. C. K. Spiggle

Rev. Spiggle came to Trinity Lutheran Church June 1, 1937. He stayed with this congregation until his death, July 5, 1949.

He was a very vigorous man who employed a business-like administration of the church. A conservative in practice, he supplied the church at Westernport while they were without a pastor; he tried to reorganize a Lutheran Brotherhood; he revived the men's choir, and was active in Luther League activities. During his tenure here, the pipe organ was bought and installed with Mrs. Coffman as the organist.

The Rev. L. E. Bouknight

Rev. Bouknight came to Trinity Lutheran November 15, 1949 and stayed with us until February 1, 1952. He was our only pastor from the South Virginia Synod. He put emphasis on thoroughness in catechetical instruction, in finance, and in conservative Lutheran practice.

He was the first pastor to wear a cassock and stole in the Trinity pulpit. He demanded thorough instruction before reception of new members.

Plans were gone over for the construction of a Parish House while he was here, but the building itself was not built until after he left our church.

The Rev. Donald Anderson, D.D.

Rev. Anderson came to Trinity Lutheran June 1, 1952, after graduating from Gettysburg Seminary. He was with our congregation until June 1, 1963, when he accepted a position as an officer of the Western Pennsylvania – West Virginia Synod. During his eleven-year stewardship, we built the present Parish House, which was completed in 1953 at a cost of $46,000.00. Payments were completed and the mortgage burned in 1962. These years also saw great improvement in the church building and parsonage. Fabrics, walls, steps, doors, furnaces, etc., were kept in good repair.

During his term a new Common Service Book was adopted. There was also the reorganization of the Church School, the Ladies' Aid, and two women's missionary societies, which became one organization and was called Lutheran Church Women. New and improved methods of church administration were introduced. The financial administration of the church was much improved. A new constitution was adopted, and for the first time we had a paid church secretary.

ANNIVERSARY BANQUET

Vo-Tech Center
New Creek Drive
Keyser, West Virginia
October 6, 1973
6:00 P.M.

-o-

The Table Prayer

Dinner Menu

Fruit Cup

| Ham | | | Roast Beef |

Potatoes   Peas   Green Beans
Cole Slaw
Rolls and Butter
Coffee or Iced Tea
Anniversary Cake

Group Singing   Leader, Mr. William Rogers

Introduction of   by Mr. Kenneth Matlick
Toastmaster -   Vice President of
Mr. James Terry   Trinity

Introduction of Guests   by Toastmaster
and Remarks

Introduction of Speaker   Pastor Moore

Address   "WHY THE CHURCH"
The Rev. Hartland H. Gifford
Editor for Adult Parish Resources
Division of Parish Services, LCA

Expression of Appreciation   Toastmaster

The Benediction   Pastor Moore

TRINITY   EVANGELICAL   LUTHERAN   CHURCH
The Rev. Donald W. Moore, Pastor
76 North Davis Street   Church - 788-3200
Keyser, West Virginia   Parsonage - 788-3614
Church School - 9:30 a.m.
The Service - 10:45 a.m.

70TH ANNIVERSARY CELEBRATION
THE SIXTEENTH SUNDAY AFTER TRINITY
October 7, 1973

Prelude   "The Pilgram's Song of Hope"   Batiste
Processional   "Holy, Holy, Holy"   No. 131
The Confession of Sins   Page 247
Introit   Page 101
Gloria Patri   Page 17
Kyrie   Page 18
Gloria in Excelsis   Page 20
The Collect   Page 101
Old Testament Lesson   Job 5:17-26
Solo   "The Lord Is My Shepherd"
                                 arr. Maxwell-Feibel
The Epistle   Ephesians 3:13-21
The Alleluia   Page 24
The Gospel   Luke 7:11-16
The Nicene Creed   Page   4
The Hymn   "I Love Thy Kingdom,
                    Lord"   No. 158
The Sermon   The Rev. Donald D. Anderson
The Offering
Anthem   "Make A Joyful Noise"   Young
The Offertory   Page 27
The Prayer of the Church   Page   6
Hymn   "Bread Of The World"   No. 279
The Thanksgiving - The Preface   Pages 29ff
    The Sanctus - The Prayers - Agnus Dei
    The Communion
The Post Communion and Benediction   Pages 38ff
Recessional   "Guide Me, O Thou Great
                    Jehovah"   No. 520
Postlude   "Onward, Christian Soldiers"
                                           Sullivan

The Rev. R. J. Westerberg

Rev. Westerberg came to Trinity Lutheran Church November 1, 1963, and left December 31, 1965.

He was a former Augustana Synod pastor, who became a member of the Lutheran Church in America through merger. Prior to his Keyser tenure, he had been in Iowa. It was during Rev. Westerberg's term that the church built a new parsonage, costing $29,000.00. He had thorough catechetical instruction. He purchased Bibles for every confirmand for the first time.

The Rev. Gerald Huhn

Rev. Huhn came to Trinity Lutheran Church from his graduation at Gettysburg Seminary on June 15, 1966. He was installed on July 17, 1966, and he terminated his pastorate here on July 31, 1970, to accept a call to Holy Trinity Lutheran Church, Hershey, Pennsylvania.

While he was pastor of Trinity Lutheran, it was decided to build a new church. The ground-breaking ceremony was held August 3, 1969. The cornerstone was placed October 12, 1969. The dedication of the new building, which cost $100,000.00, was held on June 14, 1970.

Rev. Huhn was very interested in contemporary worship and ministry to the youth. He introduced singing of the Introit and Gradual into the service.

The Rev. Donald W. Moore

Rev. Moore came to Trinity July 15, 1971. He is an experienced pastor, solid Lutheran, and extremely approachable. He was formerly Dean of Pittsburgh East District of Western Pennsylvania-West Virginia Synod. He is very active in calling on members and those who are ill.

Pastor Moore was graduated from Shepherd College, Shepherdstown, W. Va., and from the Lutheran Theological Seminary in Philadelphia, Pennsylvania. He holds the degrees of Bachelor of Arts and Master of Divinity.

The Altar Guild

The Altar Guild was organized during Rev. Huhn's term as pastor. Mrs. Roland Staggs was elected president, Mrs. Carl Avers, vice-president, and Mrs. Clarence Jackson as secretary-treasurer.

The members belonging are as follows: Mrs. Carl Theis, Mrs. Carl Avers, Mrs. Donald Moore, Mrs. Kenneth Matlick, Mrs. A. D. Wells, Mrs. William Knott, Mrs. Roland Staggs, Mrs.William Manns, Mrs. Frank Fitzgerald, Mrs. William Walker, Mrs. William Rogers, Mrs. Rudy Sites, Mrs. Ernestine Golden, Miss Mary Riggleman and Mrs. Bruce Bradford.

The Altar Guild purchased the white paraments, altered the red Altar hanging with the help of Mrs. Bruce Bradford, made linen napkins for the baptismal services, and made some of the altar linens.

This group is very active. They take care of the Communion Service and baptisms in addition to arranging for flowers and providing candles for the altar.

Until this group was organized, the altar was in the care of Mrs. Charles Broome, Mrs. Elizabeth Schultz, Mrs. Arvella Fisher, Mrs. Georgiana Goldsworthy, and Mrs. Jane Athey. Mrs. Athey had the Altar job for thirty years. At her retirement a dinner was served in her honor. A gift from the church was given her for her long and faithful service.

Sunday School Superintendents

The Sunday School was organized in 1903, even before the formal organization of the congregation. They met in the afternoon at two o'clock. There is no record of who first acted as superintendent, although it is thought that Mr. Parker Spangler occupied that office.

In 1905 or 1906, John T. Sincell became the superintendent of the school and also taught the Ladies' Bible Class. He continued in both offices until 1921, in which year Mr. William W. Wolfe was elected Superintendent and teacher of the Men's Bible Class. After 1921, Mr. W. E. Coffman was the teacher of the Women's Bible Class.

During the period from 1915 to 1930, the Sunday School attained its maximum attendance, which was highest at Easter when from 210 to 230 were in attendance.

Mr. Wolfe was succeeded as superintendent by William Coffman in 1935. He in turn was succeeded by Romaine Kephart who held the position until 1943 or 1944. Then James Goldsworthy became superintendent. In the early 1950's, Ray Virts became the head of the school. He held this office until the departmentalization of the school made the office unnecessary. Since that time each department has had its own superintendent.

Among the early teachers were Mrs. Spangler, Miss Anna Carl, Mrs. H. A. Sliger, Mrs. Claude Clevenger, Mr. Louis Bomberger, Mr. Joseph Shaffer, Mr. C. W. Souder, Mr. George H. Loy, Mr. George E. Smith, Mrs. Edith Geldbaugh, Miss Mona Rittenhouse, Mrs. Nyta Greenwade, Mrs. Edith S. Workman, Miss Ruth Bill, Miss Myrtle Berry, Mrs. Minnie Bright Kolkhorst, Mrs. Charles McDaniels, Miss Ella Wolfe, and many others to whose faithful service this church is deeply indebted.

The following is a copy of the Sunday School report from February 1954 through the 19?2-73 minutes:

"The officers and Teachers Conference (which was the name then} was composed of the following people: Mr. Ray Virts, Superintendent; Mr. Arnold Athey, Assistant Superintendent; Mr. Walter Kephart, Recording Secretary; Mr. James (Dock) Athey, Treasurer and Literature Secretary; Mrs. Virginia Kolkhorst, music Director; Mrs. Dorothy Wertman, Conference Secretary, and Mr. Romaine

Kephart, Superintendent of the entire school. Teachers were Mrs. Elizabeth Stoutamyer, Mrs. Nellie Wells, Mrs. Lorna Anderson, Mrs. Rubye Rawlings Sanders, Mr. and Mrs. Charles Blackburn, Mrs. Edith Workman, Mrs. E. A. See, Mrs. Dorothy Wertman and Mr. William Wolfe. In 1965 the name of this Committee was changed to the Christian Education Committee and has remained that as of this date. Some of the general superintendents have been Mr. Romaine Kephart, Mrs. Edith Workman, Mr. George Chidester, Mr. Richard Virts, Mr. Donald Heare, Mrs. Sally Wilson and Mr. James W. Goldsworthy.

(Quite a few names have been added to the list above as teachers since the building of the Parish House as well as to the list of worship directors and other officers in this organization.)

The men's Bible Class met in the green building in back of the church for a while after the Parish House was built. Mrs. Ernest See taught the ladies' Class in the Sunday School room of the old church building.

Vacation Bible School has been held each year with an average attendance of between fifty and sixty children and adults.

Christmas programs have been given each year both in the Parish House and in the Church.

Sunday School and church picnics also have been held each year in August or September.

The Ladies' Aid

The Rev. Luther Miller, pastor of Calvary Lutheran Church of Westernport, Maryland was invited by our Lutheran women to organize an Aid Society on March 5, 1903. Pastor Miller and the ladies met at the home of Mrs. P. M. Spangler, where Mrs. Spangler was appointed president and Miss Anna Carl was chosen secretary-treasurer.

During the years that followed, Mrs. Arvella Fisher, Mrs. Seatta Lewis, Mrs. J. E. Goldsworthy and Mrs. Martha Lee Blackburn have served as president.

The Ladies' Aid Society did much for the church, furnishing many items that were needed in the church and the kitchen. They also took care of cleaning the church.

Christian Endeavor

Pastor Baughman organized the Christian Endeavor Society. The officers elected in 1915 were Miss Josephine Miers, president; Mr. Winifred Shaffer, vice-president; Miss Carmen Whipp, corresponding secretary; and Miss Elsie Kesner, recording secretary.

Music

The first organ in the church was donated by Mr. M. P. Moller, of Hagerstown, Maryland. Mr. D. T. Greenwade was the first choir director. He was followed by Mr. Lawrence Kolkhorst, who directed the choir until he left Keyser to reside in Cumberland. Mr. Kolkhorst was followed by Mrs. Virginia Kolkhorst. In 1946, Mrs. Kolkhorst and Mrs. Evelyn Shinn went to interview Prof. Leonard Withers, who was head of the music Department of at Potomac State College, to see if he would take over the direction of the Lutheran choir. He agreed to try it for a while and remained director until 1970.

With this excellent direction, the choir grew in spirit and understanding of church music. Concerts and cantatas were given, the best loved one being Harvey Gaul's "The Babe of Bethlehem".

The following is a letter written by Mr. George M. Loy to Rev. William C. Ney:

Keyser, W. Va. 12/50

William C. Ney, D.D.
Brookline, Pa.

Dear William C:

You are about to see a picture of a group that has developed from your first pastorate. Emmett Kolkhorst and my son William could not be present for the picture – hence they said I should robe for my Son's chair. We are very fond of this group and their accomplishment.

In the fullness of time; Mr. Withers, head of Potomac State Collage Music Department, came to direct the choir and lured them into heavier work, and they have practically outgrown the church in presenting a number like "The Babe of Bethlehem". During the past three years – four performances.

Mr. Withers is a fine character, the son of a Baptist minister, and believes in hard work. Not long ago he mentioned to me something like this: Many years ago I decided to have nothing to do with a volunteer choir, but this group caused him to change his mind. He has given this group quite a bit of spare time in the past three or more years. I have learned that "The Babe of Bethlehem" is one of Gaur's top scores for church choral music.

I should like also to mention William Wolfe, U.S. Mail carrier and teacher-preacher, an unusual product in self-education. Also, a son of Trinity. Further a couple of other sons, well worked in Surgery and Educational work.

Trinity Ev. Lutheran Church, when I think of the faithful flock, and some of the shining lights that have come forth from her sanctuary, it touches me very deeply, indeed. I'm sure that we have been favored with the best of Divine Guidance.

Walter Coffman, formerly of Elkins, W. Va., said I should mention his best regards.

My eyes are not good, writing is rather difficult, but I trust you can decipher this without too much trouble. We think of you often – very often, hence this prompting.

Sincerely,
George Loy

The Church organists have been Miss Gay Greenwade, Mrs. Nyta Greenwade, Mrs. Ernest See, Mrs. Robert Coffman, Mr. Leonard Withers, assistant, Mrs. Phyllis Coffman, assistant, and Mrs. Ruth Goldsworthy, assistant. Mrs. Goldsworthy is the director of the choir at present and is doing a fine job.

Mrs. Nyta Greenwade organized a fine Junior Choir; Mrs. Mary Evelyn Coffman organized a Young Peoples Choir. Besides participating at regular services, these groups also sang at Christmas and Palm Sunday.

A woman's quartet came from the Senior choir and sang at many services. The quartet was composed of Mrs. Marie Farley, first Soprano; Mrs. Anna Montgomery Mott, second soprano; Mrs. Virginia Kolkhorst, first alto; and Mrs. Nyta Greenwade, alto. These women traveled all over the United States and won national championships three years in succession at Legion conventions.

Women's Missionary Society

November 6, 1921, at Trinity Lutheran Church of Keyser, W. Va., a meeting was called for the purpose of organizing a Women's Missionary Society. Rev. Drawbaugh acted as Chairman and called the meeting to order. The constitution was adopted and the following officers were elected: Mrs. C. E. McDaniels, president; Mrs. Harry Burkhart, vice president; Mrs. Dalton Sheets, recording secretary; Mrs. Edith Workman, treasurer; and Mrs. Nyta Greenwade, historian. There were twenty-eight charter members. Miss Nellie Wiley and Miss Ruth Bill were the first delegates from the Society to attend a missionary convention at Bittinger, Maryland, in 1922.

Mrs. C. E. McDaniels was the only member from our Missionary Society to hold the office of president of the Women's Missionary Society of West Virginia Synod. Her term of service was 1926, 1927, and 1928.

Mrs. Edith Workman has been chairman of the Education Committee of U.L.C.W. and is presently a member of the Christian Education Committee.

Young Women's Missionary Society

In April 1926, the Young Women's Missionary Society was organized with Miss Eloise Scherr as president. On April 2, 1954, the two missionary societies merged. The Young Women's Society, named the Mary Schultz Missionary Society, and the Women's Missionary Society, named the Elizabeth McDaniel Missionary Society, became the Mary Elizabeth Society and retained the name until it and the Ladies' Aid Society formed the United Lutheran Church Women in January 1959.

United Lutheran Church Women

United Lutheran Church Women was organized in January 1959. The officers elected were Mrs. James Watson, president; Mrs. Earl Ebert, vice president; Mrs. R. A. Stoutamyer, recording secretary; Mrs. Roy Leatherman, statistical secretary, and Mrs. Carl Theis, treasurer.

Through these years, the LCW has been active in all phases of church endeavors, including the following:

1. Book Reviews, sharing these with Lutheran Church Women of Westernport.
2. Baby Layettes were made for the mission fields.
3. White choir robes were purchased for the Junior Choir.
4. School bags and Supplies were made and sent to the mission fields.
5. Special offerings made to church and mission fields.
6. Refreshments were provided for Vacation Church School each year.
7. Participates in World Community Day programs.
8. Supplied materials for Christmas tree ornaments.
9. Annual bazaars have provided fellowship and fun.

Current officers of Lutheran Church women are as follows: Mrs. Clarence Jackson, president; Mrs. Roland Staggs, vice president; Mrs. Ernestine Golden, secretary; and Mrs. F. E. Workman, treasurer. Mrs. Carl Theis serves as Program Chairman and Mrs. James Terry as Christian Action Chairman.

Light Brigade

The Children's Light Brigade was organized in November 1922, under the sponsorship of the Women's Missionary Society. The leaders of this group were Miss Nellie Wiley and Mrs. Edith Workman. This group was very active for quite some time.

The Junior Missionary Society

In the fall of 1922, Miss Nellie Wiley organized the Junior Missionary Society for girls seven to fourteen years of age. They had a membership of thirty-one girls and met twice a month.

Luther League

In 1926 during the pastorate of Dr. Vorberg, the Luther League was formed. The officers were Mr. Robert Scherr, president. Mr. William Wolfe was Luther League president of West Virginia Synod in 1927, 1928 and 1929.

Girl Scouts

In 1926, the Women's Missionary Society sponsored a Girl Scout troop with Miss Nellie Wiley, Captain; Mrs. Edith Workman, First Lieutenant; and Mrs. Bertha Chapman Smith, Second Lieutenant.

There was also a Brownie Troop which was sponsored by the church. Leaders were Mrs. Eugene Athey and Mrs. Thelma Stewart, assistant.

Events, Celebrations, Parish Relationships, Affiliations with General Bodies, Forms of worship, etc.

Trinity Evangelical Lutheran Church of Keyser, West Virginia, has always been a separate parish since its founding. It was founded as a mission of the Maryland Synod until October 1911, when it became a part of the newly formed Synod of West Virginia.

Its relation to the General Synod continued until 1918 when it merged with other general bodies in forming the United Lutheran Church in America.

The first worship services were very informal. Old time gospel hymn books were used. With the building of the church, the Book of Worship of the General Synod was introduced and the simple form of service known as the "Washington Service" was used. In 1922, the Common Service Book of the United Lutheran Church in America was made the service book by the parish. This service book was superseded by the Service Book and Hymnal in 1959.

In June 1962, the parish became part of the newly formed Western Pennsylvania – West Virginia Synod of the also newly formed Lutheran Church in America.

Offering envelopes have been used during the entire life of the congregation. Benevolence has been stressed and substantial Easter offerings have been made. The Every Member Canvass for pledges for church support has been made since 1922.

Many, many anniversaries have been celebrated in the church.

Part II of the origin of Trinity Memorial Lutheran Church, Keyser, West Virginia, was compiled by Mrs. Anna Montgomery Mott, 1973.

The History Committee was composed of Mr. William Wolfe, Chairman, Mrs. Anna Mott, Mr. W. E. Coffman and Mr. Walter Kephart.

Gifts in Memoriam To
New Trinity Lutheran Church 1970-

The Lectern and Rail in memory of Mr. J. A. Athey by family and friends
A Nave Chandelier in memory of Mr. T. W. Chapman by Mr. and Mrs. Thomas Smith
A Nave Chandelier in memory of Mr. and Mrs. Thomas Smith, Sr., by Mr. and Mrs. Thomas Smith, Jr.
A Silver Paten in memory of Mrs. Edna Ravensoraft by Mrs. Madge Briggs and friends
Two Bud vases in memory of Mr. and Mrs. Luther Kesner by Mrs. Buenna Defibaugh
The Processional Cross and Dossal Curtain in memory of Mr. John Koelz by his son, Mr. Fred Koelz
The Silver Chalice in memory of Mr. and Mrs. V.T. Rohrbach by daughter, Mrs. Romaine Shepp
The Altar in memory of Terry Lee Virts by his parents, Mr. and Mrs. Richard Lee Virts
The Hanging Cross in memory of Deborah Ann Fuller by her parents, Mr. and Mrs. Paul Fuller
The Baptismal Font and Ewer in memory of Mr. A. W. Heare by family and friends
The Narthex Chandelier in memory of Henry C. Endler by his wife, Mrs. Margaret Endler
The Book of Remembrance and Repository Bracket in memory of William H. Feaster, by his parents, Mr. and Mrs. William H. Feaster, Sr.
One Nave Window and one Nave Chandelier in memory of Mr. and Mrs. H. A. Sliger by friends
One Exterior Light in memory of Sgt. Rex Wertman by his wife, Mrs. Dorothy Wertmen
One Exterior Light in memory of Mr. T. W. Chapman and son by Mrs. T. W. Chapman and Mrs. Dorothy Wertman
The Lectern Bible in memory of Mr. and Mrs. V.F. Rohrbach by Mr. and Mrs. James Ferrebee
A Silver Ciborium in memory of Harold Kephart by his parents, Mr. and Mrs. Walter Kephart
The Prie Dieu in memory of Mr. Bruce Bradford by his wife, Mrs. Bruce Bradford
A Nave window in memory of Mr. and Mrs. Jacob Wiley; sons Otto and Arthur; and daughter, Eloise, by Miss Nellie Wiley
Altar and pulpit hangings in memory of Emmett Kolkhorst by his wife, Mrs. Elsie Kolkhorst Jackson
Lectern hangings and stole by Ladies of the Church.
Parament Cabinet in memory of Clem E. Montgomery by his wife, Mrs. Anna Montgomery Mott
Fair Linen in memory of Mr. Charles Staggs by Mr. and Mrs. A. D. Wells
Sound System in memory of their parents, by Mr. and Mrs. Thomas Smith, Jr.
Red Pulpit and Lectern hangings in memory of Terry Lee Virts by his parents, Mr. and Mrs. Richard Virts

Cash Gift Memorials

Rev. Dr. Robert Vorberg by Mrs. William Summers

Mrs. Ray Kephart, by friends

Mr. Warren Kolkhorst and Mr. and Mrs. W. I. Knott by Mrs. Virginia Kolkhorst

Mrs. Nellie Tasker by Mrs. R. T. Coffman

Mr. Charles Farley, by friends

Mrs. Olive Mott by Mr. and Mrs. Carl Theis

Mr. Harry Dawson, by Mrs. Harland Ridder

ADMINISTRATION

Pastor:
    The Rev. Donald W. Moore
    310 Valley View Avenue
    Keyser, West Virginia
    Telephone: 788-3614

Church Secretary:
    Mrs. Clarence Jackson
    Office: 76 North Davis Street
    Telephone: 788-3200

Church Treasurer:
    Mrs. Thomas Harman

Church Financial Secretary:
    Mrs. Richard Virts

CHURCH COUNCIL

Vice President:	Mr. Kenneth Matlick
Secretary:	Mr. William V. Knott
Members:	Dr. James Courrier
	Mrs. Carl Theis
	Mr. Donald Heare
	Mr. James Terry
	Mrs. Thomas Harman
	Mr. Richard Virts
	Mr. William Walker

1973
STANDING COMMITTEES

Christian Education
    Chairman: Mr. Donald Heare

Evangelism:
    Chairman: Mr. Kenneth Matlick

Finance
    Chairman: Mr. William Walker

Property
    Co-Chairmen: Mr. Richard Virts
                   Mr. Carl Avers

Social Ministry
    Chairman: Mr. James Terry

Stewardship
    Chairman: Mr. William V. Knott

Worship and Music
    Chairman: Mrs. Carl Theis

Appendix III

Trinity Lutheran Church Records of the 1920s

(lightly edited to correct obvious spelling errors)

Name	Address	Accessions By	Accessions Date	Losses By	Losses Date	Miscellaneous
A						
Adams, Nannie G.	Richmond, VA			R		
Adams, Leona	W. Piedmont			R		
Adams, Zimri	35 A.			R		
Adams, Mrs. Z.	"			R		
Amtower, Harry	U.S. Army			R		
Ambrose, Mrs.	F		1922			Formerly Mrs. Olive Foley
Arnold, Mrs. J. E.	McCoole, MD			D	10/17/25	
Arnold, Georgia E.	Willow Ave.	B	4/12/25			
Arnold, George J.	S. Water	B	4/12/25			
Arnold, Mrs. G. J.	"	B	4/12/25			
Allen, Mrs. Lee	Davis	L	7/4/20			Nee Margaret Hoffman
Aronholt, A. M.	Washington, DC					
Aronholt, Mrs. A. M.	98 Spring					
Athey, Miss Sydney	S. Main					
Athey, James A.	Virginia Ave.	B	3/27/21			
Athey, Mrs. J. A.	"	C	3/27/21			
Avers, Jacob	32 Spring			D	12/22/25	
Avers, Mrs. Jacob	"			D	[3/11/22]	
Avers, W. J.	"	C	4/16/22			
Avers, J. H.	"	C	4/16/22			
Avers, Clifton	"					
Avers, George W.	Mozelle					
Avers, Carl	32 Spring					
Albright, Mrs. Catherine	"	L	4/23/22	L	11/5/23	St. Luke's, Youngstown
B						
Baker, Henry W.	Davis					
Baker, Mrs. H. W.	101 N. Main			D	5/28/23	
Barraclough, Maude	39 W. Piedmont					Married E. E. Umstot
Baughman, Mrs. Harry	Pittsburgh, PA			L		
Batdorff, Mrs. Beulah	New Creek					
Batdorff, Francis	"					
Barnett, Mrs. Roberta	A Street			L	11/17/24	M.E. South, Keyser
Bell, Dr. M. R.	123 S. Main		1923			
Berry, Myrtle	124 N. Water		1924			
Bill, Ruth H.	E Street		1923			
Bill, Clifton H.	"	B	4/20/24			
Bill, Mrs. Perry	"	C	4/16/22			
Bitner, Mrs. S. B.	Armstrong			D		
Bitner, Eugene	"			R		
Bolen, E. F.	46 Spring					
Bolen, Mrs. E. F.	"					
Bomberger, Mrs. L. M.	Beryl, WV			R		
Bomberger, L. M.	"			R		
Boor, Mrs. A. J.	N. Main					
Boor, Wm.	"					
Boor, Wayne	"	C	3/28/20	R		
Bosley, Scott	S. Main		1922			
Bosley, Mrs. Scott	"		1922			

177

Name	Address	Accessions By	Accessions Date	Losses By	Losses Date	Miscellaneous
Bower, Mrs. Charles	S. Water					[Nee Leah Wolf]
Bowers, Mrs. Pauline	D					
Bradford, Bruce W.	Fort Ave.	B	7/20/19			
Bradford, Mrs. B. W.	"	R	7/20/19			
Broome, Charles E.	26 Spring					
Broome, Mrs. C. E.	"					
Burkhart, Harry D.	121 S. Main					
Burkhart, Mrs. H. D.	"					
Burkhart, Gladys	"			L	9/8/24	Married J. H. Withers
Butler, Beulah	Covington, Va.			L		
Butler, Phylis	"			L		
C						
Caldwell, Esther	Mozell St.		1925			
Cheshire, Wm. P.	James St.		1922	R		
Cheshire, Mrs. W. P.	"		1922	R		
Clay, Mrs. R. W.	Glassport, Pa.					Nee Flora Rohrbaugh
Clevenger, Mrs. M. V.	213 N. Water	B	3/27/21	D		
Clem, J. M.	199 W. Piedmont					
Clem, Mrs. J. M.	"					
Clem, Ada	"					
Clem, Alvin B.	Cumberland, Md.			D	4/16/24	
Clem, Robert D.	S. Main	C	1923			
Clem, Mrs. R. D.	"	B	3/30/23			
Clevenger, Claude C.	Painesville, O.	L	3/27/21	L	1/18/22	
Clevenger, Mrs. C. C.	"	L	3/27/21	L	1/18/23	
Clevenger, Catherine	"	C	7/4/20	L	1/18/22	
Clevenger, Christine	"	C	7/20/19	L	1/18/22	
Cook, Mrs. H. C.	41 A	L	4/30/23			
Cook, Leonard C.	"	C	4/30/23			
Cook, Viola G.	"	L	4/30/23			
Chapman, Mrs. T. W.	Virginia Ave.	C	3/28/20			
Chapman, T. W.	"	C	4/20/24			
Chapman, Bertha V.	"	C	3/27/21			
Coffman, W. E.	S. Main	L	10/16/21			
Coffman, Mrs. W. E.	"	L	10/16/21			
Constable, Mrs. J. W.	230 Hughes					
Crooks, Bernard B.	N. Main			R		
D						
Dayton, Esther	Piedmont, W.Va.	L	5/30/20	L	5/30/21	
Dayton, Ethel M.	McCoole, Md.	C	3/28/20			
Dayton, Mrs. Lewis	22 Orchard		1923			
Davis, Mrs. Della	102 N. Main	C	3/27/21			
Davis, Albert W.	88 South					
Davis, Mrs. A. W.	"					
Davis, F. Wright	213 N. Water			D	3/25/21	
Davis, Mrs. F. W.	224 Mozell					
Davis, Raymond S.	"		1921			
Davis, Bertrand C.	" -		1923			
Davis F. G.	57 Orchard	B	4/12/25			
Davis, Mrs. F. G.	"	B	4/16/22			
Davis, Madge M	"	C	4/18/24			

Name	Address	Accessions By	Accessions Date	Losses By	Losses Date	Miscellaneous
Davis, Maxine B	"	C	4/18/24			
Diehl, Parley	104 Gilmore	B	4/16/22			
Diehl, Mrs. Parley	"	C	3/27/21			
Diehl, Wm. H.	"	C	3/27/21			
Diehl, Sadie A,	"	C	4/18/24			
Drawbaugh, Mrs. J. W.	86 Davis	L	10/16/21	L	10/16/25	St. Luke's, Baltimore
Davis, Mrs. Welton	Westernport			L	1/25/24	Calvary Lutheran
Drawbaugh, J. W.	86 Davis		10/5/21			
E						
Eady, J. W.	Cumberland.	P	3/30/23			
Eady, Mrs. J. W.	"	P	3/30/23			
Ebert, Wm.	41 E	B	4/16/22			
Ebert, Mrs. Wm.	"	C	3/28/20			[Nee Anna Irene Whipp]
F						
Farley, Charles	Center					
Farley, Mrs. Charles	"					Nee Marie Knott
Farthing, Mrs. George				L	3/5/21	
Fisher, Robert L.	35 Church					
Fisher, Mrs. R. L.	"					
Fletcher, Chas. M.	226 S. Main					
Fletcher, Mrs. C. M.	"					
Foley, Mrs. Olive	N. Water					[Nee Olive Robey]
Fox, Mrs. A. W.	Headsville, W. Va.					
Fellers, Miss Lola	W. Piedmont	L	7/12/25			
G						
Gank, Mrs. John	McCoole, Md.					
Gank, Hazel	"			L	1/25/24	Married Welton Davis
Gank, Wealthy	"	C	3/28/20			
Geldbaugh, J. Edward	98 Spring					
Geldbaugh, Mrs. J. E.	"					
Gerstell, Mrs. E. H.	Gerstell, W. Va.					
Gerstell, Hannah	"					
German, G. G.	Main			R		
German, Mrs. G. G.	"			R		
German, Fletcher	"			R		
Gillum, J. B.	23 Spring	P	4/4/20			
Gillum, Mrs. J. B.	"					
Gillum, Virgil	Armstrong	C	4/10/25	R		
Gillum, Mrs. Virgil	"	P	4/10/25	R		
Gilpin, E. C.	32 Gilmore					
Gilpin, Mrs. E. C.	"			R		
Gilpin, Lola	"	C	3/27/21			
Gilpin, Catherine	"	C	3/27/21			
Gilpin, Wm. E.	"	C	3/27/21			
Greenwade, D. T.	Davis			D	4/6/25	
Greenwade, J. P.	119 S. Main					
Greenwade, Mrs. J. P.	"					Nee Nyta Shaffer

Name	Address	Accessions By	Accessions Date	Losses By	Losses Date	Miscellaneous
Greenwade, Mrs. Frank	S. Main					
Gift, Edith	"	L	5/23/20	L	5/23/21	
Greenholt, Mrs. Floe	W. Piedmont			L		M. E. Church
Gull, Elizabeth D,	Armstrong	C	4/12/25			
Gull, Mrs. Harry	"					
Gilpin, Mrs. E. C.	32 Gilmore			R		
H						
Hardy, Mrs. Delia	W. St. Cloud			R		
Harmon, W. Lynn	S. Main	B	3/27/21			
Heare, A. W.	Virginia Ave.	P	3/30/23			
Heare, Mrs. A. W.	"					Nee Miss Verna Kesner
Hedrick, A. A.	134 Chestnut	P	4/20/24			
Hesen, Mrs. George	22 Orchard	P	7/20/19			
Hesen, Hazel Marie	"	C	3/27/21			
Hilster, L. B.	32 Spring	P	4/16/22			
Hilster, Mrs. L. B.	"	P	4/16/22			
Hoffman, W. H.	535 S. Main	L	7/4/20			
Hoffman, Mrs. W. H.	"	L	7/4/20			
Hoffman, B. May	"	L	7/4/20			
Hoffman, Margaret	"	L	7/4/20			Married Lee Allen
Hixenbaugh, Laura	"			D	5/11/23	
Holmes, Miss E.	Hoffman Hospital	P	10/16/21	R		
Holy, Dr.	Piedmont, W.Va.			R		
Hott, Frank	Church					
I						
J						
K						
Keller, W. S.	S. Main	C	3/27/21			
Keller, Mrs. W. S.	"					
Kesner, David A.	New Creek					
Kesner, Mrs. D. A.	"					
Kesner, Orin	"			D	11/23/22	
Kesner, W. B.	63 S. Water					
Kesner, Mrs. W. B.	"					
Kesner, L. O.	Sharpless					
Kesner, J. S.	New Creek					
Kesner, Mrs. J. S.	"					
Kesner, Lona Jane	"	C	4/16/22			
Kesner, Buena May	"	C	4/16/22			
Kesner, Martin S.	Mozelle					
Kesner, Mrs. M S.	"					
Kesner, Miss V. B.	S. Main					Married A. W. Heare
Kesner, Mrs. Sarah C.	New Creek			D		
Kephart, J. C.	Limestone					
Kephart, Mrs. J. C.	Spring					
Kephart, Esther	Limestone					
Kephart, Lena	"					
Kephart, Ruth	"					Married Roy Markley
Kephart, L. A.	"					

Name	Address	Accessions By	Accessions Date	Losses By	Losses Date	Miscellaneous
Kephart, R. A.	"					
Kephart, Mrs. R. A.	"	P	4/16/22			
Kephart, Walter G.	"					
Kephart, Mrs. W. G.	"	P	4/16/22			Nee Georgia McGee
Kight, Mrs. Harry T.	66 S. Water					Nee Myra Wolf
Kight, Mrs. Wm. E.	W. St. Cloud					Nee May Rittenhouse
Kight, Enoch	90 E.					
Kight, Mrs. E.	"					
Knott, Marie E.	Center					Married Chas. Farley
Knott, Virginia K.	"	C	3/28/20			Married Warren Kolkhorst
Knott, Wm. C.	"	B	4/18/24			
Kolkhorst, E. C.	Maple Ave.					
Kolkhorst, Mrs. E. C.	"					
Kolkhorst, Laurence E.	23 Spring					
Kolkhorst, Mrs. L. E.	"					
Kolkhorst, Warren	131 Center					
Kolkhorst, Mrs. W.	"					Nee Virginia Knott
Koelz, J. G.	N. Main			D		
Koelz, Fred	"	L	2/12/22			

L

Name	Address	Accessions By	Accessions Date	Losses By	Losses Date	Miscellaneous
Lark, Franklin, G.	89 W. Piedmont	P	10/16/21			
Lark, Mrs. F. G.	"		1921			
Leatherman, Mrs. Emma	New Creek			L	3/23/20	
Legore, Miss Emma	Water					
Lichliter, Daisy	"			R		
Liller, Porter	Davis	C	3/28/20			
Liller, Mabel K.	"	C	3/28/20			
Lotspeich, J. W.	W. Piedmont					
Lough, Miss Etta	New Creek					
Loy, George M.	Halde					
Loy, Mrs. G. M.	"					
Louther, Wm. P.	A. E. F.			R		
Lytle, B. G.	Maple Ave.					
Lytle, Mrs. B. G.	"					

M

Name	Address	Accessions By	Accessions Date	Losses By	Losses Date	Miscellaneous
Matlick, Ada Lee	McCoole, Md.	C	3/28/20			
Matlick, Wayne	"					
Merkle, Mrs. Ed	"			R		
Michael, Mrs. J. H.	Gilmore			R		
Miers, Josephine	222 Mozell					
Mills, Mrs. Isaac	S. Mineral					
Mohler, Hugh	N. Main	P	4/16/22	R		
Mohler, Mrs. Hugh	"	P	4/16/22	R		
Montgomery, Mrs. C.	Center					
Moomau, Roland	McCoole. Md.		1923			
Moomau, Mrs. R.	"		1923			
Markley, Mrs. Roy	Cleveland, Ohio					Nee Ruth Kephart

Mc

Name	Address	Accessions By	Accessions Date	Losses By	Losses Date	Miscellaneous
McDaniel, Chas. E.	Fort Ave. & A					

Name	Address	Accessions By	Accessions Date	Losses By	Losses Date	Miscellaneous
McDaniel, Mrs. C. E.	"					
McDaniel, Harold	"		1922			
McDaniel, Marjorie	"					Married S. L. McGee
McGee, Mrs. S. L.	Morgantown, W.Va.		1922			[Nee Majorie McDaniel]
N						
Neville, Albert	142 W. Piedmont					
Neville, Mrs. A.	"					
Nefflin, Gladys	Mineral					
Nefflin, Emil H.	S. Main	C	3/28/20	D		
Newhauser, Henry	Lancaster, Pa.			L		
Newhauser, Mrs. H.	"			L		
Newhauser, Katherine	"			L		
Newhauser, J. C.	Sharpless			L	4/5/22	
Newhauser, Mrs. J. C.	"			L	4/5/22	
Newhauser, I. S.	Davis St.					
Newhauser, Mrs. I. S.	"					
Newhauser, Katherine H.	"	C	4/18/24			
Newhouse, W. J.	Argyle					
Newhouse, Geo. B.	S. Main					
Nicholas, Henry	G St.					
Nicholas, Mrs. H.	"					
O						
Oyerly, P. W.	37 W. Piedmont	B	4/12/25			
Oyerly, Mrs. P. W.	"	P	4/16/22			
P						
Parker, Opal C.	Church	B	4/20/24			
Parsons, Mrs. Edith	McCoole, Md.					[Nee Edith Steiding]
Pifer, W. C.	Sharpless					
Pifer, C. S.	115 Orchard	C	4/16/22			
Pifer, Mrs. C. S.	"					
Pifer, Graham	"	C	3/27/21			
Pifer, Aleene May	"	C	4/16/22			
Pollock, Willis C.	150 E. Piedmont	B	4/18/24			
Pollock, Mrs. W. C.	"					
Purington, Russell	Mozelle					
Purington, Florence	"			L	6/27/19	M. E. Church
Powell, Mr. John	E. Piedmont	P	10/16/21	R		
Powell, Mrs. John	"	P	10/16/21	R		
Q						
R						
Ravenscroft. Mrs. Roy	6 Sharpless		1924			
Ravenscroft, Mrs. Roland	66 S. Water					
Ravenscroft, Ira	S. Main					
Rittenhouse, Dora	St. Cloud					Married A. W. Fox
Rittenhouse, May	"					Married W. E. Kight
Rohe, Mrs. Howard	57 Caroll St.	L	4/16/22			
Rohe, Evelyn		L	4/18/24			
Robey, Catherine	N. Water					

Name	Address	Accessions By	Accessions Date	Losses By	Losses Date	Miscellaneous
Rohrbaugh, N. F.	G. St.					
Rohrbaugh, Mrs. N. F.	"					
Rorhbaugh, Florence	"					Married R. W. Clay
Rohrbaugh, Romaine	"	C	3/30/23			
S	"					
Santmyer, Mrs. R. S.	104 C.					
Scherr, Dr. A. A.	S. Mineral	L	3/27/21			
Scherr, Mrs. A. A.	"	L	3/27/21			
Scherr, Eloise	"	L	4/16/22			
Sheetz, Mrs. Dalton	Limestone					[Nee Elsie Kesner]
Shaffer, Joseph H.	159 W. Piedmont			D	10/26/25	
Shaffer, Mrs. J. H.	"			D	8/15/23	
Shaffer, Winifred M.	"					
Shaffer, Nyta C.	"					Married J. P Greenwade
Shaffer, Margaret A.	"					
Shaffer, Chester	Cumberland, Md.			L	3/11/23	
Shaffer, Mrs. Chester	"			L	3/11/23	St. Paul's Cumberland
Shafferman, Mrs. Jennie	46 Spring			D	2/19/20	
Shafferman, Charlotte	"					
Shultz, J. B.	116 E. Center	C	4/18/24			
Shultz, Mrs. J. B.	"	L	8/3/19			
Sincell, John T.	Overton Place			L	2/25/23	Presbyterian – Keyser
Sincell, Mrs. J. T.	"			L	3/6/23	
Sliger, Harry A.	37 N. Water					
Sliger, Mrs. H. A.	"					
Sliger, Richard	"					
Sliger, Arnold T.	"	C	3/27/21			
Smith, Mrs. J. C.	Armstrong	L	9/21/19	L	3/5/21	
Souders, Benj.	Milam, W.Va.					
Souders, Mrs. B.	"					
Salyard, Mrs. Stella	Spring					Married M. T. Virts
Spangler, P. M.	Pen Mar, Md.			R		
Spangler, Mrs. P. M.	"			R		
Spangler, Elsa	Washington, D.C.			R		
Staggs, Chas. H.	New Creek	P	4/16/22			
Staggs, Mrs. C. H.	"		1922			
Stanhagen, Mrs. W.	33 N. Water	L	4/18/20			
Stanhagen, Anna	"			D		
Stanhagen, John	33 N. Water	C	3/27/21			
Stewart, Lillian	125 Orchard	L	10/26/19			Married W. R. Wildemann
Stone, Mabel	Davis					
Stoutamyer, R. A.	Mozell	C	3/28/20			
Stoutamyer. Pauline	"	B	4/10/25			
Stoutamyer, W. L.	S. Main	B	3/30/23			
Stoutamyer, Mrs. W. L.	"	P	3/30/23			
Steiding, Albert	McCoole, Md.		1922			
Steiding, Ruby	"					Married Paul Shobe
Steiding, J. B.	110 Mozell		1922			
Steiding, Mrs. J. B.	"	B	5/4/19			
Shobe, Mrs. Paul	Morgantown, W. Va.					Nee Ruby Steiding
Snider, A. R.	442 N. Main	L	3/30/23			

Name	Address	Accessions By	Accessions Date	Losses By	Losses Date	Miscellaneous
Snider, Mrs. A. R.	"	P	3/30/23			
T						
Tasker, Ruth V.	Sharpless St.	B	4/12/23			
Tasker, Mrs. B. E.	34 W. Piedmont	L	4/1/23			
Tasker, C. Bernard	"	L	4/1/23			
Tasker, Leona E.	"	L	4/1/23			
Tasker, Helen	"	C	4/1/23			
Triplett, Wm. L.	486 W. Piedmont					
Triplett, Mrs. W. L.	"					
Triplett, Cora E.	"	C	3/28/20			
Turnley, Frank B.	Baltimore, Md.	L	10/16/21	R		
Turnley, Mrs. F. C.		L	10/16/21	R		
U						
Umstot, Mrs. E. E.	RFD #1 Box 61					Nee Maude Baraclaugh
V						
Virts, W. H.	West St.			L	11/17/24	M.E. – Keyser
Virts, Mrs. W. H.	"			L	11/17/24	
Virts, Harry	Heskett		1922			
Virts, Mrs. H.	"	P	5/4/19			
Virts, Marshall	Maple Ave.	C	3/28/20			
Virts, Mrs. M.	"					Formerly Mrs. Salyard
Virts, Ray W.	"	C	3/27/21			
Virts, Mrs. R. W.	"	C	3/27/21			
W						
Waldron, Henry C.	125 Orchard	L	11/16/19			
Waldron, Mrs. H. C.	"	L	11/16/19			
Wagoner, Mrs. Russell	"					
Wagoner, Mrs. M. B.	Orchard					
Watson, M. L.	Bloomington, Md.	C	3/28/20			
Watson, Mrs. M. L.	"	L	4/16/22			
Watson, Martha	New Creek			L	9/28/21	Plainfield, Penna.
Wiley, Mrs. Jacob	31 G.					
Wiley, Nellie	"					
Wiley, Wilda	"	C	3/28/20			
Wiley, Winona K.	"	C	4/16/22			
Wiley, Bruce O.	"	C	4/16/22			
Wiley, Arthur C.	"	C	4/16/22			
Wildemann, Mrs. W. R.	125 Orchard	L	10/26/19			
Wilt, W. T.	600 W. Piedmont	L	4/16/22			
Wilt, Mrs. W. T.	"	L	4/16/22			
Wilt, Mrs. A.	39 N. F.	C	4/16/22			
Wilt, Edna K.	"	C	4/18/24			
Whipp, Carmen	41 Willow Ave,			R		
Whipp, Anna Irene	"	C	3/28/20			Married Wm. Ebert
Whipp, Edna K.	"	C	3/28/20			
Whipp, Lowell L.	"	C	3/28/20			
Wolf, A. S.	66 S. Water			D		
Wolf, Mrs. A. S.	"					
Wolf, Georgia	"					Married Roland Ravenscroft
Wolf, Myra	"					Marry Harry T. Kight

Name	Address	Accessions By	Accessions Date	Losses By	Losses Date	Miscellaneous
Wolf, Thomas	"					
Wolf, Ella	"					
Wolfe, Wm. W.	213 N. Water					
Workman, Glenn	Mozell		1921			
Workman, F. O.	23 Spring	C	4/16/22			
Wright, C. Laco	60 S. F.	L	4/16/22			
Wright, Mrs. C. S.		L	4/16/22	R		
Whitehouse, Francis	66 S. Water	L	7/13/24			
Whitehouse, Wilbur	"	L	7/13/24			
Withers, Mrs. J. H.	Buckhannon, W.Va.			L	9/8/24	Episcopal Church
X						
Y						
Z						

Notations:

    B – Baptism
    C – Confirmation
    D – Death
    L – Letter
    P – Permission
    R – By Request, or Removed